"Interpreting deep unconscious conflicts to a couple or to a family can vex even the most experienced of mental health practitioners. Fortunately, Timothy Keogh and Elizabeth Palacios have assembled an internationally renowned community of sagacious psychoanalysts who share their extensive clinical wisdom in generous fashion. I only wish that I had access to such a magnificent text when I began my training. This book would have been the perfect road map."

Professor Brett Kahr, *Senior Fellow, Tavistock Institute of Medical Psychology, London, and Trustee of the Freud Museum London*

"This book will have immediate relevance to clinicians. It represents an edited collection of papers from a conference organised by the International Psychoanalytical Association's Couple and Family Psychoanalysis Committee (COFAP) hosted by the Madrid Psychoanalytical Association (MPA) in Madrid in 2017. The conference was not only a high level scientific meeting, but one wherein there was a real debate of ideas from different cultural perspectives. This excellent book captures the theoretical and clinical plurality, which enriched the exchanges between colleagues at the conference that emphasised respect for thought, difference and creativity. It provides the reader with an exciting and accessible text on the important topic of interpretation."

Teresa Olmos de Paz, *President of the Madrid Psychoanalytical Association*

Interpretation in Couple and Family Psychoanalysis

This collection of contemporary clinically-oriented papers covers a range of theoretical approaches to the fundamentally important technical issue of interpretation. It offers thought-provoking, cross-cultural clinical perspectives about interpretation with illustrations from cutting edge clinical practice with couples and families.

Divided into three sections, the first part of the book examines interpretation within the broader field of psychoanalysis, and notes how it has been applied to couple and family psychoanalysis. Part II considers the current use of interpretation with couples, including how it informs assessment, while Part III focuses on its application with families and considers a broad range of key topics, including the nature of family, social and intergenerational links, the arrival of a newborn, same sex couples' families, bereavement in a family, and families with adolescent children. Each chapter includes a lively discussion piece.

Interpretation in Couple and Family Psychoanalysis: Cross-Cultural Perspectives represents a major contribution to the field of couple and family psychoanalysis. It reflects the fruits of an unparalleled era of global collaboration and the resultant re-shaping of approaches to clinical practice with couples and families. Mental health professionals dealing with couples and families will find it to have immediate relevance to their clinical work, either in their institutional or private practice.

Timothy Keogh is a Training Analyst with the Australian Psychoanalytical Society, Senior Lecturer, Medical School, University of Sydney, Co-chair for Australasia of the IPA's Committee on Couple and Family Psychoanalysis, a Vice President of the International Association of Couple and Family Psychoanalysis (IACFP) and the Vice President, Australasian Confederation of Psychoanalytic Psychotherapies (ACPP).

Elizabeth Palacios is a Psychiatrist and Psychoanalyst with the Madrid Psychoanalytical Association and the International Psychoanalytical Association. She is Co-chair for Europe of IPA's Committee on Couple and Family Psychoanalysis (COFAP), and President of the Aragonese Association for the Investigation of Child and Adolescent Psychic Life (AAPIPNA) and a member of FEAP.

The Library of Couple and Family Psychoanalysis

The library consolidates and extends the work of Tavistock Relationships, and offers the best of psychoanalytically informed writing on adult partnerships and couple psychotherapy.

Series Editors: Susanna Abse, Christopher Clulow, Brett Kahr and David Scharff

Recent titles in the series:

Interpretation in Couple and Family Psychoanalysis: Cross-Cultural Perspectives
Edited by Timothy Keogh and Elizabeth Palacios

Engaging Couples: New Directions in Therapeutic Work with Families
Edited by Andrew Balfour, Christopher Clulow and Kate Thompson

A Couple State of Mind: The Psychoanalysis of Couples—The Tavistock Relationships Model
Mary Morgan

Psychoanalytic Approaches to Loss: Mourning, Melancholia and Couples
Edited by Timothy Keogh and Cynthia Gregory-Roberts

Couple Stories: Application of Psychoanalytic Ideas in Thinking About Couple Interaction
Edited by Aleksandra Novakovic and Marguerite Reid

Clinical Dialogues on Psychoanalysis with Families and Couples
Edited by David E. Scharff and Monica Vorchheimer

Family and Couple Psychoanalysis: A Global Perspective
Edited by David E. Scharff and Elizabeth Palacios

Interpretation in Couple and Family Psychoanalysis

Cross-Cultural Perspectives

Edited by Timothy Keogh
and Elizabeth Palacios

Routledge
Taylor & Francis Group
LONDON AND NEW YORK

First published 2019
by Routledge
2 Park Square, Milton Park, Abingdon, Oxon OX14 4RN

and by Routledge
52 Vanderbilt Avenue, New York, NY 10017

Routledge is an imprint of the Taylor & Francis Group, an informa business

British Library Cataloguing-in-Publication Data
A catalogue record for this book is available from the British Library

Library of Congress Cataloging-in-Publication Data
A catalog record has been requested for this book

ISBN: 978-0-367-22000-6 (hbk)
ISBN: 978-0-367-22006-8 (pbk)
ISBN: 978-0-429-27027-7 (ebk)

Typeset in Garamond
by Swales & Willis Ltd, Exeter, Devon, UK

Contents

Acknowledgements

This book, which is the eleventh in the Library of Couple and Family Psychoanalysis Series, represents the hard work of a group of couple and family psychoanalysts and therapists who wrote and presented papers which demonstrated their contemporary clinical approach and way of theorising about interpretation with couples and families. We are thus primarily indebted to these practitioners for their hard work and enterprise.

We are also grateful, and wish to express our thanks to, the International Psychoanalytical Association's Couple and Family Psychoanalysis Committee (COFAP) and the Madrid Psychoanalytical Association (APM) who jointly organised the Madrid conference where these papers were presented. In particular, we acknowledge the APM President Teresa Olmos and Valentín Barenblit, the Chair of COFAP David Scharff and the local committee of the Second International Congress on Couple and Family Psychoanalysis: Pedro Gil, Alicia Monserrat, Alberto Carrión and Elizabeth Palacios, as well as the secretaries from APM, Arantcha Vidal and Ana Sánchez.

We also wish to acknowledge Gabriela Hechter for her translation from Spanish into English of a significant number of the papers, and editorial and translation support from Thomas Murphy. We also acknowledge the valuable advice and input from the series Editor in Chief David E. Scharff.

Finally, we wish to express our gratitude to the couples and families featured in the clinical presentations in this book. We hope that couples and families seeking help in the future will benefit from the developments in thinking emerging from these presentations.

Editors and contributors

Editors

Timothy Keogh, PhD, is a training analyst, full member of the Australian Psychoanalytical Society and a senior lecturer, Medical School, University of Sydney. He is co-chair for Australasia of the IPA Committee on Couple and Family Psychoanalysis, a vice president of the International Association of Couple and Family Psychoanalysis (IACFP), vice president of the Australasian Confederation of Psychoanalytic Psychotherapies (ACPP), English editor of its journal *The Review* and a member of the editorial board of the *International Journal of Couple and Family Psychoanalysis*. He is also the president of a psychoanalytic charity (which he co-founded) for couples (Penthos – *Penthos.org.au*) that offers free short-term psychoanalytic therapy for couples and families. His most recent publication is a co-edited volume: *Psychoanalytic Approaches to Loss: Mourning Melancholia and Couples*.

Elizabeth Palacios, MD, is a psychiatrist trained in Buenos Aires. She is a full member of the Madrid Psychoanalytical Association (APM) and the International Psychoanalytical Association (IPA) and an IPA child and adolescent psychoanalyst. She is president of the Aragon Association for Child and Adolescent Psychic Investigation (AAPIPNA), member of the Spanish Federation of Associations for Psychotherapists (FEAP) and co-chair for Europe of the IPA Committee for Couple and Family Psychoanalysis (COFAP). She is professor in postgraduate studies for the AAPIPNA Psychotherapy School and the co-director of the Couple and Family Working Group in APM. She is also the author of several books and papers on child, adolescent, couple and family psychoanalysis and the Director of *Thinking Psychoanalytically*.

Contributors

Carl Bagnini, LCSW, BCD, is a founding member and senior faculty member of the International Psychotherapy Institute in Washington, DC and Long

Island, New York. He is also on the faculties of the Adelphi University Post-Graduate Program in Psychoanalysis and the St John's University Post-Doctoral Program in Integrative Family Therapy. He is a featured presenter at national and international conferences and has authored and co-authored many book chapters and papers on psychoanalytic child, couple and family treatment. His book, *Keeping Couples in Treatment: Working from Surface to Depth*, was published by Jason Aronson in 2012. He is in private practice with individuals, couples and families in Port Washington, New York and conducts in-person and internet supervision.

Barbara Bianchini is a psychologist and psychotherapist, an international affiliate member of the Tavistock Institute of Medical Psychology (London), a member of the International Association of Couple and Family Psychoanalysis (IACFP) and a full member of Associazione di Psicoterapia Psicoanalitica di Gruppo (APG) (Milan). She teaches couple and family therapy and is a supervisor at the COIRAG postgraduate School of Psychotherapy (Milan).

Pedro Gil Corbacho is a psychiatrist, a full member and training analyst with the Asociación Psicoanalítica de Madrid (APM) and its former vice president, and former director of the Albacete Psychiatric Hospital. He is also former coordinator of the Preventive Health Retiro Center and a family and couple therapist at this centre and at the Psychiatric Hospital of Albacete. He is also a former mental health consultant at the Madrid Town Hall.

Lia Cypel is a psychoanalyst and a full member and training analyst at the Sociedade Brasileira de Psicanálise de São Paulo (SBPSP) and the International Psychoanalytic Association (IPA); a full professor of the program in Family and Couple Studies at SBPSP; former chair of the Family and Couple Psychoanalysis Committee of the Latin American Psychoanalysis Federation (FEPAL); and a member of the International Association of Couple and Family Psychoanalysis (IACFP).

Roberta Gorischnik is an Argentine psychologist, a graduate of the master's programme in couple and family psychoanalysis at the Instituto Universitario de Salud Mental of the Asociación Psicoanalítica of Buenos Aires and the master's programme in Family and Community Health of UNER. She is a college professor at the IUSAM and AAPPG. She is also the director of the Litoral Psychology and Psychoanalysis Institute and a member of IACFP.

Cynthia Gregory-Roberts is a couple and family psychoanalytic psychotherapist in private practice in Sydney, Australia. She is a member of the Australian Association of Social Workers and College of Social Work and an accredited Mental Health Social Worker. She is also a member of the

Couple, Child and Family Psychotherapy Association of Australasia. She has extensive experience working with couples and families and as a teacher and supervisor of general practitioners and mental health professionals.

Rosa Jaitin is a doctor of psychology (clinical psychopathology), professor at the University of Buenos Aires, an associate of the Laboratory of Psychopathology and Clinical Psychology at l'Université Paris Descartes, and a couple, family and group psychoanalyst. She is also the president of the International Association of Couple and Family Psychoanalysis (IACFP) and the scientific director of Apsylien, Lyon, France.

Sonia Kleiman, PhD, is a past president of the International Association of Couple and Family Psychoanalysis (IACFP); a member of the APdeBA (Psychoanalytic Association of Buenos Aires); an IPA (International Psychoanalytic Association) specialist in the psychoanalysis of children, adolescents and families; and degree director at the Instituto Universitario del Hospital Italiano. She is a director of the Master in Links, Families and Socio-Cultural Diversity, and Family, Child and Adolescent Assistance team coordinator of the Children and Adolescents Mental Health Services, Hospital Italiano Paediatrics Department. She is a lecturer in the Family and Couple Master's Degree at the APdeBA (National and Foreign Universities) as well as Social Sciences and Health Investigation Committee coordinator, Instituto Universitario Del Hospital Italiano Research Department.

Alicia Leisse de Lustgarten is a full member and a training analyst with the Caracas Psychoanalytical Society (SPC) and guest member of the Psychoanalytical Madrid Society and the Valencia Psychoanalytical Centre (Spain). She is ex-president, scientific director, Training Institute (SPC), an ex-director of the Latin-American Psychoanalytical Institute and an ex-board member of IPA and a clinical supervisor and teacher of psychoanalysis. She is also the author of regular publications in the journal *Trópicos* (SPC). She is also an honorary consultant in Valencia and Zaragoza (Spain).

Antònia Llairó is a psychoanalyst and member of the IPA, a psychotherapist and family therapist and co-director of the Parent-Infant Psychotherapy Seminar of the Spanish Psychoanalytical Society Training Program. She is also director of the Bruc Salut SCP Clinical Psychology Center and the leader of a research project to be carried out in perinatal depression, funded by the IPA.

Daniela Lucarelli is a psychoanalyst, a full member of the Società Psicoanalitica Italiana and of the International Psychoanalytical Association (IPA), as well as an IPA-recognised expert in child and adolescent psychoanalysis. She is also a founding member of the Society for Psychoanalytic

Psychotherapy for Children and Adolescents (SIPsIA) in Rome; a teacher and supervisor for Istituto Winnicott (IW) and the Italian Society of Psychoanalysis of Couples and Families; chair of the Couple and Family Section of the EFPP (European Federation for Psychoanalytic Psychotherapy); and a member of the International Association for Couple and Family Psychoanalysis (IACFP) board of directors. She is also the editor-in-chief of the IACFP *Review*.

Jeanne Magagna, PhD, is a child, adult and family psychotherapist and head of Psychotherapy Services at the Great Ormond Street Hospital for Children. She trained at the Tavistock Clinic. Her most recent books include: *Being Present for Your Nursery Age Child* and *The Silent Child: Communication Without Words*. She works privately in London and internationally at the Centro Studii Martha Harris in Florence and Venice, Italy.

Hanni Mann-Shalvi, PhD, is a psychoanalyst and an IPA research fellow and director of the Psychoanalytic Couple and Family Center in Israel, affiliated to the International Psychotherapy Institute in Washington, in which she is an adjunct faculty member of the Child, Couple and Family Program. She was the vice president of the International Association of Couple and Family Psychoanalysis (IACFP), a board member since 2006 and member of its scientific committee for five international conferences. She is a psychoanalyst at the Israeli Psychoanalytic Institute and teaches at the Hebrew University of Jerusalem. She is also the author of several books on the Israeli unconscious, intergenerational transmission of trauma and couple and family psychoanalysis. Hanni is based in Tel Aviv where she is in private practice and offers individual and couple psychoanalysis, psychotherapy and supervision.

Damian McCann, D. Sys. Psych, is a couple psychoanalytic psychotherapist working as head of learning and development at Tavistock Relationships, London and an adjunct faculty member of the International Psychotherapy Institute (IPI), Washington, DC. Dr McCann has a particular interest in working with same-sex relationships and his doctoral research was concerned with understanding the meaning and impact of violence in the couple relationships of gay men. His most recent publications include an exploration of open relationships and couples where one of the partners is in the process of transitioning from one gender to another.

Carmen Monedero Mateo is a clinical psychologist, psychoanalyst and family and couple therapist at the Psychiatric Hospital of Albacete, the Mental Health Unit in Toledo and the National Health Institute of Madrid in the Area II District and also teaches in these institutions. She is also an associate member of the Psychoanalytic Association of Madrid (APM), as well as secretary of the Department of Children and Adolescents of the APM and actively participates in its scientific activities.

Alicia Monserrat Femenía, PhD, is a clinical psychologist (Universidad Complutense, Madrid) and a full member of the Asociación Psicoanalítica de Madrid and the IPA. She is a well-known IPA psychoanalyst in the field of child and adolescent psychoanalysis, a postgraduate professor and author of several books and papers on family and child psychoanalysis. She co-directs the Couple and Family Working Group of the Asociación Psicoanalítica in Madrid.

Mary Morgan is a psychoanalyst and couple psychoanalytic psychotherapist and Fellow of the British Psychoanalytical Society. At Tavistock Relationships she is a Reader in Couple Psychoanalysis and is head of the Master's in the Couple Psychoanalytic Psychotherapy course. She is also the European member of the IPA Committee on Couple and Family Psychoanalysis (COFAP). She has written many papers in the field and her book: *A Couple State of Mind: Psychoanalysis of Couples and the Tavistock Relationships Model* was recently published by Routledge.

Susana Muszkat is a psychologist and psychoanalyst, full member and faculty of the Brazilian Society of Psychoanalysis of São Paulo. She is a member of COFAP (the IPA Committee on Couple and Family Psychoanalysis), former co-chair of the Latin American Psychoanalytic Federation (FEPAL) Family and Couple's Work-Group (2010–2012), and of the Family and Couple psychoanalytic study and clinical group of the São Paulo society (2001–2017). She is the author of *Violence and Masculinity* (Casa do Psicólogo, 2011) and *Family Violence* (Blucher Publishing House, 2016). She has published articles, chapters and short essays in Portuguese, Spanish and English, in books and specialised journals on the topics of gender violence, family and couples' analysis. She has a private psychoanalytic practice in São Paulo, Brazil since 1983 seeing individual patients, families and couples.

Anna Maria Nicolò, MD, is a neuropsychiatrist with children and president of the Italian Society of Psychoanalysis (SPI). She is an IPA-recognised expert on children and adolescents. She has been chair and is currently a member of the Committee for the Forum on Adolescence of the European Psychoanalytical Federation (FEP). She is also co-founder of the International Association of Couple and Family Psychoanalysis (IACFP), co-founder and former editor of the *International Review of Couple and Family Psychoanalysis* and the director of the journal *Interazioni/Interactions* (Franco Angeli Ed., Milan).

Diana Norsa, PhD, is an adult and child psychoanalyst. She is a full member of the Società Psicoanalitica Italiana (SPI) and the International Psychoanalytical Association (IPA), a member (2007–2017), now an adjunct member of the IPA Committee on Couple and Family Psychoanalysis (COFAP), the European Federation of Psychoanalytic Psychotherapy in the Public Sector and a member of the International Association of Couple and Family Psychoanalysis (IACFP).

Carles Pérez Testor is a Doctor of Medicine and Surgery and a specialist in psychiatry. He is director of the University Institute of Mental Health "Vidal i Barraquer", Ramon Llull University (URL) and full professor in the FPCEE Blanquerna, URL. He is Principal Investigator of the Research Group on Couple and Family (GRPF) of the URL, a psychotherapist and a co-ordinator of the Couple and Family Unit, in the Vidal i Barraquer Foundation and President of the European Network of Institutes of the Family (REDIF).

Karen Proner is an adult and child psychoanalyst who trained in England. She now resides in New York and is a faculty member of the Contemporary Freudian Society (CFS) and a faculty member of the Institute for Psychoanalytic Training and Research. She is a member of the American Psychoanalytic Association. She has been a training supervisor for the CFS child analysis training and the International Psychoanalytic Institute (IPI) child analysis training and is also a faculty member of CAPA and the Si Chuan He Guang Clinical Psychology Institute in China. She also teaches in Florence and is on the faculty, as well as a training supervisor of the Centro Studii Martha Harris in Florence and runs a workshop in Rome on working with infants and parents. She has written and published papers on primitive defences and borderline states and the Tavistock training method of infant observation. She is a member of the IPA Committee for Health and a former member of the IPA Committee on Couple and Family Psychoanalysis (COFAP).

Pilar Puertas Tejedor is a clinical psychologist, a training psychoanalyst and full member of Madrid Psychoanalytic Association (MPA). She is a member of the IPA and Director of the Northern Psychoanalytical Center in Bilbao where she has her private practice. She is also a psychotherapist with the Spanish Federation of Associations for Psychotherapists and a group psychotherapist. She has published multiple papers on different psychoanalytical subjects.

Janine Puget, MD, is a psychoanalyst, emeritus professor and ex-director of the Couple and Family Master's Degree at the University Institute of Mental Health (IUSAM). She is a full member of the IPA, the Latin American Psychoanalytic Federation (FEPAL), the Psychoanalytical Association of Buenos Aires (APdeBA) and the director of its Department of Family and Couple Psychoanalysis. She is the recipient of the prestigious Sigourney Award (2011), Doctor Honoris Causa of the University of Buenos Aires (2018) and author of numerous publications in various national and international journals.

Juan González Rojas is a psychoanalyst and a clinical psychologist in public mental health services in Madrid. He is a full member of the Spanish

Federation of Psychotherapists, and the Sociedad Española Para el Desarrollo del Grupo and the Psicoterapia Psicoanalitica (SEGPA). He is the founder of the Asociación Creadora del Dispositivo de Tratamiento de Familias (AEIPPS) en Riesgo (1993–2011), Parla y Pinto, Madrid. He is a member and co-founder (2007) of the International Association for Couple and Family Psychoanalysis (IACFP). He has been a group, family and multiple family psychotherapist in Spanish public institutions since 1991.

Anna Romagosa Huguet, is a clinical psychologist, psychoanalyst and a psychotherapist with SEPYPNA. She is a full member of the Spanish Federation of Psychotherapists, a psychoanalyst of Sociedad Española de Psicoanálisis and the IPA. She is a couple and family psychoanalyst and a member of IACFP. She is also co-editor of the *Revista Catalana de Psicoanàlisi* and a member of the editorial board of *Monografies de Psicoanàlisi, Psicoteràpia i Salut Mental*.

Jill Savege Scharff, MD, is the co-founder of the International Psychotherapy Institute (IPI) (Washington DC [www.theipi.org]) and faculty member of its Couple, Child and Family Program. She is a founding chair and supervising analyst at its International Institute for Psychoanalytic Training and its Child Analytic and Psychotherapy Training Programs and clinical professor of psychiatry, Georgetown University, Washington, DC. She is the co-author of numerous books and chapters on object relations individual, couple and family therapy including *Object Relations Couple Therapy* and *The Interpersonal Unconscious*; co-editor of *New Paradigms in Treating Relationships, Psychoanalytic Couple Therapy*, and *Psychoanalysis Online 1, 2, 3 and 4*; and an analyst and child, couple and family therapist in private practice in Chevy Chase, Maryland.

David E. Scharff, MD, is the co-founder of the International Psychotherapy Institute (IPI), chair, IPA Committee on Couple and Family Psychoanalysis (COFAP), a teaching analyst, Washington Baltimore Centre of Psychoanalysis in Washington DC and supervising analyst at the International Institute for Psychoanalytic Training, Chevy Chase, Maryland; a clinical professor of psychiatry at Georgetown University and at the Uniformed Services University of the Health Sciences, Washington DC; founder and chair of the Continuous Course in Couple and Family Therapy in Beijing and in Moscow. He is co-author of *Object Relations Family Therapy, Object Relations Couple Therapy* and *The Interpersonal Unconscious*, co-editor of *New Paradigms in Treating Relationships and Psychoanalytic Couple Therapy* and the editor of the journal *Psychoanalysis and Psychotherapy in China*.

Amita Sehgal is a couple psychoanalytic psychotherapist accredited by the British Psychoanalytic Council. She is a visiting lecturer at Tavistock Relationships (London) and a consultant psychotherapist at the Balint

Consultancy (London). She has a special interest in the neurobiology of contemporary attachment perspectives in couple psychotherapy, in the psychological process of separation, divorce and in resolving family disputes constructively and out of court. She also consults with family lawyers regarding strengthening client–lawyer relationships, as well as on the emotional impact of family work on legal professionals. She has published in the field of couple psychotherapy and maintains a private practice in central London.

Caroline Sehon, MD, is a child and adult psychoanalyst and psychiatrist, Chair and Supervising Analyst of the International Institute for Psychoanalytic Training (IIPT) at the International Psychotherapy Institute (Washington, DC), and associate clinical professor of psychiatry at Georgetown University. She is also an editorial board member of the journal *Couple and Family Psychoanalysis*. Dr Sehon maintains a psychoanalytic practice in Bethesda, Maryland.

Miguel Alejo Spivacow, MD, is a psychiatrist, a psychoanalyst and former assistant professor of psychiatry (Universidad de Buenos Aires). He is a full member of the International Psychoanalytical Association (IPA) and the Asociación Psicoanalítica Argentina. He is author of *Clínica Psicoanalítica con Parejas* and *La Pareja en Conflicto*.

Anastasia Tsamparli, PhD, is a professor of clinical psychology at the University of the Aegean, Greece, and a couple and family psychoanalytic psychotherapist. She is an adjunct faculty to the Couple Program of International Psychotherapy Institute (Washington, USA) and a member of the International Association of Couple and Family Psychoanalysis and the SFTFP.

Mónica Vorchheimer is a training and supervising analyst with the Buenos Aires Psychoanalytic Association (APdeBA), a member of the Latin American Psychoanalytic Federation (FEPAL), the European Federation of Psychotherapy (FEAP) and a full member of the International Psychoanalytical Association. She is co-chair for Latin America of the IPA Committee on Psychoanalysis with Families and Couples (COFAP) and co-editor (with David E. Scharff) of *Clinical Dialogues on Psychoanalysis with Families and Couples* (Karnac, 2017). She is in private practice in Argentina.

Janine Wanlass, PhD, is a director of the International Psychotherapy Institute (IPI) in Washington, DC, founding chair of the Master of Mental Health Counseling Program at Westminster College, and a psychoanalyst and psychologist in private practice in Salt Lake City, Utah. She specialises in the treatment of trauma in children, teens, adults and families. She teaches couple and family therapy in ongoing training programs in the United States, China, and Russia.

Series editor's foreword

Christopher Clulow

The *Library of Couple and Family Psychoanalysis* was established in 2009 to assemble and track state of the art developments in thinking about, framing and working with couple and family relationships from a psychoanalytic perspective. This book, the eleventh in the Series, focuses on the change agent most commonly associated with psychoanalytic practice: interpretation. Most importantly, it takes a cross-cultural approach in illuminating what we mean by interpretation. What is revealed is no narrowing down of definition or prescriptive technique but an invitation to extend our horizons as practitioners and enlarge the space within which meaning might be encouraged to emerge from shared experience.

There has been a direction of travel in the psychoanalytic literature concerning interpretation since Strachey's (1934) seminal paper, which I have represented as six interconnected developments (Clulow, 2017):

1 a move away from focusing on individuals as entities and towards one that focuses on their relationships, and how these become internalised and structured into a sense of self;
2 a shift in understanding what happens in the key transference relationship – that between patient and therapist – as bi-directional rather than uni-directional phenomena, reflecting a growing interest in understanding therapeutic process as something jointly created by interactions between the different subjectivities of patient and therapist;
3 regarding the analytic encounter as the theatre in which everything a patient brings can be viewed as part of the transference (but not in a reductionist way) so that the influence of intergenerational trauma and socio-cultural context may be gathered into the transference and become the object of analysis;
4 a conception of the therapeutic process, less in quasi medical terms of "cure" and more in terms of exploring what constitutes a caring environment, and how that might be affected by what each party brings to the relationship;

5 a heightening awareness of the role of countertransference in accessing unconscious communication;
6 a focus on the myriad ways in which people communicate about themselves, often quite unconsciously, challenging our capacity as therapists to tune into the "chatter" that takes place outside as well as within the domain of language.

Couple and family therapists will immediately identify an omission that is central to their practice: the potential site of transference and countertransference is not limited to the patient–therapist relationship but occurs in couple, family, work, and, indeed, any social configuration where two, three or more people are gathered together. Because of the emotional proximity between early developmental experiences and couple or family relationships the intensity of the intersubjective encounter is likely to be particularly pronounced in these contexts. This volume is therefore especially timely, focusing, as it does, on the intersubjective fields created by couples, families and therapeutic encounters. What quickly becomes apparent to the reader is that interpretation is not the exclusive domain of therapists, is not constrained by language and, to have a mutative effect, must do more than generate insight. Effective interpretations interfere with prevailing rules, roles and beliefs, often unconsciously prescribed, and confront us with difference. Indeed, the very act of proposing couple or family therapy may, in itself, constitute an interpretation, signposting relationships as the seat of discord – the patient in need of therapy – rather than a symptom presented in other terms.

What this book also does is address cultural differences in bringing together psychoanalysts and psychoanalytically informed psychotherapists from Australasia, Europe and the Americas to debate the nature of interpretation from their clinical experience and different theoretical standpoints. Two theoretical threads are prominent in this enterprise: first, the object relations tradition emanating from central Europe (in the work of Melanie Klein) connecting intrapsychic and interpersonal experience; second, Link theory, emanating from Latin America (especially through the work of Pichon Rivière), and extending the range of therapeutic vision to encompass intersubjective and socio-cultural realities that impact on relationships and so on personal identity. It is hard to escape the conclusion that our theories, both personal and professional, are highly context dependent. Moreover, as we look around we become aware that what we see and interpret can be seen and interpreted by others in very different ways.

This reality was brought home to me when reading anthropological perspectives on attachment theory (Otto & Keller, 2014), a conceptual framework I have found personally illuminating and professionally useful. What we in the WEIRD world (Western, Educated, Industrialised, Rich, Democratic, comprising about 12% of the global population) take for granted – that the cradle of emotional security and thought is rooted in maternal sensitivity – does not necessarily apply to other cultures with different mores, socio-economic challenges and parenting practices. The thought of applying the Strange Situation procedure (Ainsworth et al., 1978), a gold standard test of attachment security that exposes infants to a sequence of separations and reunions with their primary caregivers (usually mother), as a means of assessing emotional security and future mental health to some populations living outside the WEIRD world, were it even to be tolerated by them, may be as mad as the potential madness it is designed to capture.

This is a sobering reality check, and a curb on any tendency towards the indiscriminate application of any one theory to all situations. It requires us to take seriously different ways of understanding the problems we wrestle with, different approaches to tackling them, and to become acquainted with knowledge generated by disciplines other than our own that are relevant to understanding the predicaments of those we seek to help. In short, we have to be open to doing what we ask of those consulting us: engage with perspectives different from our own. Interpretation is not a one-way street; we must be as open to learning from our patients as we encourage them to be open in learning from us. Interpretation then moves from the realm of explanation to exploration, from identifying therapist-led linear causal chains of connection to creating the conditions in which something new and unexpected might emerge from the therapeutic encounter. This is what makes psychotherapy interesting and valuable.

The papers assembled in this book, so ably edited by Timothy Keogh and Elizabeth Palacios, are a truly interesting and valuable collection. They come out of a conference initiated by the International Psychoanalytical Association's Couple and Family Psychoanalysis Committee and hosted by the Madrid Psychoanalytical Association. It is the third of a trilogy of publications instigated by this Committee to promote dialogue between psychoanalytic couple and family practitioners across the world, the earlier two also appearing in the *Library of Couple and Family Psychoanalysis* (Scharff & Palacios, 2017; Scharff & Vorchheimer, 2017). The book is divided into three parts. The first considers the concept of interpretation from different socio-cultural perspectives. The second examines different ways of applying the concept through psychoanalytic psychotherapy with couples. The third covers the same territory in relation to work with families. The last two parts form the core of the book and provide detailed illustrations from clinical practice of interpretive work, providing a stimulating and thought-provoking excursion into the minds of therapists as much as their patients. Indeed, it is clear that the mind-set of the therapist often *is* the interpretation, an orientation that derives not just from learned theory but from the experience of encountering many diverse "theories" held by partners and family members.

That is not the end of the story. Most chapters are followed by reflections from one or two discussants who engage in a dialogue with the authors, allowing different thoughts to emerge in relation to the material. The editors' brief introduction to these responses helps the reader make connections between the two. In this interplay of thought, affect and experience the structure of the book demonstrates its key message: the value that follows from the link arising from engaging with difference.

When the first book in this international trilogy was published, just two years ago, I had the privilege of writing the Series Editor's Preface. I commented on how it linked us to ourselves as well as to global perspectives on couple and family psychoanalysis. Its successor developed this clinical dialogue in rich and multi-textured ways. This third volume takes us further and deeper into what it means to be a psychoanalytic couple and family psychotherapist, and all of us practising in this field will learn much from it.

Christopher Clulow
Series Editor
St Albans, United Kingdom

References

Ainsworth, M. D. S., Blehar, M., Waters, E., & Wall, S. (1978). *Patterns of Attachment: A Psychological Study of the Strange Situation*. Hillsdale, NJ: Lawrence Erlbaum.

Clulow, C. (2017). Before, between and beyond interpretation: Attachment perspectives on couple psychoanalytic psychotherapy. *Psychoanalytic Inquiry*, *37*(5): 343–354. DOI: 10.1080/07351690.2017.1322435.

Otto, H., & Keller, H. (Eds.) (2014). *Different Faces of Attachment. Cultural Variations on a Universal Human Need.* Cambridge: University of Cambridge Press.

Scharff, D., & Palacios, E. (Eds.) (2017). *Family and Couple Psychoanalysis. A Global Perspective.* London: Karnac.

Scharff, D., & Vorchheimer, M. (Eds.) (2017). *Clinical Dialogues on Psychoanalysis with Families and Couples*. London: Karnac.

Strachey, J. (1934). The nature of the therapeutic action of psychoanalysis. *International Journal of Psychoanalysis*, *15*: 127–159.

Editors' preface

Timothy Keogh and Elizabeth Palacios

The establishment of international organisations and committees whose aim is to promote and develop couple and family psychoanalysis has been a tremendously important catalyst in consolidating the identity of this increasingly important and valued area of psychoanalytic practice.

One of the key outputs of such organisations and structures has been the establishment of collaborative international meetings and congresses, which have facilitated the sharing of ideas concerning the theory and practice of couple and family psychoanalysis. These events, which are usually organised around a particular theme, allow for participants to hear about a range of theoretical viewpoints and techniques and provide the opportunity for the expansion of the field of contemporary theory and practice. This book will have immediate relevance to clinicians. It represents an edited collection of papers from a Conference organised by the International Psychoanalytical Association's Committee on Couple and Family Psychoanalysis (COFAP) which was hosted by the Madrid Psychoanalytical Association (MPA) in Madrid in 2017. The conference was not only a high level scientific meeting, but one wherein there was a real debate of ideas from different cultural perspectives. This book captures the theoretical and clinical plurality, which enriched the exchanges between colleagues at the conference that also emphasised respect for thought, difference and creativity.

An overview of this range of thinking and approaches is provided in the first part of the book. This introductory chapter firstly discusses the historical developments in thinking and practice with interpretation within the broader field of psychoanalysis, noting the impact of developments of thinking about psychoanalysis as representing an inter-subjective field and then looking at the impact of these developments on both couple and family psychoanalysis. In order to provide a broad-brush outline of the major cross-cultural perspectives on interpretation, European, British, North American, South American and Australasian perspectives are then presented. Elizabeth Palacios traces the unique and substantial contribution in theory and practice that has resulted from the enterprise of psychoanalysts in Europe. She highlights the multiple ways of considering, theoretically and clinically, our bonds with others.

Next, Mary Morgan traces the developments in psychoanalysis as they have been practiced in Britain, highlighting how this has shaped the approach to couple and family work. She underlines the focus on working in the here and now and the use of countertransference. David and Jill Scharff then provide a North American perspective using a clinical vignette, which illustrates the attention they pay to generational and cultural influences on families and their difficulties. They stress how their approach is one in which interpretation is seen to be multi-faceted and to operate at various levels. They suggest it is a process of sharing understanding with the family, not of imposing conjecture. Janine Puget, in providing her perspective on interpretation, a view from South America, highlights the relevance of the "link" that the couple co-create. In particular, Puget stresses the importance of understanding that what happens between two subjects is a consequence of the contact with otherness and with the alienness of the other. Timothy Keogh adds to the cross-cultural perspective by identifying the factors influencing the development of the approach to interpretation within the Australasian region and most recently in the broader Asian region. He acknowledges the British heritage that is evident in the practice of couple and family psychoanalysis in Australia and New Zealand, but notes how in the last decade link theory and inter-subjectivity have shaped practice.

The second part of the book examines the subject of interpretation in relation to couple work and describes the type and range of interpretations used. In Chapter 2, Mary Morgan firstly suggests how the field of psychoanalytic couple interpretation is not only complex, but also potentially creative. She describes the nature of interpretation of intervention with couples and discusses how interpretations come together in the mind of the analyst and specifically what is meant by a "couple interpretation". Morgan suggests that all interpretations gradually build into couple interpretations which are important because they can bring about a different state of mind in the couple – their own capacity for a "couple state of mind". In the discussant papers that follow, Hanni Mann-Shalvi explores the analyst's role in the interpretative work and Roberta Gorischnik explores the issue of interpretation from the perspective of link theory.

In Chapter 3, Timothy Keogh and Cynthia Gregory-Roberts examine the use of interpretation in assessment with couples and an approach to interpretation from a link theory perspective. It is proposed that interpretation is an important and effective aspect of the couple assessment process, particularly when it is seen as iterative and stemming from an evolving container–contained relationship. The unique challenges faced in the conjoint assessment of a couple are also discussed as are the use of *mutative couple interpretations* and the technique of *reflective interpretation* by conjoint couple or family therapists. In their commentary on the chapter, Damian McCann firstly considers the issue of when interpretations might arise from a selected fact, rather than from an over-valued idea and use of history. Alicia Leisse de Lustgarten then discusses the chapter in terms of the value of co-therapy, especially (in terms of the unconscious parental situation it represents) with disturbed couples, and the value of the reflective interpretation as representing an important third position.

In Chapter 4, Pedro Gil Corbacho and Carmen Monedero Mateo describe how the conjoint analytical treatment of couples, such as those representing borderline disorders, not only present special complexities but also important therapeutic possibilities. They consider the transference matrix with conjoint couple treatment, which they see as containing diverse primitive idealised or denigrated objects that can generate turbulence in the setting, favouring "acting out" and testing the analyst's capacity for containment. In her discussion of the chapter, Rosa Jaitin takes up the author's argument from the perspective of the paradoxical bonds in the couple relationship and by considering the lack of separation and individuation in the couple presented, which she suggests impacts on their ability to resolve satisfactorily their Oedipal complexes.

In Chapter 5, Miguel Alejo Spivacow, arguing for the term intervention rather than interpretation, suggests there should be a focus on the exchange between the two partners, in particular on the conscious and unconscious, as well as the voluntary and involuntary, aspects of their exchange. He sees the purpose of the intervention as the clarification and working through in the treatment of the way in which both partners contribute to the shaping of their psychic functioning or suffering.

The third part of the book presents a range of clinical situations to demonstrate the contemporary use of interpretation with families. It examines the nature of family, social and intergenerational links that may need to be interpreted in family work. It also considers a range of contemporary clinical family presentations, including the arrival of a newborn, same sex couples' families, bereavement in a family and families with adolescent children.

In Chapter 6, Diana Norsa and Anna Maria Nicolò propose that it is by observing the "economic policy" of the functioning of the family at the fantasy level, that the analyst can investigate the family's mental life in terms of the inter-exchange and distribution of suffering. They note that as a result of the mental work brought to these observations, interpretation is only one of the tools that will be useful. They note the importance, above all, of the multiple associations activated by the analyst in families that are emotionally blocked. In the discussant papers that accompany this chapter Carl Bagnini highlights the value of dream interpretation in family psychoanalysis as well as the role of children's play in communicating the family's difficulties. Janine Puget suggests that it is the link, as it is experienced along with the alienness of the analyst, that facilitates the expression of something previously unheard in the family.

In Chapter 7, David and Jill Scharff present the script of a video assessment session with a family and demonstrate how they use ordinary language with a family to explore the links into which this family unit and each of its members was born, the effect of past and current links on family attachment patterns, and the family's ways of entering into and warding off unconscious fears. In discussing their chapter Anastasia Tsamparli explains how the Scharffs use their countertransference, noting that it acts as a platform for effective interpretations concerning the intra-psychic and inter-personal difficulties that are impacting on this family.

Again, from the perspective of link theory, in Chapter 8 Mónica Vorchheimer considers the effect of the *presence* of the other, suggesting that the presence of the members of the group allows one to conjecture about how meaning is borne out of what they do in the presence of the other and *with* the presence of the other. She also raises the question of how this presence impacts on the members of a family group and how these effects result from being part of a specific relationship, something that the participants of the link cannot view. The discussants, Jeanne Magagna and Pilar Puertas Tejedor, take up quite different issues arising from the chapter. Jeanne Magagna suggests that the family's main issue is a protest, an anger and hostility regarding their unmet needs for nurturance and understanding and that she might have included interpretations concerning the need for wealth and achievement which appear to have superseded some of the requirements for emotional satisfaction of needs within the family. Pilar Puertas Tejedor suggests that it is the interactive dynamic of the drive in the here and now which needs to be the main focus of the intervention and this requires an adaptation of the traditional approach to interpretation.

In Chapter 9, Alicia Monserrat Femenía and Elizabeth Palacios discuss a homoparental family as an example of contemporary presentations and how they see that the suffering which triggers such consultations is essentially inspired by the manner in which the links play out among the members of the families. They propose that psychic change is achieved with such families by means of intervening (including interpreting) in the conflict and suffering observed between the subjects in the group. In discussing the chapter, Carles Pérez Testor focuses on the lack of a parental mental space in this family whose dynamics result from widespread use of projection. From another perspective Caroline Sehon incisively identifies the primitive nature of the defences in this family, looking at how interpretation in such a family can be seen as an attempt to transform a static closed system into an open, dynamic one in which the family's interactional matrix might be re-patterned.

In Chapter 10, Janine Wanlass provides the reader with a moving account of unresolved parental loss in a family with young children. She describes how play therapy and parental guidance sessions are combined to help the family address painful affects, mourn the family they have lost, and form a new family. In the commentaries on this chapter, Susana Muszkat firstly supports the value of psychoanalytic family therapy for such a family where aspects of the reaction to loss are split off and projected into the children. Daniela Lucarelli then focuses on how the author's management of the therapeutic setting was helpful in dealing with this family's presenting problems, along with the interpretation of links between the mother and her children.

In Chapter 11 of the book, Antònia Llairó provides a clinical case of family therapy in the perinatal stage and describes the fear of chaos and misunderstanding in the sessions connected with the arrival of a newborn. The author notes how the child's drawings illustrate the course of the therapy and how the work enables the family to reflect and connect with aggressiveness and sadness, which ultimately lead them to again find pleasure in their relationships. In discussing the chapter, Sonia Kleiman considers, from the perspective of link theory, how the best starting point with such a family might be a position of uncertainty, rather than a focus on their origins and causality. Juan González Rojas focuses on the *inter-fantasmatisation* in this family, which he sees as a response to something shameful, which cannot be thought about. He also highlights how effectively the therapist utilises the daughter's drawings as a starting point of representation, or *figurability*.

In Chapter 12, Karen Proner describes a case she supervised, of a couple who presented with a failure to mourn the loss of their baby. In this chapter she considers the relevance of Meltzer's concept of the *Aesthetic* to work with couples, in particular noting how the complexity of the early infantile experience of each partner can influence the couple's relationship, especially in terms of intimacy and sexuality. In their commentaries, Amita Sehgal and Anna Romagosa Huguet take up different aspects of the chapter. Amita Sehgal examines the role of the analyst in being able to contain the grief of the parents. She focuses on how the analyst, whose work Karen Proner describes, comes to understand this by paying attention to the mirroring of affect between the partners. Anna Romagosa Huguet, with a creative reference to Dali's painting of the *Angelus*, notes how important the third position, whom the analyst represents, is to the facilitation of the mourning process in such a couple. She provides a link theory perspective to the material presented, especially noting the impact of trans-generational links.

In Chapter 13, Lia Cypel returns to link theory and considers the value of the concept of inter-subjectivity in couple and family psychoanalysis, noting that an approach that stems from a theoretical framework of inter-subjectivity, focuses on interpreting the links in couple and family relationships where interpretations are focused more on meaning than causation. In discussing the chapter, Barbara Bianchini notes how such an approach is characterised by uncertainty and unpredictability. She notes that, from this perspective, transference also acquires a broader meaning, in particular, that it is part of an emotional field with its own specific and potentially transformative functioning.

The Epilogue of the book underlines the enormous enterprise in the field of couple and family psychoanalysis. It considers that many areas of difference in theory and practice have the potential for integration and how all contemporary couple and family psychoanalysts have in common a focus on working with the here and now and use their countertransference as a means of working with the psychic process of couples and families.

Throughout the book the cases presented highlight the contemporary nature of couples and families; the ability to relate to the current problems facing them across cultures also speaks to the universal applicability of psychoanalytic concepts. We believe that the chapters in this book provide many stimulating ideas and considerations for clinical practice, which will have an immediate relevance and applicability for the clinician. In reading the very human stories represented by the case material presented in the book, it is noted what a privilege it is to work in this field.

Part I

Introduction

Chapter 1

Approaches to interpretation with couples and families

INTRODUCTION

Timothy Keogh and Elizabeth Palacios

Although interpretation is central to the practice of psychoanalysis, the way it is conceived and applied varies considerably. In general terms Berenstein (2007) notes:

> Psychoanalysts usually belong to different schools and surely from each one of them they will have similar expressions to describe the world of links. But these similarities do not hide, however, marked conceptual differences. There is no monolithic thinking and a border separates and unites, unites and discriminates conceptions based on the psychic apparatus and those based on the link . . . reformulations of some psychoanalytic concepts need to be posed . . . as well as the practices stemming from them.
>
> (Berenstein, 2007, p. 22)

Within couples and family psychoanalysis the nature of the patient – the couple or the family – fundamentally affects the way in which interpretations are conceived and applied.

This book, the eleventh in the series on couple and family psychoanalysis, provides a contemporary cross-cultural perspective on the role of interpretation in the applied field of couple and family psychoanalysis. The papers gathered in this book were presented at the Second International Congress on Couple and Family Psychoanalysis held in Madrid in 2017, organised by the International Psychoanalytical Association's Couple and Family Psychoanalysis Committee (COFAP) and the Madrid Psychoanalytical Association.

In terms of the broad developments in thinking about interpretation, Freud (1899) originally applied it as a technique to elucidate meaning in the psychoanalytic process as outlined in his classic work *The Interpretation of Dreams*. His intention was to apply it in the sense that Aristotle had, as a term that denotes a means by which hidden meaning could be uncovered. As a more general concept, interpretation has had a long history linked to the field of hermeneutics. Hermeneutics as the theory and methodology of interpretation, especially the interpretation of biblical texts, wisdom literature, and philosophical texts, has also extended its reach to other forms of language and communication, including the spoken. Freud saw dreams representing a language: that of the unconscious. To him they represented the "Royal Road" to the unconscious and he regarded their interpretation as achieving one of the central aims of psychoanalysis, that is to bring into consciousness that which is unconscious and in the neurotic patient, that which he saw as being the source of that patient's distressing symptomatology. He was at pains to show that the language of the unconscious was structured in particular ways and its symbolic language was governed by certain mechanisms, such as displacement and condensation. Interpreting dreams, and moreover all unconscious communication, he saw as requiring a special knowledge about its functioning. As he elaborated the process of classical psychoanalysis, Freud highlighted the central role of interpretation of resistances and defences against unconscious wishes when conducting an analysis. He noted the important link between dream thoughts and those occurring in waking states. He suggested:

> By interpretation in the waking state we are actually opening a path running back from the dream-elements to the dream-thoughts. The dream-work has followed the contrary direction, and it is not at all probable that these paths are equally passable in opposite directions . . . We can see how the recent thought-material of the day forces its way into the interpretation-series, and how the additional resistance which has appeared since the night probably compels it to make new and further detours.
>
> (p. 534)

Whilst a defining feature of contemporary psychoanalysis remains its privileging of such unconscious processes and the interpretation of these processes (especially unconscious transferences), the role played by interpretation and its definition has changed a great deal. Culture, in particular, by influencing the development of different schools of psychoanalytic thought, has had an important role in shaping the meaning and views about the way in which interpretation might contribute to the therapeutic change achieved in psychoanalysis as it is practiced with individual patients. The definition of interpretation as an activity that makes conscious that which is unconscious (Gabbard, 2004) still provides a broad-church definition that encompasses these varied perspectives.

Theoretical developments arising in different cultures have spawned various definitional perspectives. In this regard Schermer (2011) has argued that these definitions can be seen to evolve from one of four perspectives that link to different schools of psychoanalytical thought. In addition to the above-mentioned Aristotelian approach which Freud adopted, he notes that there are those approaches which adopt a phenomenological view of interpretation which aims to expose objectified overlays of meanings, a dialogical existential vertex which focuses on interpretation in the context of a relationship and/or an approach which regards interpretation as transforming both parties in the analytical relationship.

From this framework one can see that the changed view of interpretation has resulted from a view of psychoanalysis which has moved from a one-person psychology to a more phenomenological and existential vertex, whereby the analytical relationship is seen as transformative by virtue of the inter-subjectivity that it involves.

These views have arisen in reaction to the original propositions that psychoanalysis is a process that should be focused on exposing the role of unconscious drives and instincts and later on identifying the role of internal representations of self and (attachment) objects articulated as Object Relations Theory, as either described by Klein (1945), who retained her allegiances to instinct theory, or by Fairbairn (1944), who divested himself from it and focused on the need for relationship as the primary driving force.

Developments in psychoanalytical thinking concerning interpretation arising from other schools of thought have acknowledged variously an existential and/or phenomenological heritage, placing emphasis on the influence of the relationship between the analyst and analysand. Some schools of thought, such as the relational school, have highlighted how both are changed by the psychoanalytical relationship and influence what is interpreted and the impact of this. Schermer (2011) argues that a contemporary approach to interpretation can in fact encompass all these perspectives. He notes, "A key to integrating these approaches to interpretation within the psychoanalytic session is for the analyst to attend to how he or she orients to him or herself, the patient and the material" (p. 838). He suggests that this involves the analyst being able to adopt an appropriate analytic stance, to be able to attend to the patient's empathic needs and, most importantly and relatedly, to the acknowledgement of the relationship existing between the analyst and analysand, especially the need to attend to the mutual impact in interpretation of both analyst and analysand.

Others have suggested that it is the level of psychopathology that should determine the approach to interpretation. For example, it is argued that there is little point attempting interpretations based in transference with patients operating at a psychotic level of functioning where there is little capacity for symbolic thinking. In terms of such primitive states of mind, Ogden (1989) describes an "autistic-contiguous" level of functioning where there is an absence of a "psychic skin" that allows for a sense of separateness from the other. In this instance it is thought that factors such as the sound of the analyst's voice, which provide a sense of containment, are the most important factors in producing change, not classical interpretive method.

Approaches to psychoanalysis which have stressed the role of the analytic relationship in producing change have also de-emphasised the traditional approach to interpretation in the process. The relational emphasis, in contrast, is on the interpretation of the affective state of the analysand and being attuned to it. If ultimately making the unconscious conscious is what creates therapeutic change, it is important to be clear how one makes contact with the unconscious in a way that generates change. Psychoanalysts who privilege the relationship see that it is an experience with the analyst which contradicts their unconscious assumptions or self-object relations that make for the change. In this regard Wolf (1993) notes:

> Simple dynamic explanations about what is going on unconsciously are usually ineffective, even if they make good sense to the patient. Insight contained in a verbal statement rarely reaches the analysand's unconscious. It is necessary to provide an experience for the analysand that is contrary to the unconscious expectation . . . As the analyst gets to know his patient better, he can gradually address the specific fears, the so-called resistances. I want to stress, however, that it is not an analysand's fear of their own impulses, sexual or aggressive or otherwise, that motivates their resistance. It is a fear that past experiences will be repeated.
>
> (p. 28)

All of these developments relate to the changing views and approaches to interpretation with individual analysands. When it comes to the application of these ideas to interpretation with couples and families in psychoanalysis, one has to contemplate how such approaches may manifest in this particular mode of work. This is determined by several factors which characterise interpretation in couples and family psychoanalysis which include the fact that:

1. Interpretation with couples and families is a more complex phenomenon than with an individual analysand in that interpretation can focus not just on the individual, but also the couple and the family.
2. Interpretation with couples is also often *couples-focused* such that interpretations are made about the interplay of internal object relations within the couple dyad or about the nature of the couple link.
3. With family work the play of children is often interpreted to demonstrate how the couple is malfunctioning. Interpretation of their play is therefore a family-based interpretation.
4. Interpretation requires the therapist to be able to relate to the couple or the family as the patient.

In the field of couple and family psychoanalysis the concept of inter-subjectivity has seen an increasing focus amongst object relations-based couples therapists on the countertransference to the couple or family psychoanalyst and amongst those psychoanalysts who have applied link theory to their work, to the value of seeing themselves as not only transference figures, but an actual "interference" to a couple's determination to have their archaic inner world representation of themselves and others confirmed.

Clinical practice has shown us that certainties don't last forever. Freud's unique contribution, as well as the enrichment of the theoretical and clinical thinking added by many other followers, needs to be brought into consideration so as to include the inter-subjective dimension, including a group and social perspective. A review of the foundational psychoanalytical concepts, including setting variations, needs to be taken into account in order to lodge links, both of the couple and the family. A review of such foundational concepts is stimulated by the exchange of different culturally determined approaches to clinical work.

The chapters in this volume represent the frontier of developments in thinking about interpretation with couples and families across cultures in the context of the above-mentioned developments on thinking. There is little doubt that inter-subjectivity has had a significant impact on technique. In this book cultural perspectives on interpretation with couples and families in North and South America, Europe, Britain and Australasia reveal the ways in which culture is shaping the contemporary approach to this particular field of psychonalaysis and in particular to interpretation. Each region has a particular perspective on interpretation.

References

Berenstein, I. (2007). *Del ser al hacer. Curso sobre vincularidad.* Buenos Aires: Paidós.

Fairbairn, W. R. D. (1944). Endopsychic structure considered in terms of object relationships. *International Journal of Psycho-Analysis*, *25*: 70–92.

Freud, S. (1899). *The Interpretation of Dreams*, J. Strachey. New York: Basic Books, 2010 (a member of the Perseus Books Group).

Gabbard, G. O. (2004). *Long-Term Psychodynamic Psychotherapy: A Basic Text.* Washington, DC: American Psychiatric Press.

Klein, M. (1945). *Love, Guilt and Reparation*. London: The Hogarth Press.

Ogden, T. H. (1989). On the concept of an autistic-contiguous position. *International Journal of Psycho-Analysis*, *70*: 127–140.

Schermer, V. L. (2011). Interpreting psychoanalytic interpretation: A fourfold approach. *Psychoanalytical Review*, *98*(6): 817–842.

Wolf, E. S. (1993). The role of interpretation in therapeutic change. In: A. Goldberg (Ed.), *The Widening Scope of Self Psychology: Progress in Self Psychology*, Vol. 9 (pp 15–30). Hillsdale, NJ: The Analytic Press.

EUROPEAN PERSPECTIVE

Elizabeth Palacios

In order to address the subject of interpretation in European couple and family psychoanalysis nowadays, I need to give some background ideas on how psychoanalysis has developed to consider some levels of understanding of what happens in inter-subjective and trans-subjective processes which are beyond its initial object of study.

Some background notions

Historically psychoanalysis, from within its epistemological approach to its object of study, has addressed the processes of constitution of the psychic space of the singular mind. There is no explicit theory in Freud's approaches to the idea of inter-subjectivity. Although the subjectivity of the object is required for the constitution of the drives, identification and unconscious alliances are the key processes in subjectivity.

If we want to address the psychic reality of inter-subjective links, or even trans-subjective ones, we need to extend our knowledge to those fields and revise our hypothesis creating new ones from an intra-psychic level to a level of organisation in which links between subjects are recognised and addressed. We need to consider what happens unconsciously between two or more subjectivities when acting together. This means that an epistemological dimension of our given knowledge needs to be put forward, since we are addressing a new dimension of phenomena not dealt with from within the concepts and clinical setting in which we were initially trained as psychoanalysts. The psychic reality of the link needs to include many levels of interaction, such as unconscious alliances that give way to the suffering and the psychopathology of the link.

Our initial knowledge comes from the interest in understanding the inner world and its conflicts, the different levels of understanding of the personal history and the processes of individuation within a family, a couple or a group. To be part of all these links, there is a need for unconscious identification between the different subjects which are part of these inter-subjective experiences.

Different perspectives in different European countries

Psychoanalytic theory in English-speaking countries has viewed couple relationships from the vertex of self-object relationships motivated either by drives or the need of attachment. Klein gives rise to a new way of thinking about the mind and its mechanisms, stressing the importance of the introjection processes, the ego structure and the integrated nature of the objects within the infant's mind. From this perspective, all psychic activity follows unconscious phantasies which establish a logical structure that organises and codifies experience and influences the internalisation of experience with external objects as internal objects. These constitute the foundation of psychic reality; interpretations of the external world will come from this internal source and the type of relationship that the ego will have with the external objects depends on it. External objects are considered mere conjectures cloaked by projections which are influenced by the way each subject deals with his anxieties which in turn determines his ability to perceive external objects as independent and his desire to gain knowledge about them.

Couple and family psychoanalysis inspired by Kleinian and post-Kleinians such as Dicks (1967), Pincus & Dare (1978), Ruszczynski (1993), Pick (1985), Scharff and Scharff (1987) and Scharff (1989, 1992) hold this view. As you will be able to read in Mary Morgan's approach to interpretation, the idea that new concepts needed to be created and others extended is present. The notions of shared unconscious phantasies (Fisher, 2009) and shared unconscious beliefs (Britton, 1998; Morgan 2010), defensive projective systems that are shared, unconscious complementariness (Dicks, 1967), the unconscious choice of partner, the couple's co-created shared inner world and its influence on the couple's shared everyday life and the projective gridlock (Morgan, 1995) or the claustrum type relationship (Meltzer 1992; Feldman 2014) – just to mention a few – can be addressed in the here and now of the session. How interpretation is addressed in clinical material is discussed in Chapter 2.

The work of Tavistock Relationships and the Tavistock Clinic is highly influential in this field and has provided a great deal of training among European psychoanalysts and psychotherapists interested in this clinical area and all around the world.

The notion of link is much used in this field of knowledge. It is highly polysemic, having different meanings according to the psychoanalytical context in which it is formulated. During the fifties and sixties, Bion's (1961, 1967, 1970) and Winnicott's theories (1951, 1953, 1960) addressed the need to explain how another mind played a role in the development of a new mind.

Several French psychoanalysts addressed diverse levels of interaction, trying to understand and describe the psychic reality of inter-subjective and trans-subjective links. Inter-subjectivity and all its levels of interaction are concepts developed by post-Freudian authors coming from non-psychoanalytical fields, but taken up by some psychoanalysts. The subject was a term used in other areas of knowledge, such as philosophy or linguistics. Jacques Lacan (1966) imported that notion into psychoanalysis from philosophy and linguistics.

Concepts such as the narcissistic contract (Aulagnier, 1975), unconscious alliances, prohibitions, common ideals, shared imaginary and symbolic representations come from these investigations. René Kaës is an outstanding figure in this field, together with some other French psychoanalysts. Kaës (1993,

2007, 2008, 2009) made an important contribution to the understanding of groups and inter-subjective links, opening the idea of a third topic in order to deal with the inter-subjective space between subjects in a clinical situation in which several subjects interact, not only how the inter-subjective space affects the internal world. Trans-generational links have been addressed by different authors (Faimberg, 2005; Aubertel, 1990, 2007).

Latin America contributed to the understanding of the link (el vínculo). The parents and the family were thought by Pichon Rivière (1980) and his disciples (Losso, 2009) as having a defining role in the individual psychic constitution. His concept of the spokesperson in the family as the least mentally disturbed and an informer of what was going on in the family group's dynamic was truly original. The Oedipus configuration was thought of as external to the individual subject. The family's structure began to be considered important in diagnosis, prognosis, treatment and thus prophylaxis. García Badaracco (2000, 2001, 2002) studied how a psychotic mind could be created within a family and that the non-resolution of the Oedipus Complex in one generation was repeated in the next. Ill members were thus considered emergents of a pathological family dynamic. Janine Puget and Isidoro Bernstein (1997; Berenstein, 2001a, 2001b, 2004, 2007) studied the inevitable suffering experienced by anyone involved when sharing a link.

The idea that subjects live in several worlds, not only the inner one with its representations but also an inter-subjective world and a socio-cultural world that determine social identifications and make us be subjects of our time, is an example of this.

All these different ways of thinking have influenced European clinical approaches in couple and family psychoanalysis in different countries.

Apart from the British and French groups, an important group of Italian psychoanalysts (Nicolò, 1992, 1996, 1997, 2000) have developed a particular approach to interpretation using British, French and Latin American theorists and blending their own theoretical ideas in a particular way that defines their clinical practice. Spanish approaches (Palacios & Monserrat, 2017) have been shaped by authors from Latin America as well as object relations theorists from the Tavistock, as well as French theorists. In this volume, the reader will be able to see how each of these groups work clinically and addresses the subject of interpretation.

On interpretation

Each psychoanalytical theory gives its own definition of what an interpretation is. Each theory and each author operate with their own ideas about cure and thus interpretation, about the relationship between analyst and analysand and their transference–countertransference. One of the difficulties for most psychoanalysts working with different types of settings to the individual one is that we are all originally trained as individual psychoanalysts with little personal experience in multi-personal settings which always activate unconscious conflicts derived from everyday aspects of our life connected with the family, the couple and the group life. These aspects cannot be completely addressed in individual personal analysis.

The concept of reality is a different one in this type of setting since the other is a real one, present in the room and not a product of the unconscious fantasy of one of the members. Here the interpretation will not have the aim to investigate the internal world of each of the subjects present in the room; the presence of the other members limits the expression of internal fantasies. From the link perspective the contents that could be conveyed by means of interpretations are the narcissistic contract, the pacts and alliances that are held unconsciously between the members of the group. These produce mental suffering, but simultaneously give stability to the members of the group.

We consider interpretation as an explanatory verbalisation that conveys information on the unconscious motivations of a patient and provides meanings to acts and thoughts and has to do with the type of unconscious agreement that analyst and patient have been able to establish. The analyst will be able to formulate his knowledge on the meanings he is able to understand about the unconscious of the patient. According to the type of training the analyst has had (theory of repression, the unconscious and his laws, psychic organisation, technical approach), the content and type of interpretation will vary substantially.

When making a link interpretation the analyst will focus on a certain sequence of what is expressed by the members of the group. The sequence chosen and the new way of looking at it will be conveyed according to the theoretical model of the analyst. Giving a new perspective and a new meaning to the group may also facilitate new associations by the members of this grouping. If interpretations provide new meanings to the link organisation a possibility for change for the group as a whole, and for each ego will be possible; new meanings may also derive from their mutual interaction.

The different ways of being within the link, unconscious alliances, pacts, identifications and kinship issues that are expressed in the exchanges of members of the group and how these interact at different times during the analysis, become part of what is interpreted. The group creates a space in which the members can think together and become observers of their own interactions.

Individual interpretations thus differ in an important way from those we use when trying to convey the meaning present in a link interaction (link interpretation) (Puget & Berenstein, 1997).

References

Aubertel, F. (1990). Les fonctions de l'idéologie familiale. *Dialogue, 108*: 72–87.

Aubertel, F. (2007). L'idéologie familiale. In: J.-G. Lemaire et al. *L'inconscient dans la famille*. Paris: Dunod.

Aulagnier, P. (1975). *La violencia de la interpretación* (p. 54). Buenos Aires: Amorrortu editores, 1977.

Berenstein, I. (2001a). *El sujeto y el Otro*. Buenos Aires: Paidós.

Berenstein, I. (2001b). *Clínica familiar psicoanalítica. Estructura y acontecimiento*. Buenos Aires: Paidós.

Berenstein, I. (2004). *Devenir otro con otro(s): ajenidad, presencia, interferencia*. Buenos Aires: Paidós.

Berenstein, I. (2007). *Del ser al hacer. Curso sobre vincularidad*. Buenos Aires: Paidós.

Bion, W. R. (1961). *Experiences in Groups and Other Papers*. London: Tavistock.

Bion,W. R. (1967). *Second Thoughts*. London: Heinemann.

Bion, W. R. (1970). *Attention and Interpretation*. London: Heinemann.

Britton, R. (1998). Belief and psychic reality. In: R. Britton, *Belief and Imagination: Explorations in Psychoanalysis* (pp. 8–18). London: Routledge.

Dicks, H. (1967). *Marital Tensions*. London: Routledge and Kegan Paul.

Faimberg, H. (2005). *The Telescoping of Generations: Listening to the Narcissistic Links between Generations*. London and New York: Routledge.

Feldman, T. (2014). From container to claustrum: Projective identification in couples. *Couple and Family Psychoanalysis*, *4*(2): 36–39.

Fisher, J. V. (2009). Macbeth in the consulting room: Proleptic imagination and the couple. *Fort Da*, *15*(2): 33–55. Reprinted (2017) in S. Nathans & M. Schaefer (Eds.), *Couples on the Couch: Psychoanalytic Couple therapy and the Tavistock Model*. London: Routledge.

García Badaracco, J. E. (2000). *El padecimiento humano y la cura psicoanalítica. La presencia de los otros en el sufrimiento psíquico*. Buenos Aires: Paidós.

García Badaracco, J. E. (2001). *Naturaleza de los problemas del psicoanálisis con los así llamados 'pacientes difíciles'*. Buenos Aires: Paidós.

García Badaracco, J. E. (2002). Comentario sobre el trabajo de Enrique Kaës R., (1989) Le pacte dénégatif dans les ensembles intersubjectifs. In: A. Missenard et al. *Le négatif. Figures et modalités*. Paris: Dunod.

Kaës, R. (1993). *El grupo y el sujeto del grupo*. Buenos Aires: Amorrortu editors, 1995.

Kaës, R. (2007). *Un singulier pluriel. La psychanalyse à l'épreuve du groupe*. Paris: Dunod.

Kaës, R. (2008). Pour une troisième topique de l'intersubjectivité et du sujet dans l'espace psychique commun et partagé. *Funzione Gamma, 21*. http://www.funzionegamma.edu

Kaës, R. (2009). *Les alliances inconscientes*. Paris: Dunod.

Lacan, J. (1966). *Écrits*. Paris: Les Editions du Seuil.

Losso, R. (2009). Presentation at International Psychoanalytic Congress, Chicago, IL.

Meltzer, D. (1992). *The Claustrum: An Investigation of Claustrophobic Phenomena*. Perthshire, Scotland: Clunie Press.

Morgan, M. (1995). The projective gridlock: A form of projective identification in couple relationships. In: S. Ruszczynski & J. V. Fisher (Eds.), *Intrusiveness and Intimacy in the Couple* (pp. 33–48). London: Karnac.

Morgan, M. (2010). Unconscious beliefs about being a couple. *Fort Da*, *16*(1): 36–55. Reprinted (2017) in S. Nathans & M. Schaefer (Eds.), *Couples on the Couch. Psychoanalytic Couple Therapy and the Tavistock Model*. London: Routledge.

Nicolò, A. M. (1992). Mondo interno e interazioni reali nella seduta familiare. Manuscrit présenté au congrès organisé à Buenos Aires par l'Associacion Psicoanalitica Argentina Tercerasjornadas de psicoanalisis de la familia y la pareja,

'La dimension familiar del psicoanalisis – Clinica psicoanalitica de la familia', 28–29 août 1992.
Nicolò, A. M. (1996). *(a cura di), Curare la relazione*. Milano: Angeli.
Nicolò, A. M. (1997). L'importanza diagnostica delle interazioni nella valutazione della famiglia e delle sue difese transpersonali. *Interazioni*, *10*(2): 53–66.
Nicolò, A. M. (2000). La memoria nella trasmissione generazionale della famiglia. *Psiche*, *2*: 111–122.
Palacios, E., & Monserrat, A. (2017). Contribution to the link perspective in interactions with families: theoretical and technical aspects and clinical applications. In: D. Scharff & E. Palacios (Eds.), *Couple and Family Psychoanalysis: A Global Perspective*. London: Karnac.
Pichon Rivière, E. (1980). *La teoría del Vínculo*. Buenos Aires: Paidós.
Pick, I. B. (1985). Working through in the countertransference. *International Journal of Psycho-Analysis*, *66*(2): 157–166.
Pincus, L., & Dare, C. (1978). *Secrets in the Family*. London: Faber & Faber.
Puget, J., & Berenstein, I. (1997). *Lo vincular teoría y clínica Psicoanalítica*. Buenos Aires: Paidós.
Ruszczynski, S. (1993). *Psychotherapy with Couples: Theory and Practice at the Tavistock Institute of Marital Studies*. London: Karnac.
Scharff, D. E. (1989). An object relations approach to sexuality in family life (pp. 399–417); Transference, countertransference and technique in object relations family therapy (pp. 421–445). In: J. S. Scharff (Ed.), *Foundations of Object Relations Family Therapy*. Northvale, NJ: Jason Aronson.
Scharff, D. E. (1992). *Refinding the Object and Reclaiming the Self*. Northvale, NJ: Jason Aronson.
Scharff, J. S., & Scharff, D. E. (1987). *Object Relations Family Therapy*. Northvale, NJ: Jason Aronson.
Winnicott, D. W. (1951). Transitional objects and transitional phenomena. In: *Through Paediatrics to Psycho-Analysis* (pp. 229–242). London: Hogarth Press.
Winnicott, D. W. (1953). Play and Reality. *International Journal of Psycho-Analysis*, *34*(2): 11–17.
Winnicott, D. W. (1960). Ego distortion in terms of true and false self. In: *The Maturational Processes and the Facilitating Environment* (pp. 140–152). London: Hogarth Press, 1965.

BRITISH PERSPECTIVE

Mary Morgan

Fundamental to interpretation in the British couple psychoanalytic tradition is enabling the couple to understand what they unconsciously create together. Difficulties in the couple's relating are thought about from the perspective of their intersecting internal worlds, what they bring from their past, what they newly create in the present and from their difficulties simply (or not so simply) in being a couple.

Psychoanalytic interpretation is embedded in conceptual frameworks and within the British psychoanalytic tradition this has developed and changed over time. Although the early work of clinicians used psychoanalytic concepts drawn from individual work, the new clinical situation of working with a "couple" analytically challenged previous analytic mindsets. Psychoanalytic concepts became extended and gradually new ones created to take account of what happened unconsciously between two. In what follows I identify some of the key analytic and couple analytic concepts that form the basis of interpretations within the British perspective.

Psychoanalytic concepts extended and newly created

Transference

Working with couples highlights that transference, as Freud pointed out, is ubiquitous. It does not only occur between patient and analyst but between the members of the couple. Interpreting the transference, wherever it is having a distorting effect on a "new" relationship that appears to the subject a version of an "old" relationship, is helpful. In a couple relationship that has become a "mutual transference relationship", it can be hard for either partner to relate more "realistically". Interpreting transference to the therapist, who attempts to be more of a neutral object, can inform an interpretation made to the couple on their transference dynamics.

Unconscious phantasy and shared unconscious phantasy

Unconscious phantasy can form the basis of an interpretation to either member of a couple. This is because of the way in which their unconscious phantasies colour their perception, especially of the other – partner or the analyst. Couples, however, also develop shared unconscious phantasies together as an outcome of their relating – particular ways they always see things, borne out of past interactions but now shaping and being shaped by present interactions. Fisher (2009) expressed the idea of "proleptic imagination" to describe the way that couples can get into a state of mind in which they are predicting the other's behaviour and relating to the other in this light. Britton (1998) described how certain unconscious phantasies do not develop in relation to external reality and become fixed in the unconscious as "beliefs". In a previous article I have suggested that couples develop unconscious beliefs about the *meaning* of being a couple (Morgan, 2010). Interpreting phantasy, shared phantasy and beliefs becomes progressively more difficult as we move from the spectrum of unconscious phantasy towards belief. Beliefs, which can unconsciously grip a couple, are often in the background of a session, not verbalised but felt and often only available for interpretation, when an elusive countertransference or subtle enactment is understood.

Projective identification and the couple projective system

Projective identification is a rich concept and seen as valuable in understanding a couple relationship. From early on in the work of Tavistock Relationships and the Tavistock Clinic, projective identification was seen as a developmental and defensive force in relationships. The idea that one might choose a partner who can represent some split off part of the self, and that gradually in the intimacy of a couple relationship these aspects can be reintegrated, has been an important way of understanding a couple's attraction, and is a fertile area for interpretation. So too is the defensive version of this in which one person is required to carry a "double dose" of an unwanted aspect of the other. In this way the couple form a defensive projective system that binds them together, but not necessarily happily. Dicks (1967) described it as:

> unconscious complementariness, a kind of division of function by which each partner supplied part of a set of qualities, the sum of which created a complete dyadic unit. This joint personality or integrate, enabled each of the dyad to rediscover lost aspects of their primary object relations, which they had split off or repressed and which they were, in their involvement with the spouse, re-experiencing by projective identification.
>
> (p. 69)

More recently interpretation of the projective system is focused not only on what is projected between the partners, but the nature of the projective system, how flexible, potentially containing and integrative or how defensive, rigid and narcissistic (Morgan, 2018).

Links between past and present

Understanding and interpreting links between the past and present is an important strand in psychoanalytic work. In British couple analytic work this helps to understand the unconscious choice of a partner and the attempt to repeat aspects of the past in the present relationship. Contemporary British psychoanalytic thought might think of a patient's history more in terms of their living inner world, one that is built up from past object relations but also changed by lived experience, including with the present partner. The couple's co-created shared inner world also itself influences the couple's relating. It is also important that interpretations that link the past connect with the lived experience of the here and now in the analytic session, otherwise the more specific, and therefore meaningful aspect of the link, may not be discovered.

Containment – the relationship as a psychological container

Interpretation is linked closely with containment (Bion, 1959, 1962) – the containment of anxiety – anxieties that the couple bring in the minute-to-minute process of the sessions, anxieties that might be part of a presenting problem and also anxieties about being a couple, something that has become harder than the couple imagined and has taken them by surprise. Colman (1993) described the way the relationship if functioning well can be a psychological container for the couple where the *relationship itself becomes* the container, the creative outcome of the couple's union, to which both partners can relate (p. 89). Those couples seeking help need the temporary container that the therapist provides.

Narcissistic relating and the otherness of the "other"

Since the 1990s there has been more of a focus on interpreting narcissistic difficulties. This includes both the ordinary difficulties in facing the otherness of the "other" and more pathological and fixed versions of this, as seen in a "projective gridlock" (Morgan, 1995) or in a claustrum type relationship (Meltzer, 1992; Feldman, 2014). This is challenging in terms of interpretation as the therapist can find it difficult to establish a separate space. Her "otherness", expressed in her own separate mind and the interpretation she makes, can be felt as a threat to the pathological system.

Creative couple relating

The opposite to the turning away from "otherness" is the capacity that the couple might find to engage with the otherness of the other and to create something valuable and new between them. This is part of the work of the couple psychoanalytic process and interpretation here may focus on the couple's difficulty in allowing the coming together of their two individual minds. This might also be represented in their sexual difficulties and the creation of alive intimacy. The therapist may note and interpret that the coming together of two minds is, for example, one incorporating the other, instead of allowing the mating of two separate and different minds, with the outcome yet unknown.

The process of interpretation

The careful monitoring of countertransference is considered an essential part of the psychoanalytic process and part of what informs interpretation. There have been some important papers in recent years within British psychoanalysis which have had an effect on all modes of psychoanalytic treatment. Brenman Pick's (1985) attention to "working through in the countertransference" argues that for interpretations to have emotional depth, the analyst needs to make emotional contact with the experience the patient projects into her and which is conveyed in the interpretation that is made. She notes "The contention that the analyst is not affected by these experiences is both false and would convey to the patient that his plight, pain and behaviour are emotionally ignored by the analyst" (Pick, 1985, p. 166).

Britton and Steiner's (1994) work on the "selected fact" in interpretation addresses the analyst's state of mind in interpretation. They suggest interpretation rests on a capacity for not knowing and allowing something to come together. As Bion (1967) observed:

> from the material the patient produces, there emerges, like the pattern from a kaleidoscope, a configuration which seems to belong not only to the situation unfolding, but to a number of others not previously seen to be connected and which it has not been designed to connect.
>
> (p. 127)

Following Bion, Britton and Steiner describe this process as "the emergence of a *selected fact*", which they see "as a creative integration of disparate facts into a meaningful pattern". In a couple interpretation, this process is complex and can be thought of as a "conjoint selected fact" as Pickering (2011) describes. "There is a selected fact which serves to sublate both selected facts, if not a series of selected facts. The word 'conjoint' refers to the *third* entity created by the combination of the two individual selected facts" (Pickering, 2011, pp. 59–60).

Without this negative capability and filled with collections of facts, thoughts, feelings and no sense of how they fit together, an alternative phenomenon can occur, which Britton and Steiner describe as an "overvalued idea". They suggest this can "be used by the analyst to give a sense of integration to otherwise disparate and confusing experiences" and "forced to fit a hypothesis or theory which the analyst needs for defensive purposes". This is part of the difficult work of analysis, whether with a couple or an individual.

For this reason, having made an interpretation, it is then important to see how it lands, how the couple respond to it, and also how the therapist feels about having made it. This is an integral part of the process as it helps the therapist assess whether the interpretation was valid.

Roth's creative article on different levels of transference interpretation is helpful in describing the process in an analytic session "mapping the landscape", where to locate the transference not only at what level but in what place (Roth, 2001). Interpretations can range from the patient's experience of external objects, internal objects and the experience of what is happening at that moment in a session in relation to the analyst as an object and to the analyst's internal experience. In this topographical exploration – roaming freely over the psychic landscape, there is a structural exploration as we move from more surface to depth, more conscious to unconscious. In couple analysis there is a process of interpreting different relationships in the room: each partner's internal world, their shared internal world, the couple's relationship with each other and their relationship separately and together to the analyst.

Both Steiner and Roth address the types and levels of interpretation which rely on how the patient is functioning psychologically and where the material can be most usefully taken up. Interpretations have to be modulated depending not only what the analyst might understand and have worked through in herself, but crucially on gauging the patient's capacity and receptiveness. Steiner (1993) suggests that sometimes patients may not be able to take a classical patient-centred interpretation, and the focus might have to be an analyst-centred interpretation, which might give the patient a sense of being understood, if not yet much understanding of himself (Steiner, 1993). In couple analytic work one might think about when a couple are able to move into a state of mind in which they can be receptive to a "couple interpretation", what they are creating together, rather than how they are experiencing the other. As the work develops it becomes possible to make more couple interpretations which are important in helping the couple develop a couple state of mind.

The articles by Pick (1985), Britton and Steiner (1994) and Roth (2001) are examples of developments in British psychoanalysis which give a greater emphasis on working in the here and now of the session, monitoring the transference and countertransference, thinking not only about what interpretation to make, but where to make it (in which relationship) and when to make it, considering what the patient or couple is able to take in.

Finally, it is important in any discussion of interpretation to acknowledge that this is not the only therapeutic action. The couple analytic setting and the analyst's couple state of mind not only support the couple analyst in making an interpretation but can be thought of as other forms of therapeutic action in themselves. The analyst making couple interpretations brings change not only through what is said, but by offering another way of thinking and perspective that can be internalised by the couple into their relationship.

References

Bion, W. R. (1959). Attacks on linking. *International Journal of Psycho-Analysis*, *40*: 308–315.

Bion, W. R. (1962). The psycho-analytic study of thinking. *International Journal of Psycho-Analysis*, *43*: 306–310.

Bion, W. R. (1967). *Second Thoughts*. London: Heinemann.

Britton, R. (1998). Belief and psychic reality. In: R. Britton, *Belief and Imagination: Explorations in Psychoanalysis* (pp. 8–18). London: Routledge.

Britton, R., & Steiner, J. (1994). Interpretation: Selected fact or overvalued idea? *International Journal of Psycho-Analysis*, *75*(5–6): 1069–1078.

Colman, W. (1993). Marriage as a psychological container. In: S. Ruszczynski (Ed.), *Psychotherapy with Couples: Theory and Practice at the Tavistock Institute* (pp. 70–96). London: Karnac.

Dicks, H. V. (1967). *Marital Tensions. Clinical Studies towards a Psychological Theory of Interaction*. London: Karnac (reprinted 1993).

Feldman, T. (2014). From container to claustrum: Projective identification in couples. *Couple and Family Psychoanalysis*, *4*(2): 136–154.

Fisher, J. V. (2009). Macbeth in the consulting room: Proleptic imagination and the couple. *Fort Da*, *15*(2): 33–55. Reprinted (2017) in S. Nathans & M. Schaefer (Eds.) *Couples on the Couch: Psychoanalytic Couple therapy and the Tavistock Model*. London & New York: Routledge.

Meltzer, D. (1992). *The Claustrum: An Investigation of Claustrophobic Phenomena*. Perthshire, Scotland: Clunie Press.

Morgan, M. (1995). The projective gridlock: A form of projective identification in couple relationships. In: S. Ruszczynski & J. V. Fisher (Eds.), *Intrusiveness and Intimacy in the Couple* (pp. 33–48). London: Karnac.

Morgan, M. (2010). Unconscious beliefs about being a couple. *Fort Da*, *16*(1): 36–55. Reprinted (2017) in S. Nathans & M. Schaefer (Eds.), *Couples on the Couch. Psychoanalytic Couple Therapy and the Tavistock Model*. London & New York: Routledge.

Morgan, M. (2018). *A Couple State of Mind: Psychoanalysis of Couples and the Tavistock Relationships Model*. London & New York: Routledge.

Pick, I. B. (1985). Working through in the countertransference. *International Journal of Psycho-Analysis*, 66(2): 157–166.

Pickering, J. (2011). Bion and the couple. *Couple and Family Psychoanalysis*, *1*(1): 49–68.

Roth, P. (2001). Mapping the landscape: Levels of transference interpretation. *International Journal of Psycho-Analysis*, *82*(3): 533–543.

Steiner, J. (1993). Problems in psychoanalytic technique: Patient-centred and analyst-centred interpretations. In: J. Steiner, *Psychic Retreats: Pathological Organisations in Psychotic, Neurotic and Borderline Patients* (pp. 131–146). London: Routledge.

NORTH AMERICAN PERSPECTIVE

David E. Scharff and Jill Savege Scharff

Interpretation is the workhorse of the psychoanalytic couple and family therapy approach used in the English-speaking countries. The concepts underlying interpretation come from psychoanalysis and group theory, but we avoid theoretical terms, even if we find them useful with professionals when teaching technique. Instead we prefer everyday, simple, short, direct language for therapy, close to the family's way of talking and symbolising their experience. If the family has young children our way of communicating with them will include play. In our view an interpretation is not a single, oracular pronouncement imposed on the family. Interpretation is multi-faceted and operates at various levels. It is a process of sharing understanding with the family, not of imposing conjecture. Rather it develops in concert with the family working toward understanding over time.

Early interpretive comments of fear of exposure simply open a safe psychological space for the couple or family to tell us more about themselves. As they talk they develop more empathy for one another. We intervene to ask for clarity. We share our observations. We note their, and our, responses and comment on those. Some interpretations are more effectively conveyed not in words, but in the therapist's behaviour that interrupts a pattern, for instance in his calmness in the face of chaos, or in setting a boundary. An action mode of intervention, what we call a *behavioural interpretation*, is at times more effective than words.

Working as a group with our outside perspective, we recognise ingrained patterns that have limited the couple or family's capacity to achieve intimacy and growth. Then we can ask ourselves why they are necessary, and move on to interpret the reasons for these fixed patterns. At the same time, interpretation expresses the *meta-communication* from us as therapists, namely that we are there for them as a family and trying to understand their issues, their patterns, their history and their goals for growth. We offer a container for their experience. There is no reason to think that what we say has to be right all the time. It is part of the process that family members should be able to set us straight, and that we should work with their modifications of what we have to say and with their overt disagreement among themselves and with us.

Interpretation is part and parcel of joining with the family in the process of understanding. In our broad use of the term, interpretation covers a range of activities, from marking an affect, behaviour or pattern, finding the unconscious link between disparate phenomena, clarifying ambiguity and misunderstanding, peeling away the defence against revealing family secrets and explaining the underlying anxiety, all of which have led to a pattern becoming set in the first place. In this way interpretation is part of *a spiral process* of observing repetitive patterns and going deeper and deeper into the cycles of defence and acknowledgement of anxiety in order to interrupt the patterns by our encounters and interventions with the family. Which of these modes of interpretive intervention will be most helpful in any given moment is a matter of clinical intuition. We are drawn to intervene at *a point of urgency* that shows us when to speak and what to focus on. Multiple currents of experience past, present and future, out there in the real world and in here in the therapy session, come together into what we have called a *core affective moment*. When memory, awareness, and capacity to tolerate strong feeling have ripened in this moment, we can reach for greater understanding than had been possible until then.

A moment like this occurred when David Scharff was interviewing a family that was concerned about an 18-year-old girl who was depressed and perfectionistic, always crying, expecting too much of herself, and complaining about the lack of understanding by the men in her family. The family consisted of her mother and father, her elder sister and brother-in-law, along with their 14-month-old baby. The mother and elder sister hovered over this 18-year-old girl, caressing her, trying to soothe her incessant tears, while her father and brother-in-law sat by silently looking uncomfortable. The 14-month-old baby stole the show, making everybody laugh. The 18-year-old girl felt that she was always compared to her more excellent older sister, who not only was good in school but was now married, with a baby, whereas the 18-year-old girl had nothing to show for herself and felt weak and imperfect. David turned to her assertively on behalf of the men, and said, "Toni, I think you're actually not the weakest and most incompetent member of the family, but the strongest. You have everybody taking care of you as though you were a little baby, even younger than your nephew. They're patting you on the shoulder and your sister's even stroking your chest. Meanwhile your brother-in-law and father are sitting hopelessly by, accused of not understanding how sad you are and how much care you need from them. But through all of this you are really in charge of the family." At this, the sister and brother-in-law began to nod vigorously and smile. Then the mother said, "Yes, that's true. We don't know what to do for her, and she has us in the palm of her hand."

In this episode, David interpreted the moment, interrupting a family pattern that had been going on for two years, a pattern in which this girl accused her father of not understanding her and her needs, while commandeering her mother and sister to take care of her in an anxiously attentive manner. He said that she was proving everybody incompetent because they couldn't cure her depression. At this intervention, everybody sat up and took notice. The baby began to throw toys away for others to retrieve, as if to distract us from what might feel like an assault on his teenage aunt and also to break up the clinging mother–girl couple at the centre of the family's attention until then. The intervention opened the way for a more empathic exploration of the pattern of endless depression that had pulled the family into a sinkhole, capturing the undying attention of Toni's mother and sister and disabling the two men.

Toni moved away from tears to speech. She became able to express anger, and seemed much less depressed. Her father was able to acknowledge trauma in his early life that left his family scared and sad. Toni, uncoupled from her mother, and relieved of pent-up anger at her father, began to flirt with him as repressed Oedipal longings began to emerge.

We cite this example to show that an interpretation in the moment of an observable dynamic among family members and its emotional impact on the therapist who could speak to it led to an interruption of that repetitive pattern in the family. Of course, this single interpretation would not change things by itself, but it did serve to change the pattern in the room that day. It led the family to talk more freely and understand more of the roots of this behaviour, both in the present family configuration and in traumatic, ancient family history that could now be talked about and integrated into current understanding.

Toni had been unable to grow into being a sturdy adolescent who could steer her own way into her future as a young adult. Instead she had been held back, and had held her family back, by her demand for babying because she felt so incompetent and by the family's need to project incompetence into her. The therapist pointed out that she had plenty of competence, if it were not so hobbled by the collusion between her family and her to baby her. Now even in this interpretation, the spoken words were not really the most effective part. The intervention met its mark because of the sincerity of the affective tone that David brought to it, not produced by a contrived strategy, but prompted by his emotional reaction to the destructiveness of this girl's stubborn, repetitive clinging to her depressed mood while accusing the men like him, for not understanding. It was the whole situation that made him feel anger (his own and that projected into him by the girl) that lent therapeutic energy and force to his remarks. We tend to privilege verbal intervention in therapy, but the most successful interventions are those conveyed both verbally and affectively.

It takes a while before we can safely speak to defensive behaviours of couples and families without their feeling misunderstood. If we can offer a reason for the way they operate, they will find our interpretation easier to accept. To find the reasons, we look at the way they operate as they relate to us at progressively deeper levels of examination – at 1) the way they repeatedly behave; 2) the way they avoid behaving as they would if they were to face their hidden fears; and 3) at the deepest level, totally falling apart. We identify these three parts of the group transference, which are parcelled out among group members, and then we have to reassemble them in order to understand the complete group transference. Putting it all together like that can only happen after many prior partial comments as we ask the family to work with us toward understanding.

Our intention is to build a better holding environment for the management of anxiety, loss, and trauma than the couple or family has been able to do so far. We aim to help them contain unmanageable pain by putting it into words and developing a way of thinking about experience together. We speak to the direct problem of the moment to one person, to the relationship between the couple, to the family as a whole, to the family in its socio-cultural context and in relation to earlier generations. We deal with the way members become defensive and angry and show how this connects to shared anxieties about being abandoned, damaged, or unloved. We note the way they become controlling when they are being misused or feeling unloved and we connect that to their personal and family group histories. In short, we interpret the unconscious couple or family-wide forces that cause them to relate to one another as though they were yesterday's objects instead of today's real family members. All of these activities contribute to the interpretive mode of engaging the family in establishing a better shared holding capacity as we work toward deeper group-wide understanding and insight, which will offer relief to symptomatic individuals and strengthen the family's capacity to develop and implement goals.

SOUTH AMERICAN PERSPECTIVE

Janine Puget

New everyday problems and tools

It is necessary to become aware of how technology creates new problems and in some way emphasises the importance of learning how to communicate with our patients, and investigate the tools we need to discover concerning "links". Something happened in the world which obliges us to be able to accept that some walls of our theoretical and clinical corpora have fallen down but have not disappeared; but just do not occupy the same important position.

Fallen walls: encounter as a whole, encounter and multiplicity

Fallen walls have to do with all those things which avoid the radical otherness and alienness of the other/s, as well as the unpredictability of any encounter. They concern, for example, transference and countertransference, identificatory processes in their various forms, the recalling of past history, the prediction. Introducing the specific meaning of links leads to highlighting the importance of *Radical Difference*, in capital letters, as a necessary concept that is related to multiplicity. Dealing with what happens when two or more subjects establish a link concerns the work that emerges from the space in between which is this unavoidable empty space that increasingly separates the members of any link. This depends on the effect of a presence creating a new concept called "presentation", which differs from what belongs to the order of what we name "representation".

The specific meaning of Difference

Radical Difference is the basis of what I call a link. Consequently, we discover what members of links do to avoid the work of recognising the otherness and alienness of the other, and the effect of the increasing separation of each member. Any hypothesis which reduces the otherness to similarity or complementarity will avoid the linkage work based on the effect of the presence of the other, since the presence of the other is always an excess which disturbs the organisation of the inner world of each one. Of course, couple and family psychoanalysis gives us the opportunity to highlight this struggle between the same and the always alien.

What I have learned working with couples and families

Little by little I became aware that even in individual psychoanalysis the work that emerges from the *Radical Difference* must be taken into account as a constitutive part of the relationship between analyst and patient that doesn't concern only transference and countertransference. The psychoanalyst will have to deal with two overlapping logics, one of the inner world and one of the linkage. In one of them crude otherness can be avoided and in the other it's impossible. To work with the complexity of links as it happens with family and couple psychoanalysis has to do with the difficulty to accept the unavoidable otherness and alienness of each one. This is the richness of the link; it also requires that they accept that the other will never be a complementary part of oneself, nor will it be a similar part. The majority of conflicts have to do with that kind of suffering and the major complaints, and sometimes violence, emerging from this, that is, for example, a need to accuse the others whoever they are, because they don't fulfil the necessity of the subject. In the family structure, it is very difficult to accept that the link is not only based on complementary function but should also be based on the necessity to recognise that being together requires a permanent work that awakens curiosity and accepts the unpredictability of each encounter. So, the main suffering is "why did he/she not tell me? Why does he/she never do what I expect? Why is it impossible to go back to the first love? Why . . ." and so on. Little by little the members of a couple or family have to accept the disappointment and the discovering of belonging to a space created by them, but which doesn't respond exclusively to the rules of what happens in a structural system. They have to move along without the support of identificatory processes and complementary functions. They also have to discover that they never know the other forever. Knowing is a continuous discovering. "He or she was so kind when we first met . . .! When our first baby was born it was such a delightful experience and now it's such a disappointment! Our family life is so complicated" and so on . . .! "Our sexual life is so complicated that it tends to disappear." "I feel alone when we are together! That is worse than being alone!" "We have no time to talk." "The other day we went to a tearoom to talk and we realised that we had forgotten to do it."

Interpretation and intervention

Undoubtedly, to be alone or to create a link awakens different feelings. Couples and families give rise to very complex situations in which unpredictability is a necessary condition. By analysing couples and families we become aware that the emphasis must be placed on what they do together to create a dynamic relationship. Listening to the other/s is always surprising. In consequence, we'll have to look for what they are able to do together as well as for the effort they do to look for single definitions, placing the other/s in a complementary position or similarities instead of discovering what stimulates curiosity and, therefore, the desire to meet.

I hypothesise that we need to find a new sense to what is happening and here we have all kinds of interpretations depending on the frame of reference of each psychoanalyst. We also have to be able to formulate interventions which have the purpose of giving room to think together, that is, with patients. On some occasions patients could tell us, "That is not what I think or what we are talking about and I will object to that of course; this is how I listen to what you say."

My purpose is to lead families and couples to become aware that it's impossible to avoid conflicts, but it's possible to become friends with them. However, the patient has to awaken what should sustain a link, that is Love, and what love means. My work consists of helping couples, families and individuals to become friends with conflict . . . and in the majority of cases I observed that this is not what happens. All that surprises is quoted as a disturbance, and on the other hand, if we cannot accept the alienness of the other's life, loses part of its vitality.

AUSTRALASIAN PERSPECTIVE

Timothy Keogh

Interpretation in couples and family psychoanalysis in Australasia has been linked to the developments in the broader practice of psychoanalysis in Britain and Europe, with the establishment of the Australian Society and psychoanalytic psychotherapy in New Zealand being supported, especially by analysts who arrived from central Europe at the time of World War II (Keogh & Gregory-Roberts, 2017). Consequently, it was largely influenced by the developments that followed from Freud's initial articulation of the Topographical and Structural Models and his later Metapsychology, which included a prescient view of an internal world that was to later spawn Object Relations Theory (Freud, 1900, 1923). As such, the Australasian approach to psychoanalysis was influenced by developments in thinking about the nature of the psychoanalytic relationship based on a one-person psychology involving a neutral analyst towards whom the patient was seen to develop a transference, which then became the focus of interpretative work.

Countertransference and inter-subjectivity

The subsequent development of ideas by theorists, especially Heimann (1950) and outside of Britain by Racker (1968), brought into focus the notion of the analyst's countertransference to the patient. This development in thinking also brought into the foreground the idea that there may be something transformative about the relationship between the patient and the analyst that involved the person of the analyst, in bringing about change in the analysand. The concept of countertransference, the importance of which was not embraced by all analysts at the time, progressed the idea of psychoanalysis as involving an inter-subjective dimension which could inform technique, including interpretation. The ideas of Bion developed this thinking even further as his theory highlighted the importance of the analyst as a mind, playing a role in developing the mind of the other, particularly through the capacity for reverie and containment.

Specific influences on the practice of couple and family psychoanalysis

The development of specifical couple and family psychoanalysis in Australasia was very influenced by such developments in thinking. A particular influence on its development was through its connection to theoretical developments emanating from the theory and practice amongst psychoanalytic colleagues at the Tavistock Clinic. Against the backdrop of the broader developments in psychoanalysis, Australian analysts and psychoanalytic psychotherapists who worked with couples and families were originally strongly influenced by the ideas of theorists such as Dicks (1967), Byng-Hall (1985) and Box (1998). Australian analysts were influenced by Dicks's notion of a conjoint marital personality, that is, the idea that the couple relationship represented an intersection of two internal worlds or sets of self-object relationships. In turn this approach also privileged the concept of projective identification as a means of understanding how split-off parts of the self that could not be integrated were lodged in the other partner or family members. With family work this also meant understanding that children's play was seen as part of the latent unconscious communication of the family. This approach meant that children who were presented with pathology could be seen as expressing a problem in the family or a "symptom bearer". This was initially seen as something of a radical idea when it was first introduced into clinical practice in Australia by Dr Charles Enfield (who had himself trained at the Tavistock Clinic), who had come to Australia at the suggestion of John Bowlby (Enfield, personal communication).

Approaches to interpretation

The approach to interpretation with couples and families, following developments in individual psychoanalysis, also later included a focus on the analyst's countertransference. This brought with it an emphasis on interpreting in the "here and now" of the session. In more recent decades Scharff and Scharff's development of the dyadic version of Fairbairn's Endopsychic Model was also embraced and provided a helpful way to think about splitting and projection and how these might be interpreted in the couple context. Another helpful concept that has taken root in the Australasian context is the notion of the couple state of mind introduced by Morgan (2018). This enabled an important perspective of seeing the couple as the patient and the value of couple interpretations. The evolving view of couple and family psychoanalysis that these ideas have helped to shape thus facilitated a view of interpretations that could take into account the multiple transferences and countertransferences.

The last decade was a particularly important period in the history of couple and family psychoanalysis in Australasia, especially in terms of changes in thinking about interpretation with the increasing focus on inter-subjectivity that has been spawned by the sharing of cultural perspectives on interpretation in couple and family psychoanalysis. This has been facilitated by the formation of a number of associations and committees devoted to the promotion of psychoanalytically-based couple and family work. Amongst these the formation of the section of Couple and Family Psychoanalytic Psychotherapy of the European Psychoanalytic Psychotherapy Federation, The International Association of Couple and Family Psychoanalysis (IACFP) and The International Psychoanalytical Association's Committee on Couple and Psychoanalysis (COFAP) have been the most significant. These organisations have facilitated a sharing of different theoretical paradigms, especially "link theory", which has significantly enriched thinking about the approach to interpretation.

These influences have not only strongly shaped thinking about interpretation in Australasia, but are now also influencing the Asian region with Australian analysts increasingly sharing their ideas with the so-called New Groups in Asia, such as China, Taiwan, South Korea and India, along with more established societies such as the Japanese Society. This sharing of ideas about couple and family psychoanalysis, which includes the approach to interpretation, has been facilitated by the IPA's Asian conferences (Taipei, 2016 and Tokyo, 2018), with a further conference planned in 2020 in Sydney.

The sharing of theoretical and clinical perspectives has also encouraged the development of concepts from within this region, which have a direct bearing on interpretation. These have included Pickering's (2008) concept of the conjoint selected fact and reflective and couple mutative interpretation (Keogh & Gregory-Roberts, 2017) and the concept of developmental anxieties in couples and families (Keogh & Enfield, 2013; Jools, Berg & Byrne, 2018; Keogh & Gregory-Roberts, 2018).

All of these developments have stimulated the development of a very distinctive and contemporary approach to interpretation in couple and family psychoanalysis in this region.

References

Box, S. (1998). Group processes in family therapy: A psychodynamic approach. *Journal of Family Therapy*, *20*: 123–132.

Byng-Hall, J. (1985). The Family Script: A useful bridge between theory and practice. *Journal of Family Therapy*, 7: 301–305.

Dicks, H. V. (1967). *Marital Tensions. Clinical Studies towards a Psychological Theory of Interaction*. London: Karnac (reprinted 1993).

Freud, S. (1900). The Interpretation of Dreams. *S.E.*, *4–5*. London: Hogarth Press.

Freud, S. (1923). The Ego and the Id. *S.E.*, *19*: 1–66. London: Hogarth Press.

Jools, P., Berg, J., & Byrne, N. (2018). *Working with Developmental Anxieties in Couple and Family Psychotherapy: The Family Within*. London: Routledge.

Keogh, T., & Enfield, S. (2013). From regression to recovery: Tracking developmental anxieties in couple therapy. *Couple and Family Psychoanalysis*, *3*: 28–46.

Keogh, T., & Gregory-Roberts, C. (2017). The role of interpretation in the assessment phase of couple psychoanalysis. *Couple and Family Psychoanalysis*, 7(2): 168–180.

Keogh, T., & Gregory-Roberts, C. (2018). *Psychoanalytic Approaches to Loss: Mourning, Melancholia and Couples*. London: Routledge.

Heimann, P. (1950). On counter-transference. *International Journal of Psychoanalysis*, *31*: 81–84.

Morgan, M. (2018). *A Couple State of Mind: Psychoanalysis of Couples and the Tavistock Relationships Model*. London & New York: Routledge.

Pickering, J. (2008). Who's afraid of the Wolffe couple: The interlocking traumatic scene. *Journal of Analytical Psychology*, *51*(2): 251–270.

Racker, H. (1968). *Transference and Counter-transference*. London: Hogarth Press.

Part II

Interpretation in couple psychoanalysis

Chapter 2

Complex and creative

The field of couple interpretation[1]

Mary Morgan

Introduction

The field of couple interpretation is not only complex, but also potentially creative. I use the word "field" to evoke the idea of a range of different but intersecting, interrelating relationships and unconscious dynamics that can be understood and interpreted within the couple therapy setting. Beginning with some framing comments about the nature of interpretation as I conceive of it, I will then describe what I think constitutes a "couple interpretation" and then outline a range of interpretations used in analytic work with couples. As interpretation is a far from perfect process, I will also suggest some of the things that can easily go wrong with interpretations.

The nature of interpretation

Interpretation is a specific form of psychoanalytic communication to the couple that shows them what the therapist might understand about the way they relate and what is happening in their relationship. The interpretations address various aspects of the couple's conscious and unconscious relationship, for example, their projective system, transference relationship, shared phantasy, conflicts, anxieties, defences and beliefs. Particular attention is given to what the couple creates together as a consequence of their specific coupling.

Psychoanalytic interpretation attempts to make conscious aspects of the couple relationship that are unconscious or partially so; they are not final statements, but part of the developing understanding between the couple and therapist. The therapist, in different ways, puts into words aspects of, and dynamics in, the psychic life of the couple, so that there is the possibility that these can be thought about. This is a way for the couple to come to "know" their relationship, especially aspects of it of which they have been unaware. With thinking comes the possibility of understanding, rather than enactment, working through and a different perspective.

Psychoanalytic interpretation can only be made within the context of "the analytic setting". The therapist takes care of the setting and "provides a 'couple analytic space'" in which she can be attuned to, think about, and analyse the couple's relationship. The setting also supports the therapist in having a state of mind which is receptive to the couple's unconscious, giving close attention to what they bring, their passing remarks, the affective tone of what is said, what is not being said or understood, the kind of unconscious pressure the partners exert on each other, and on the therapist. The couple analytic space, encompassing continuity and boundedness, also supports the couple in being able to be receptive to the therapist, even though this might be difficult and not always possible.

Giving an interpretation is part of a process and takes place alongside other non-interpretive activities, all of which aim towards understanding. To make an interpretation, firstly something has to come together in the therapist's mind, perhaps from several sources, for example, countertransference, observation of the couple, a small enactment, or an image the couple brings that is saturated with symbolic meaning. Interpretation rests on a capacity for not knowing and allowing something to come together. As Bion (1967) observes:

> from the material the patient produces, there emerges, like the pattern from a kaleidoscope, a configuration which seems to belong not only to the situation unfolding, but to a number of others not previously seen to be connected and which it has not been designed to connect.
>
> (p. 127)

Following Bion, Britton and Steiner (1994) describe this process as "the emergence of a selected fact", which they see "as a creative integration of disparate facts into a meaningful pattern". In a couple interpretation, this process is complex and can be thought of as a "conjoint selected fact" as Pickering (2011) describes, "There is a selected fact which serves to sublate both selected facts, if not a series of selected facts. The word 'conjoint' refers to the third thing created by the combination of the two individual selected facts" (pp. 59–60).

Maintaining a state of mind in which to wait for a selected fact to emerge can be difficult and sometimes not possible as the couple recruit the therapist to intervene in various ways. Some couples, for example, can contribute to the development of an empty or stuck feeling and the therapist finds it hard to think of anything to say. Even when it is not possible to interpret, the therapist internally processes the material both consciously and unconsciously. The selected fact might then arise later when the couple use a particular word or expression, or describe a particular event, or avoid something or repeat a particular argument and so on. We know that not all interpretations are correct, but even a wrong interpretation can help if the couple are in a reflective state of mind. Interpretation, as Winnicott pointed out, shows the limits of the therapist's understanding, what the therapist does understand, but also what she does not yet understand (Winnicott, 1969, p. 711).

What is a couple interpretation?

Whilst one could say that in couple therapy all interpretations are "couple interpretations", I think of a "couple interpretation" as something specific. The interpretation is made from a "third position" about the relationship and therefore offers a perspective that is not about who is doing what to whom, but what they are unconsciously creating *together*. If effective, it should, at least for a moment, bring an alternative state of mind from that of blame and accusation, and offer the couple a different way of seeing things. Couple interpretations aim to help the couple find a place, a third position, from which they can see themselves and what they are creating or recreating between them. Many such interpretations are made over the course of the therapy and if the couple can receive them, they develop an interest in their relationship and what they create positively and negatively together, rather than maintain a focus on the other partner who is seen to be at fault. This is in contrast to the lived experience in their relationship in which they might feel blamed by the other or blaming of the other. They often expect that a version of this will take place with the therapist, who will support their view or that of their partner's. It can be met with relief by the couple when the therapist takes a third position and provides a way of thinking about what is being created between them in their relationship.

Although a couple interpretation can come as a relief, it can also be difficult for the couple to receive. The requirement to make a shift in thinking from the belief that the partner is responsible for their difficulties to the idea that they are both responsible and actively part of creating something together might be strongly resisted. Instead, they may need to continue to blame the other. If there is too much resistance, the therapist may then decide not to make such interpretations for the time being, but equally might make the judgement that the interpretation is still worth making, as although its content is not accepted, it introduces the different state of mind of the therapist, a different perspective and potentially more psychic space.

A couple interpretation: Ann and Bill

Ann, the wife in a couple, is talking about sex and the way she feels her cues about wanting sex are not responded to by her husband. Bill, the husband, in his defence then cites a few recent occasions when he has made quite a direct sexual advance to his wife and she ignored it. The wife is dumbfounded and says she cannot remember any of these occasions. There is blame and recrimination, rejection and hurt. The therapist is addressing this and perhaps helping them think about how they might communicate their wish for sex more openly, more directly. However, the complaints are repeated in the next few sessions and this time the therapist is more aware that she is being recruited by the couple to mediate, leaving her feeling that her efforts are rather fruitless. At some point she is able to find a third position, her couple state of mind, in which she can think about what is happening in the "relationship". In this case, the couple are unconsciously creating a dynamic between themselves in which they can be certain that there will be no sex. This would be the basis of the couple interpretation and by now the therapist might also have some sense of what anxieties lie behind this "no sex defence", which then might also be part of the interpretation, or be part of a later interpretation if the couple are able to connect with the idea that this is something they are creating together.

Couple interpretations are most important because they introduce a different state of mind, both the therapist's and as a possibility for the couple, which creates more psychic space. They introduce a couple state of mind that, over time, can be introjected by the couple into their relationship. So, it is not just the content of the interpretation, but also the offering of the couple state of mind in itself. Bion (1967), in his theory of containment, suggests, along with the mother processing "beta elements" through her alpha function (i.e., her ability to process emotion through thinking) and gradually transforming these un-metabolised beta elements into alpha elements that can be thought about, that over time the mother's capacity to do this, her alpha function, is introjected too. This helps the infant build up the capacity to process his own beta elements. The introjection by the couple of the therapist's "couple state of mind" is similar to this process in the couple, as it provides the couple with the capacity to think about the relationship, rather than deal with psychic pain or conflict by evacuation into, or acting out with, the partner.

Now I am going to describe some other kinds of interpretations in the field of couple analysis, showing the way they involve the therapist, either partner, and the couple.

Interpretations involving the therapist, either partner, and the couple

A fundamental difference between couple and individual therapy is that no interpretation is made to one partner alone because it is made in the presence of the other partner. If the other partner is temporarily not present for a session, the therapist is careful not to make an interpretation that she could not make again when both partners are present.

When making an interpretation that might temporarily focus on one partner or the other, the therapist is still thinking about this in relation to the couple, even though unable to formulate, or choosing not to make a couple interpretation at this point. If the couple has enough of an experience of the therapist doing this, they can build trust in the therapist's "couple state of mind" (Morgan, 2001), and can tolerate the focus on one of them. If there is not enough of a sense of "couple state of mind", such interpretations can be experienced as a "ganging up" on the partner who is in focus and the therapist needs to intervene to re-establish the couple focus. However, the fact that there are at least three in couple therapy, while having its challenges, is also something that makes the work creative in a different way to individual therapy or analysis. This triangular dynamic in which one of the partners is temporarily an observer of the partner/therapist couple increases psychic space, as that partner is able to take a third position on the dynamic in his or her own relationship (Balfour, 2016). I will describe some different uses of the transference in the triangular setting of couple therapy.

An observing partner taking a third position on the relationship: Carly and James

James, who despite having a promising future career as an academic, had very little sense of self. He had had a breakdown when, as an undergraduate, he had struggled in relationships, though had succeeded academically. He was in a relationship with Carly, who related to him very narcissistically. She told him what he thought and felt and when he did attempt to express a different thought, she told him he was lying. The couple were in their twenties, had only been together for a year and were unmarried. Despite an intense initial attraction, during which James timidly wooed Carly while both on an under-30s Club holiday in Ibiza, the relationship had since become very abusive. The couple could only be calm together when they could get themselves into a place where there were no differences. Carly could not tolerate me having any alternate perspective on things to hers, and I felt it was only when James could witness her attempt to verbally obliterate me, including my interpretation of how anxious my possibly different view made Carly feel, that he could take any kind of third position on his own relationship. The couple only came to therapy for a few months and then broke it off. I did not feel I had been able to help them with their difficulties in being psychically more separate. However, a few weeks later, James came to see me on his own and told me that following an argument in which Carly had tried to bar him from leaving their flat, he had left her. He felt that it had only been by being in the couple therapy sessions that he could "see" his relationship and realise how destructive it was for him. He was describing that with me in the room interacting with Carly he could, from a third position, see himself in the relationship with Carly. Prior to this, he was simply "in" the relationship with Carly, confused about what was he and what was she and unable to get hold of his own mind. Following this meeting I felt very concerned about Carly and contacted her to see if she would like another appointment. She accepted, but then cancelled at the last moment and did not rearrange.

Using the transference and countertransference between one partner and the therapist to understand the dynamic between the couple: Donna and Johnny

Six weeks into the therapy Donna started the session expressing anger towards the therapist who she felt had focused almost exclusively on Johnny in the previous session. She even thought that the therapist might be blaming her for Johnny's problems. The therapist responded defensively, saying she wasn't blaming Donna for Johnny's problems and acknowledged that there had been more of a focus on Johnny the previous week. However, as the session continued, the therapist noticed that each time she tried to make contact with Donna's distress she was rebuffed. When Johnny tried to talk about something that was worrying him, Donna cut across him and changed the subject. The therapist had an experience of Donna feeling angry and let down by her, but also an experience of being continuously rebuffed by Donna.

Observing the couple, she noticed that Donna couldn't bear the attention that Johnny received. It was as if there would be a repeat of the experience of the previous week, which was very painful for her. In this part of the session, the therapist was mainly focused on what was going on between Donna and herself, especially Donna's wish for her attention and the way it was rejected. She then started to think about this in relation to the couple. She asked herself, does Donna's experience of her in their relationship throw any light on a dynamic in the couple's relationship? The presenting problem is Donna's wish to leave the relationship because she can no longer bear to "mother" Johnny, but the therapist can see from her own experience the more nuanced aspects of this – Donna wants to be cared for but is fearful of it – does she not allow Johnny to provide this just as she does not allow her therapist? Does she project her neediness into Johnny and mother that part of herself in him where it's safer, but then also resent him for getting his needs met – as she experienced in the previous session and feared at one point in the current one? Does Johnny feel, like the therapist, that his attempts to get close to Donna are rejected?

This part of the therapy, largely concerning Donna, was of course only part of their relationship dynamic and at this stage an aspect of the therapist's emerging hypothesis about their relationship, but it is an example of how the therapist can work with different relationships in the room to help her understand the relationship (the couple's) that has come for help.

Interpretation bringing together transferences to the therapist and transference between the couple: Will and Tamar

Will, the male partner in a couple just starting therapy, seemed to be relating to me as if I were a judge presiding over him. He was unsure about making a long-term commitment and I felt he expected me to condemn his ambivalence and tell him to "get on with it". He also expressed irritation with what he called his girlfriend's "therapy-speak" (she was in a closely related profession and had been in individual therapy for some time). Tamar seemed more relaxed and expressed agreement with most of what I said. I had a strong countertransference response of being made into someone judgemental for Will, and an even more uncomfortable one of being misperceived by both as if in an alliance with Tamar. It was as if we were two therapists analysing him. I therefore made an interpretation to Will that he felt I was judging him in his uncertainty about the relationship, but I included an interpretation to the couple – the idea that they each felt I was getting together with Tamar to judge him. In this example, the transference of one partner to the therapist, to his partner, and from the couple to the therapist is all contained in the interpretation. It sounds complex, in some ways it is, but I think this is what happens in analytic couple therapy – we often navigate between and bring together the different experiences in the room.

A later interpretation explored Tamar's feeling that she needed to make an alliance with me. I explored why she felt she needed to do this and interpreted this as being her way of controlling me, as I was also feared by her as a potentially critical/judgemental figure. A few sessions later these thoughts came together in a couple interpretation about a dynamic in the relationship in which each feared judgement by the other and the way in which they evoked the other to play a part in this judging/judged dynamic. Once the couple had some time to think further about this interpretation, which did make sense to them, they were, over time, able to bring this together with earlier experience and I was able to help them think about a very critical object that was part of their shared couple internal world.

Moreover, these examples also illustrate the point that interpretations, wherever they are located initially, build up and gradually become more "couple" and more complete. There is a note of caution here. In this approach the therapist has quite a lot of scope to move around between the different relationships in the room, gradually building up an understanding of the couple. There are dangers in allowing oneself this flexibility, such as not being sufficiently even-handed or the possibility and even likelihood that one will get "caught up" with one partner or the other. If one is going to have the freedom to move between the different relationships and dynamics in the room, one needs the anchor of a "couple state of mind". In other words, if the couple therapist has a "couple state of mind" firmly inside her, then she does not need to concretely address everything, all the time, to the couple. Part of this analytic stance is knowing that in fact everything is indirectly addressed to the couple and the therapist's task is to take a third position in relation to all the relationships operating in the room, including her relationship to the couple.

Interpretation from the therapist's countertransference to the couple: Lois and Walt

Lois made several phone calls to the therapist before coming for a consultation. She wanted to establish that he was the right therapist, having had several failed attempts at couple therapy. After an initial brief phase of idealisation, the therapist felt under constant attack from her. In different ways Lois told him he was wrong, did not understand them and was making things worse. Walt was in the background of most sessions and was difficult to make contact with or to gauge. The therapist often wished he, Walt, could provide a third position on what was going on between himself and Lois, but he sat back. At this stage it was very difficult to understand much about the couple. The therapist dreaded seeing them but, despite threats from Lois to find a new therapist, they continued. After a lot of processing and consultation the therapist realised that he had to be kept as the "wrong therapist". This could be understood as, in Racker's terms, a complementary identification and the dread that he felt before seeing this couple was Lois's dread, and possibly more hidden, Walt's, a concordant identification (Racker, 1968). Lois was clearly desperate for containment, but had no belief in a benign containing object, so that the therapist's attempt to contain felt dangerous for fear that he would escalate her anxiety or project into her. With this couple, this issue of the right or wrong therapist had to be understood first, as this powerful dynamic threatened the possibility of even the next session. A lot of thought had to go into how to work with this fragile couple. It was only when Lois felt a measure of trust in the therapist that Walt could get more into the picture. He had to be kept by Lois as a neutral, ineffective and unthreatening object, which for his own complex reasons he was prepared to be. It will probably be of no surprise to know that Lois had a psychotic mother and Walt, a physically and emotionally abusive father, from whom he tried to keep hidden.

The transference in the couple's relationship: Jimmy and Dale

Jimmy met Dale when he was an intern and Dale was his department head. They both complained that whenever they tried to think about and discuss something important together, their communication quickly broke down. Jimmy was considering a radical career change and resigning from his current job. In one session, just before communication broke down again, Dale said he thought that every time he spoke to Jimmy, that he responded to Dale as if he were trying to stop him making his career change. I said I felt this was accurate; Jimmy related to Dale as if he was an authority figure or parent against whom he had to rebel to establish a sense of his own identity. Jimmy agreed with this interpretation but protested that this was because

Dale *was* an authority figure. It was true that Dale could behave in an angry and somewhat authoritarian way, and perhaps had done so to a greater degree earlier in their relationship. However, it would be hard for anyone else not to notice how powerless, insecure, and totally lacking in influence over Jimmy he now felt. I then took the interpretation a stage further and said to the couple that although it could look like Dale had the authority in the relationship, certainly from Jimmy's perspective, in fact it seemed they shared an experience of powerlessness and each easily perceived the other as in control. This time Jimmy was temporarily able to step outside the transference and consider this new thought.

Interpreting the projective system

When one partner is expressing something strongly, the therapist thinks about the ways in which what one partner is talking about connects with the other, but these connections are not usually obvious or straightforward. It may be that one partner is expressing something on behalf of the couple. The way the couple use the relationship to project unwanted aspects of the self into the other leaves the other carrying a "double dose" of this aspect. Again, this may be for defensive or developmental reasons, but can lead to the couple feeling very polarised, for example, one partner carrying all the dependent feelings, the other all the need for autonomy and separateness. Although one might imagine the partner with the double dose may be burdened by the projection, they may also be reluctant to return it, as unconsciously it serves a protective function for the relationship.

Kath and Christine

Kath and Christine had been in therapy for about a year and although the therapist was aware of a powerful projective system it was very difficult to shift it. Kath felt very let down by Christine, who she experienced as very chaotic when it came to making arrangements, keeping appointments they had and keeping the house in order. They had recently moved in together after five years of being unsure of their commitment to each other in order to see if they could make a go of it. Although these difficulties had been present before Christine moved in, Kath felt somehow if they were in the same place, she could feel more in control of Christine's chaos and that with her influence she would settle into a more ordered life. Instead, she felt Christine was set on driving her mad. This belief ranged from mild irritation to moments of feeling she would really lose her mind.

The therapist was aware of something rather disorganised, even chaotic in Christine, but she had also become aware of something quite disturbed in Kath. She could see, in the to and fro of the sessions, the way in which Kath projected this frightening part of herself into Christine and that Christine all too readily accepted the projection. She tried to appease Kath by acknowledging her faults and while she also protested a bit, she usually ended up promising to do better. It was as if she was aware of this disturbed part of Kath and unconsciously, for the sake of the relationship, she was prepared to take the projection, an example of the "conscious container" being the "unconsciously contained" (Lyons & Mattinson, 1993, p. 108).

In this situation, the therapist trying to help Kath see that she was projecting a very frightening chaotic part of herself into Christine would not only be refuted, but she would also feel misunderstood and perceive the therapist as trying to force something disturbing into her. When working with and interpreting the projective system, it is important to remember the defensive aspect of this process. We split off and project parts of the self that cause us conflict, but also parts we cannot manage that threaten to overwhelm us, even to destroy us. Therefore, showing the couple what they are projecting into each other is rarely enough to enable them to take this part of themselves back. I think it happens in a different way.

If we recognise that what we are witnessing in a couple is a manifestation of their projective system, a double dose of some psychic contents in one partner, we first of all have to work with it there, in that part of the relationship. We know that couples coming for help are often bringing a split-off part of themselves located in the other. In a sense that is why they have to come for couple therapy. By working with this disowned and often frightening part of the self where it is located in the relationship, it might become less frightening. The projecting partner can see that the therapist is not so frightened by it, is not judging it, and is interested in understanding it. This is one of the ways in which the third perspective afforded by couple therapy can be so effective. Over the course of the therapy, it is sometimes then possible for the projecting partner to become less frightened by this part of herself. It took a while, but Kath did start to talk about her own internal chaos and there was an increased sense of something chaotic and fragmented that they both shared. However, at times of stress, the relationship went back to its default position of Christine carrying the disturbance, but again over time the couple became aware of the dynamic even though they could not always prevent it occurring.

Interpreting unconscious phantasy, fantasy, unconscious beliefs

Couples have many ideas about what a relationship is, or should be. This is an important area in couple therapy because these assumptions, fantasies and unconscious beliefs are driving the relationship in some way and unless they can be brought into consciousness and thought about, they can lead to a sense of never-ending conflict which, in the mind of the subject is justified, but in the partner, feels irrational or unfair. It may be that each partner thinks these are shared views and discovers they are not. An unconscious belief

(Britton, 1998) exerts a powerful background influence on the relationship, usually accessed by the therapist in a difficult to process countertransference or enactment. Such beliefs can pose particular problems for interpretation. For example, it can feel very difficult for the therapist to think and to find any useful way of formulating an interpretation, or the countertransference may feel difficult to manage and there may be a pressure towards enactment. The therapist may herself respond with insistence or certainty as in an "overvalued idea" (Britton & Steiner, 1994). In a way, as long as the therapist becomes aware of it, this is also useful, as it is an indication to the therapist of the terrain she is in. It might help her monitor her interpretations to check that she is not responding to one overvalued idea with another.

Interpretation of symbols and dreams

Analytic listening is different to ordinary listening as it involves listening to latent as well as manifest communication, in other words to the unconscious and symbolic meaning of what is being said. If we can understand that the thing the couple are fighting about is not just the thing itself, but what it represents, we sometimes have the means of bringing some light into a repetitive exchange of misunderstanding. The couple finds the apparent issue they were fighting about is not quite the thing they thought it was.

Clinical example: Charlie and Erica

This couple came to see me in an urgent state as they had recently argued, and Charlie had pushed Erica aggressively. They hadn't been together long but had both felt this was the relationship to which they wanted to commit. Erica said despite what had happened she thought she loved Charlie. In the first few sessions, we tried to process how their fighting had escalated to physical violence. In a later session they told me they had argued because Charlie had not dealt with a faulty smoke alarm as he had agreed, and it went off in the middle of the night waking them. Charlie's not attending to the smoke alarm spoke to a tension between them that we were starting to become aware of, about who was looking after whom and, in particular, a wish in Erica to feel more taken care of by Charlie than he was able. But the image of the smoke alarm was most helpfully thought about in terms of its symbolic meaning – the alarm going off inside of both of them and the relationship. Working with the material symbolically in this way brought them both into contact with a panic and terror they felt about the relationship and had not been fully aware of, as they realised there was not really a relationship of any substance between them.

A dream brought to couple sessions is also symbolic material for the couple. Although one partner has the dream, we can think of it as a version of "social dreaming", the dream having its source and meaning beyond the dreamer.

Furthermore, the decision to bring the dream into the couple analytic space suggests that the dreamer is already associating to his or her relationship.

A female patient brings the following dream:

> She was at a dance. The setting was hazy, but she was able to see the grey suit worn by a man who asked her to dance. They danced around the room, and suddenly her partner steered her to a corner and pressed himself against her. She could feel his erect penis.
>
> (Giovacchini, 1982)

This is, in fact, an excerpt of a dream used by Priscilla Roth in her article "Mapping the Landscape", as an example through which she describes different levels of transference interpretations (2001, p. 533). It is interesting to think how this might be taken up in a couple session were one of the partners to bring it. Firstly, I think the couple might both associate to the dream and it could be that this kind of object relationship between someone pressurising, and another who feels pressurised, is an object relationship that both partners know about internally or externally in their families of origin (for example, perhaps either or both had oppressive, pushy or sexually inappropriate mothers/fathers).

It could also be an aspect of the way they experience each other, a relationship between a pressuring and pressurised object that might be part of the unconscious belief the couple have about the nature of relationships. It might also be a communication about their sexual relationship, an eagerness for sex, a fear of sex. Thought about in relation to the therapist, it could be that the couple experience the therapist like the man in the dream or possibly like the woman in the dream, under pressure from them as they join forces and pressurise her. It could also be what is being felt by one or both parties towards the other now in the session, rather like what Hobson (2016) calls a "self-representing event" in that what is being talked about, out there in the dream, is at the same time happening right now in the session.

Some things that can go wrong with interpretations

Sometimes the therapist makes interpretations out of anxiety, often something has been projected into the therapist that makes her uncomfortable and she wants to do something with it. The interpretation can then be more like an evacuation, as it hasn't yet been understood or brought into connection with other elements by the therapist. It is sometimes possible to recognise a pressurised feeling when the therapist is saying more than she needs to, or too quickly, or maybe putting something in a complicated way that is hard for the couple to understand. Not knowing or understanding and feeling helpless can be difficult to manage and result in the therapist interpreting based on previous knowledge or experience, which might not be close enough to this couple's experience or, as Britton and Steiner (1994) have described, as an overvalued idea.

Therapists, particularly those less experienced and with a less developed "couple state of mind", sometimes feel they have to see everything in the couple's projective system and they over-interpret this dynamic in the couple. For example, one of the partners is feeling abandoned or angry, or jealous or depressed, the other apparently not, and it may be that this partner's feeling is part of the couple's projective system, that is, that it exists in each of them and there is an unconscious agreement that one of them carries this difficult experience, a "double dose of it". But this is not always the case. This might be an example of an "overvalued idea" that gets in the way of recognising the true clinical picture. If this is the case it can make the couple, or one of them, feel very misunderstood and if repeated too often can make the couple feel something rather mad is going on.

Well timed couple interpretations usually bring some relief and enable a shift from a blaming dynamic to more reflectiveness on what the couple are creating together – a temporary couple state of mind. However, sometimes the couple cannot move into this state of mind; they want to blame and hold onto the idea of the other at fault. A couple interpretation makes them feel misunderstood. Similarly, interpreting the projective system feels unhelpful, as there is a need to evacuate, an unwanted or frightening part of the self. The couple aren't ready to re-introject something that is so split off that it feels alien and probably is part of the defensive structure of the relationship. When we think about the timing of an interpretation, we think about all the preparative work that goes before. In the case of projection, part of this is understanding the anxiety that leads to the projection. The projection needs to be understood by the therapist, felt by the therapist and worked through in the countertransference, mainly unconsciously, and this takes time.

Interpretation is an imperfect and complex process. We all struggle to understand our patients and to communicate this understanding to them in a way that they can take it in and process it. Sometimes, for a long time, they can't take it in and we have to find different ways of keeping in contact with them. Sometimes we get interpretations right and sometimes we don't; in many therapies this is tolerated, in others it is not. There is a process, but not just a developing relationship between two people, as in individual therapy, rather a relationship that allows for a third perspective (a triangular dynamic) that lends itself to understanding through the many "couples" in the room being at different times participant and observer, which helps the couple to develop a couple state of mind.

Conclusion

This chapter explores the field of couple interpretation in psychoanalytic work with couples. I suggest that a "couple state of mind" is not only crucial in being able to make a "couple interpretation", but that it informs and anchors other interpretations. It also helps the therapist process countertransference and subtle enactments. For the couple, this third perspective on the relationship, experienced both through simply being with a therapist with a "couple state of mind" as well as through receiving more explicit couple interpretations, can gradually be introjected into their relationship.

References

Balfour, A. (2016). Transference and enactment in the "Oedipal setting" of couple psychotherapy. In: A. Novakovic (Ed.), *Couple Dynamics: Psychoanalytic Perspectives in Work with the Individual, the Couple, and the Group* (pp. 59–84). London: Karnac.

Bion. W. R. (1967). A theory of thinking. In: *Second Thoughts*. London: Heinemann.

Britton, R. (1998). *Belief and Imagination. Explorations in Psychoanalysis*. London: Routledge.

Britton, R., & Steiner, J. (1994). Interpretation: Selected fact or overvalued idea? *International Journal of Psycho-Analysis*, 75: 1069–1078.

Giovacchini, P. (1982). *A Clinician's Guide to Reading Freud*. New York and London: Aronson.

Hobson, R. P. (2016). Self-representing events in the transference. *Scientific Meeting of the San Francisco Centre for Psychoanalysis*, June.

Lyons, A., & Mattinson, J. (1993). Individuation in marriage. In: S. Ruszczynski (Ed.), *Psychotherapy with Couples: Theory and Practice at the Tavistock Institute* (pp. 104–125). London: Karnac.

Morgan, M. (2001). First contacts: the therapist's "couple state of mind" as a factor in the containment of couples seen for initial consultations. In: F. Grier (Ed.), *Brief Encounters with Couples* (pp. 17–32). London: Karnac.

Pickering, J. (2011). Bion and the couple. *Couple and Family Psychoanalysis*, *1*(1): 49–68.

Racker, H. (1968). *Transference and Counter-transference*. London: Hogarth Press.

Roth, P. (2001). Mapping the landscape: Levels of transference interpretation. *International Journal of Psycho-Analysis*, *82*(3): 533–543.

Winnicott, D. W. (1969). The use of an object. *International Journal of Psycho-Analysis*, *50*: 711–716.

Note

1 Previous versions of this chapter were published in *fort da* Vol. XX1V, No. 1, Spring 2018, pp. 6–21; and in Morgan, M. (2018) *A Couple State of Mind: Psychoanalysis of Couples and the Tavistock Relationships Model* (pp. 152–175). London & New York: Routledge.

Editors' prologue to the discussant perspectives

The chapter by Mary Morgan describes the complex yet creative field of couple psychoanalysis, illustrating the range of interpretations that are involved in such clinical work and emphasising the importance of the couple state of mind. It also highlights some of the things that can go wrong with interpretation in couple psychoanalytic work. In order to explore these issues more deeply, Hanni Mann-Shalvi explores the analyst's role in the interpretative work and Roberta Gorischnik explores the issue of interpretation as described by Mary Morgan from the perspective of link theory.

Discussant perspective

Hanni Mann-Shalvi

I believe it is the author's ability to present complex theoretical and clinical material, to identify gaps in knowledge and to conceptualise the material in a clear coherent manner, that allows one to easily integrate it into one's own understanding. That is, I feel the author facilitates the necessary thinking for one to contemplate and arrive at new understandings about complex clinical presentations.

In this way the chapter evoked in me a carousel of new thoughts and ideas which I will attempt to share. I would like to use as a starting point Morgan's conceptualisation of the "creative couple" which is defined in her chapter "On being able to become a couple: The importance of a 'creative couple' in psychic life", that is, the movement towards feeling oneself to be part of a couple in which two minds come together to create something (Morgan, 2004). Related to this, Colman (1993) has noted that the relationship itself becomes the container in which the couple feels their existence and by which they are contained. The relationship is like a third party – a symbolic child.

We can trace the bedrock of Morgan's ideas to that of Freud's Oedipal conflict (Freud, 1913), Winnicott's triangular or potential space and the role of creativity as the central achievement of growth (Winnicott, 1971), Green's (2004) *analytic object* and Ogden's (1994) *analytic third*. Applying such concepts to the unconscious couple relationship, in the way the author does, seems a natural and necessary development.

This raises the question of what is the analyst's role in the possible formation of the creative couple and where does interpretation fit with this?

Mary Morgan's chapter provides an organised range of descriptions and implications of couple psychoanalytic interpretations which comprise a key component of our work. She suggests that in order to promote growth and development in a couple, the analyst needs to focus on the unconscious processes that interfere with the well-being and development of a creative couple.

As couple psychoanalysts we are accustomed to identifying the congruence between internal disturbed object relations and their manifestations in the couple relationship and in the transference. We have rich theory to assist us to understand and work with such pathological dynamics and the associated defence mechanisms. We also work with concepts such as transference, splitting, projective identifications, the conjoint personality and unconscious assumptions. The author gives us a comprehensive illustration of these concepts through the clinical vignettes she provides as she demonstrates how to work with them.

Notwithstanding this articulation there has not been a similar elaboration of such concepts as to how they might apply in the later phases of treatment when development and transformation begins to occur in the unconscious internal object relations. This is perhaps where the impact of the real relationship (not just the transference relationship) also has an impact. To expand on this idea, I would like to borrow from Greenson and Wexler's (1969) important article "The non-transference relationship in the psychoanalytic situation". The authors refer to the basic theory of schizophrenia as one which highlights the loss of object representation that Freud articulated (Freud, 1907, 1920). They suggests that the logical consequence of this theory leads to a focus on "reality" relatedness in analysis, as an effort to restore object constancy, in the relationship between patient and therapist. The degree to which interpretive measures may succeed is seen to depend on the extent to which object representation and object constancy, which are related to the nature of the real relationship, are restored as elements in the psychic structure.

Anna Freud (1954) wrote that:

> We see the patient enters into analysis with a reality attitude to the analyst; then the transference gains momentum until it reaches its peak in the full-blown transference neurosis which has to be analysed until the figure of the analyst emerges again, reduced to his true status.
>
> (Freud, 1954, p. 618)

As such we should leave room somewhere for an acknowledgement of the impact of the real relationship between the analyst and (in this case) the couple. Margaret Little (1951) noted that patients come to know a great deal of both the actual and psychic truth about their analysts. Patients, however, do not realise this and it is part of the analyst's task to bring it into consciousness. Searles (1965) also identified that "reality-relatedness always proceeds a bit ahead of, and makes possible, the progressive evolution and resolution of the transference" (p. 557).

From this perspective I agree with Greenson and Wexler's conclusion that, "only the development of a viable, non-transference relationship, no matter how limited in scope it may be, is essential to effect the resolution of the transference neurosis" (p. 37).

It is therefore important that while preserving aspects of the phantasy world, the analyst should strengthen the sense of reality through their interpretations, especially the developing real relationship with the

(continued)

(continued)

analyst and that between the couple. In this regard we need to bear in mind that once the patient can also recognise the analyst as a differentiated person, the achievement of the depressive position is being realised as the patient/couple comes to see the analyst as a real figure, not just a transference construction. In turn this can herald that the termination of the work may be in view. If this is the case one needs to consider what types of interpretation can best acknowledge this situation. In this sense interpretations that identify and encourage the tiniest signs of an emergence of symbolisation, especially the "symbolic third" in the internal and external arena, warrant special attention. Expressed in the transference in the smallest of gestures, such developments can signal the starting point of a recognition of individuality. Here a patient may ask: "How are *you*?" or if he is late, "I am sorry," where such statements represent a recognition of the analyst's separateness. It is therefore important to recognise new and productive unconscious relational patterns that have been previously blocked by un-metabolised unconscious conflicts. With sufficient emotional working through via interpretation, such blocks can be identified, and their resolution facilitated. Recovered unconscious relational patterns identified by the skilful use of interpretation also give recognition to the analysand's ownership of his or her new abilities and sense of self, which promotes separation individuation processes.

I will end with an example which illustrates the importance of interpretation of the type discussed above. Carl and Carla, a newly married couple, had a relationship that was characterised by a sado-masochistic projective identification relational pattern. Both wanted a child but then decided to wait as they did not feel ready. Nevertheless, Carla got pregnant during their honeymoon. Both described their sexual relationship on this occasion as special. Immediately after the honeymoon, however, they got into a serious fight. While consciously there was no place for a third in their relationship, unconsciously the potential to be a creative couple and produce a third had begun to sprout. Their next session was filled with sado-masochistic interactions and fantasies about the eventuality of a spontaneous abortion.

Whilst I interpreted the existence of these murderous thoughts, I also realised that something else important was manifest in this situation. I recognised the sprouting of a "creative couple" and a "third" when they commenced intercourse and the possibility of creating life. I choose to give words to that moment as something new that they created and to give voice to the anxiety aroused in them as a result of allowing themselves to live and create life, and the destructive thoughts that followed.

After this session they went for their first ultrasound test. They started the next session sharing in a way that suggested they had taken something from the previous session – an acknowledgement that they had begun to establish a third position, something new and exiting. Following this there was a further flood of destructive content.

This small vignette illustrates more of the range of interpretative work with couples that Mary Morgan has described, but this time as in the later stages of analytic couple work.

References

Colman, W. (1993). Marriage as a psychological container. In: S. Ruszczynski (Ed.), *Psychotherapy with Couples: Theory and Practice at the Tavistock Institute* (pp. 70–98). London: Karnac.

Freud, A. (1954). The widening scope of indications for psychoanalysis—Discussion. *Journal of the American Psychoanalytic Association*, *2*: 607–620.

Freud, S. (1907[1979]). Letter from Sigmund Freud to C. G. Jung, 23 May 1907. *The Freud/Jung Letters: The Correspondence Between Sigmund Freud and C. G. Jung* (pp. 46–48). London: Picador.

Freud, S. (1913). Totem and Taboo. *The Standard Edition of the Complete Psychological Works of Sigmund Freud, Volume XIII (1913–1914): Totem and Taboo and Other Works* (pp. vii–162). New York: W. W. Norton.

Freud, S. (1920). Beyond the Pleasure Principle. *The Standard Edition of the Complete Psychological Works of Sigmund Freud, Volume XVIII (1920–1922): Beyond the Pleasure Principle, Group Psychology and Other Works* (pp. 1–64). New York: W. W. Norton.

Green, A. (2004). Thirdness and psychoanalytic concepts. *Psychoanalytic Quarterly*, *73*(1): 99–135.

Greenson, R. R., & Wexler, M. (1969). The non-transference relationship in the psychoanalytic situation. *International Journal of Psycho-Analysis*, *50*: 27–39.

Little, M. (1951). Counter-transference and the patient's response to It. *International Journal of Psycho-Analysis*, *32*: 32–40.

Morgan, M. (2004). On being able to be a couple: the importance of a "creative couple" in psychic life. In: F. Grier (Ed.), *Oedipus and the Couple*. London: Karnac.

Ogden, T. H. (1994). The analytic third: Working with intersubjective clinical facts. *International Journal of Psycho-Analysis*, *75*: 3–19.

Searles, H. F. (1965). *Collected Papers on Schizophrenia and Related Subjects*. London: Karnac.

Winnicott, D. W. (1971). *Playing and Reality*. London: Routledge.

Discussant perspective

Roberta Gorischnik

The clinical material presented and the theoretical conceptualisations linked to it allowed me to reflect on interpretation as one of the modalities of intervention associated with link theory (Puget & Berenstein, 1998; Gomel, 1998; Rojas, 1991; Spivacow, 2005; Moguillansky & Nussbaum, 2013). The present work confronts us with the question: What is couple interpretation? Mary Morgan argues that in couple therapy, the interpretation is of the couple as an entity. This, however, raises a specific question concerning what actually represents a "couple interpretation". That is, what does it mean to make a couple interpretation and what are the specifics of this task? Moreover, it raises the questions: Why does the author talk about the field of couple interpretation and what is a couple state of mind?

I start from the notion that interpretation has a meaning in classical psychoanalysis which is different from how interpretation is applied in the treatment of couples. The original Freudian concept of interpretation is one in which interpretation is directed to an individual psychic apparatus via the transference and the free association of the patient in which listening has a privileged place in unveiling the unconscious (Rojas, 1991; Moscona, 2001; Spivacow, 2010).

I agree with Mary Morgan when she says that while interpretation focuses on a couple's inner world, other factors impact on their relationship and are legitimate. That is why I believe interpretations that refer to "links" and link theory constitute legitimate interventions.

The proposal here is that psychic work with couples' therapy also involves analysing problems of the couple bond, that is, that interpretations with a couple can address both. Moscona and colleagues (2010) argue that a couple session produces a "joint discourse" (Spivacow, 2011). This is a set of experiences that includes both partners as well as their words and interactions. The link or linking device is a mechanism designed to bring into play the effects of inter-subjectivity in their discourse and in the clinical setting. Consequently, the way the couple look at each other and the way the analyst looks at the couple (part of his presence) acquire a significance which has an effect on interventions in general, including interpretation (Rajnerman, 2000; Mondolfo, 2000).

In the material presented, consideration is given to a specific type of interpretation which the author calls "couple interpretation" since it is seen to introduce a different state of mind, both for the therapist/analyst and the couple, thus creating greater psychic space.

Mary Morgan notes that:

> Couple interpretations are most important because they introduce a different state of mind; both the therapist's and as a possibility for the couple and it also creates more psychic space. They introduce a couple's state of mind that over time can be introjected by the couple into their relationship. So, it is not just the content of the interpretation but also the offering of the couple state of mind in itself.
> (Morgan, 2017, p. 1)

In the specifics of interpretation with couples and in the field of couple interpretation, she includes the different transference modalities that operate (Spivacow, 2005). The couple's therapeutic space generates the emergence and development of a transferential field. Complexity is generated in the arena of transference, as the transferences are not only directed to the therapist by each member of the couple, but also involve the couple's transferences to each other and from the couple as a group to the analyst. We also need to add to the latter the countertransference responses of the therapist and those of the individuals and the couple.

Moreover, the success of analytic interventions such as interpretation are correlated with the capacities of the couple. That is, they are correlated with their capacity to allow for their co-created couple link to be analysed, which in turn facilitates an identification of the mechanisms underpinning their suffering and increases their capacity to internalise an "analytical linking function".

The author tells us that in couple therapy our interpretations are oriented towards the couple's relationship and towards what they recreate from the past and what they create at present. She notes, "The couple interpretations aim to help the couple to find a place, a third position, from which they can see each other and observe what they are creating or recreating together" (Morgan, 2017, p. 3).

In the couple presented, Ann and Bill, a transference field is created by stating "the truth" that each of them wants to convince the analyst that he/she wants to have sexual intercourse but does not because of the other partner. The hypothesis proposed by Moguillansky and Nussbaum (2014) is that a way of intervening with a couple can be achieved by the analyst building in her own mind a couple, who are able to transform two contradictory discourses, which are mutually exclusive, into a discourse that belongs to the same semantic universe. This third position is said to facilitate the analyst's task of helping the couple turn their reproaches into a rapprochement.

Mary Morgan argues similarly that the couple's introjection of the "couple state of mind" provided by the analyst gives the couple the

(continued)

(continued)

ability to think themselves into the relationship, rather than the psychic pain being drained into the other member of the relationship, as in the case of Ann and Bill. This third position allows the partners to access what they are unconsciously creating together, and in this way allows the expansion of the psychic space.

As this refers to a *couple* state of mind and not to the *couple's* state of mind, I wonder: Is the couple state of mind a tool the analyst uses and which the couple eventually uses for understanding their own state of mind, or is it the state of mind which, elucidated through analytic intervention, allows the couple to arrive at another state of mind?

References

Gomel, S. (1998). *Clínica hoy: Indicaciones y estrategias, en Ética, clínica y formación del analista* (Clinical practice today: Indications and strategies in ethics, the analyst's clinical learning). *Rev. deAEAPG*.

Moguillansky, R., & Nussbaum, S. (2013). *Teoría y Clínica vincular. Vol. I, Fundamentos teóricos del abordaje clínico de la pareja y la familia* (Theory and clinical link Volume I, Theoretical fundamentals of the clinical approach of the couple and family). Buenos Aires: Lugar.

Moguillansky, R., & Nussbaum, S. (2014). *Teoría y Clínica vincular. Vol. II, Discusiones clínicas Vinculares* (Theory and clinical link Volume II, Clinical link discussions). Buenos Aires: Lugar.

Mondolfo, N. (2000). *El despliegue de la escena: Instrumento y obstáculo* (The unfolding of the scene: Instrument and obstacle). *Jornadas de FAPCV, Vol. III*.

Morgan, M. (2017). Complex and creative: The field of couple interpretation—Congress. Paper presented at the IPA Conference, Madrid, 2018).

Moscona, S. (2001). *Construcción del dispositivo y nuevas inscripciones* (Construction of the linking device and new psychic markings). *Rev. de AAPPG, XXIV*(2): 71–90.

Moscona, S., & colleagues (2010). *Clases Seminario Actualización en la Clínica de Parejas* (Notes from Seminars attended on updating clinical practice in couples). AAPPG Buenos Aires.

Puget J., & Berenstein, I. (1998). *Psicoanálisis de la Pareja Matrimonial* (Psychoanalysis of the married couple). Buenos Aires: Paidós.

Rajnerman, G. (2000). *¿Vicisitudes? del encuadre en la clínica vincular* (Vissicitudes of the setting in clinical links). *Rev. de AAPPG, XXIII*(1): 171–194.

Rojas, M. C. (1991). *Psicoanálisis de los vínculos* (Psychoanalysis of the links). *Rev. de AAPPG, XIV*(1–2): 39–52.

Spivacow, M. A. (2005). *Clínica psicoanalítica con parejas. Entre la teoría y la intervención* (Psychoanalytical clinical practice in couples. Between the theory and the intervention). Buenos Aires: Lugar.

Spivacow, M. A. (2010). *El contexto intersubjetivo en el funcionamiento psíquico y su lugar en la clínica psicoanalítica* (The inter-subjective context in the psychic functioning and its place in the Psychoanalytic Clinical). *Rev. de AAPPG XXXIII*(2): 39–52.

Spivacow, M. A. (2011). *La pareja en conflicto. Aportes psicoanalíticos* (The couple in conflict. Psychoanalytic contributions). Buenos Aires: Paidós.

Chapter 3

The role of interpretation in the assessment phase of couple psychoanalysis[1]

Timothy Keogh and Cynthia Gregory-Roberts

Introduction

Interpretation is a fundamental component of psychoanalytic interventions with couples, yet where and how it is used varies widely. In this chapter, we make a case for its use in the assessment of couples. The authors regard assessment as a process directed at understanding the nature of the couple's presenting problem from a psychoanalytic perspective, a means of exploring a couple's ability to benefit from psychoanalytic treatment, and determining their level of psychic functioning and associated defences. These issues are illustrated in material from a conjoint couple assessment, arguing with reference to this material that as an intervention, interpretation is an important and effective aspect of the couple assessment process, particularly when seen as iterative and stemming from an evolving container–contained relationship. We also highlight the unique challenges faced in the conjoint assessment of a couple and the use of our related concept of a mutative couple interpretation and the technique of reflective interpretation.

The couple

When Joe and Olivia, a young, middle-class, professional couple with two children, attended for assessment, interpretation was primarily used as a means of engaging them in a transformative psychoanalytic process. (To protect confidentiality, the case as presented here is based on composite clinical material.) The aim of this intervention was to help them to ultimately understand how their unconscious, internalised, working models, or self-object relations, which derived from the perception of relationships formed early in their development, had come to haunt their current relationship, especially after an affair had triggered the loss of an idealised psychic representation of their coupledom. We also aimed to help them to begin to reframe the meaning of that affair in order that it could be understood, and so that this understanding might, in turn, potentially open up a new way of relating (Scharff, 2014).

The role of interpretation in couple psychoanalysis (and indeed that which is interpreted) speaks to the overall theoretical model of psychoanalysis applied in our work. For the authors, this is a model of psychoanalysis as a process, which assists the development of a mind that is individuated.

Traditionally, the definition of interpretation has referred to the verbal interventions of the analyst, aimed at bringing about the identification of the latent (i.e., unconscious) aspect of the analysand's speech and behaviour. For many, it later became, as Wolf puts it, "all those intentional activities of the analyst, that in their totality bring about a modification of the analysand's psyche" (Wolf, 1993, p. 15).

In the specialised setting of couple assessment, interpretation is aimed at understanding the couple as an entity and how it is functioning or malfunctioning. Such assessment places a premium on what Morgan (2001) has referred to as the need for a "couple state of mind" in the analyst (see Chapter 2). This, in part, means that the analyst is attempting to interpret (i.e., make conscious) how individual psychic issues contribute to couple functioning. In individual work the concept of a mutative interpretation is one that links archaic intra-psychic issues and their manifestation in the transference to bring about change. We refer to a "mutative couple interpretation" as one that takes the individual, archaic, psychic issues of each of the couple and links them to the presenting problem of the couple and, in so doing, makes conscious underpinning couple dynamics, as a means of achieving a psychic transformation in couple functioning. As with Strachey's (1934) original proposal of the concept in the individual psychoanalytic process, such a transformation emerges from the recognised difference between the original fantasmatic object and the actual object. In the couple, we see this arising out of the complex matrix of transference and countertransference processes. Such interpretations can also be facilitated in conjoint couple therapy by means of a reflective interpretation between the two therapists (Keogh & Gregory-Roberts, 2015). That is, as conjoint therapists, we purposefully reflect on connections with the couple rather than make a direct interpretation, which might otherwise be felt to be too persecutory. In doing so, we model a process of containment, mentalisation, and couple functioning where difference can be recognised. This can be particularly helpful where splitting and projection have become entrenched parts of the couple's defensive bastion, and the partners in the couple have had a poor model of coupling in their families of origin. As in the case of Joe and Olivia, during the course of the assessment, the therapists also attempt to make a psychodynamic formulation that encompasses a view about the capacity of the couple to benefit from psychoanalytic treatment. The psychoanalytic formulation, therefore, can also be seen as an implicit interpretation that is developed and held in the mind of the therapist, in response to the multiple transferences, both experienced and observed. Explicit, preliminary, interpretative statements are carefully utilised to gain an idea of the couple's capacity to benefit from a psychoanalytic intervention and to determine their level of psychic functioning and the required level of interpretations (Keogh & Enfield, 2013).

In the assessment phase, interpretation also helps to convey to the couple an ability to make sense of the unconscious dimensions of their presenting difficulties. This highlights that effective interpretation only occurs when a state of container–contained experience is achieved and that, moreover, interpretation and a deepening of the transference are intimately linked. As such, initial interpretations are pivotal in forming the all-important initial connection or therapeutic alliance with a couple.

The Referral

The referral of the couple was made by the couple's general practitioner who had become concerned about Olivia's repeated presentations, which he felt were psychosomatic. On enquiring into her current circumstances, Olivia told him that she had been arguing with her husband, whom she saw as unresponsive to her. She said that she had become concerned that the relationship might be at risk, as she felt she was "not sure who she was living with". She had become very disillusioned with her partner, adding that their children were unsettled and appeared to be responding to the tension between them. Initially, Olivia was not sure about the referral for couple psychotherapy, given that a previous one had resulted in an unsatisfactory experience. After talking about the proposal with her partner, however, they agreed it might be helpful. The general practitioner had suggested conjoint couple therapy, feeling that the couple were particularly challenging in terms of the level of their presenting anxiety and conflict. The need for, and possible value of, conjoint couple, or indeed family therapy would be a question to consider in the assessment process.

Olivia made the first contact. She said that she would like to make an appointment as soon as possible, as she felt she could not go on in a relationship where her husband "was so uncommunicative". Neither of the therapists spoke with Joe until the first session.

In the following record of our meeting, the respective psychotherapists' contributions are identified with their initials.

The first assessment session

When the couple arrived, we both had an impression of them as a young, fit, attractive-looking, professional couple. Olivia was a dark-haired, neatly presented woman. She seemed pressured and anxious in her manner of speech. We felt that this suggested that, in terms of her internal world, there was a sense of a struggle to get through to the object. She also conveyed a deprived, emotionally hungry feeling. In comparison, Joe seemed to be rather flat and disconnected. He was minimally verbal, but communicated by a lot of "knowing looks", which had to be decoded by us. He was dressed in shorts and a T-shirt and, while he looked physically robust, his ginger hair and fair skin gave him a rather boyish look.

In the initial session, TK began by noting the contents of the referral letter that their general practitioner provided. Olivia was anxious about this, expressing concern about what we might communicate back to him. Our countertransference to her behaviour had a consistency; we both experienced an uncomfortable sense of being seen as untrustworthy, as well as a feeling of something shameful that might be exposed. We made a preliminary interpretation about Olivia's worry and concern about not being able to trust us. This is an example of one type of interpretation in couple assessment, where the individual's anxiety is acknowledged and where the therapist conveys a respect and empathy for this. Such interpretations are often later linked to the couple's shared problem. It is thus a first step in an interpretative process, which is iterative. Moreover, it is the beginning of the development of an all-important container–contained relationship that, when established, becomes the platform for mutative couple interpretations.

Given the manner in which the session with this couple had started, we later wondered about their history, in terms of disappointments or abuse, which may have led to such a reaction. While it was Olivia who voiced the anxiety, we also wondered about this as an unconscious transference reaction to us as a therapist couple, representing potentially abusive parents.

We thought this might also link to their history of previous therapists whom they felt had failed them. Further, we were aware of being potentially provoked into a defensive reaction, rather than one in which we contained their anxiety. As a response, CGR asked if they could tell us a little more what had brought them to therapy and how they felt about being there.

Olivia was quick to say that, from her point of view, she felt very alone in the relationship and wondered if Joe cared about her anymore. As she spoke she became tearful and distressed. She continued through her tears, explaining that she felt things were getting worse between them, and expressed uncertainty about staying together. At this point, in addition to registering the urgency of her distress, we were becoming aware that there was little space for Joe to express his feelings. TK had a particular countertransference experience at this time that he later shared with CGR, of feeling unable to speak when Olivia was talking. Moreover, we noted to each other out of session that while we both felt her distress, we also noticed that the way Olivia behaved in relation to Joe seemed to ensure that he did not get to speak. We discussed the possibility that there was something Olivia was doing that was bringing about a self-fulfilling prophecy in the relationship, that is, that a repetition compulsion of some sort was happening. This turned out to be a prescient thought, as we later discovered that, for her, Joe represented an impermeable paternal object and that she represented a maternal object that had little space for him. In response to our countertransference feelings, TK noted how upset Olivia was, but asked Joe how he felt. There was a somewhat passively angry tone in his response. He said that he did not understand why she felt like this, that from his point of view what she said was not true and that he did respond to her, but, he added, that she was always distressed about something. He said that he felt things were a bit one-sided and that when she talked like this it felt like there was very little understanding of what was happening for him. This last point, however, was said almost apologetically. We acknowledged his feelings.

At this juncture, as a therapeutic couple, given the rather tense feeling between Joe and Olivia, we felt that it would be helpful to make a reflective interpretation to each other. TK thus said to CGR, while facing her, but also looking at each of the couple as he spoke:

> It seems that both Olivia and Joe are currently feeling very upset by the way they feel treated by the other. They both seem to see each other as behaving unreasonably.

CGR nodded and added:

> I agree, but I think it is important to try and think what has happened to them as a couple, for things to end up feeling like this.

In this interpretation, we were trying to acknowledge their splitting and projection, but also to demonstrate our interest in thinking about them with a couple state of mind. We were also assessing their ability to think from this couple perspective. This underlines how the process of assessment and interpretation go hand in glove.

Olivia said that she often saw Joe as wanting her to leave him alone and not to keep bringing up difficulties in the relationship.

Olivia: He doesn't realise that if I don't, the relationship is not going to survive.

She continued, in a way that pressured us to accept her view, that Joe was the problem in the relationship and to collude with her splitting. We also felt this to be challenging our proposal to try and think about them as a couple. We looked to Joe for a response. He replied saying that he felt that Olivia was always "under the pump" with deadlines at work and he felt she brought a lot of pressure into the relationship. He said, expressing his own aggression safely:

> Even the kids comment on it . . . Jonathon says, "Mummy is a real tense-head". Anyway, I don't know what to say to her – nothing seems to be right.

We later came to understand that this was how he also saw his mother. Olivia said that she got infuriated with Joe because he just closes down on her and "puts his head in the sand".

Olivia: Nothing ever gets resolved and from my point of view the tension just becomes unbearable, but he just carries on as if nothing has happened. When someone just stares at you when you are really feeling distressed, what are you supposed to think?

As she said this, we once again thought about what sort of an object he represented for her. She went on describing a series of incidents that she cited as proof of her complaints about Joe. Joe seemed to be increasingly less able to express himself verbally and he looked somewhat frozen, yet frustrated. We both had the feeling that he felt it was hopeless trying to defend himself, as if he experienced her as indefatigable.

Feeling a rise in the level of tension as this went on, CGR said, as a means of containing the affect: I am wondering if things have always felt like this?

They both said that this was not the case. CGR then invited them to tell us how they had met and what things were like at the beginning of their relationship.

Looking at Joe (and trying to give him some space) she asked:

> Can you tell us something about this?

Joe said that they had met ten years ago through some mutual friends in a walking club. He said he was just finishing off his architecture studies at that time and was sharing a flat with a woman who worked in Olivia's office. He said that there was a dinner arranged and they sat next to each other. They seemed to hit it off and began dating.

TK then asked Joe what it was that had attracted him to Olivia. Joe said that he thought Olivia was the first woman he had felt really "got me". He thought she was very sensitive and warm, a very caring person, but that she was also very stunning looking. He looked at Olivia affectionately as he reminisced on their meeting. Here we were reminded of Dicks's (1997) concept of the "glove turning inside out", which refers to how unresolved conflicts in a couple, often after a rather idealised start, result in the projection of internal bad objects into each other.

Olivia said that she saw Joe as a very handsome guy, intelligent and not at all like others she had dated.

Olivia: He seemed really interested in me as a person and I don't know, I just think I felt very safe with him.

She went on to say that once they started having sex, things became intensely passionate between them. She said that their sex life had remained pretty good "for the most part" until very recently. During this section of the session there was a much calmer feeling between the couple. They even smiled at each other as they related details of their initial meeting.

Olivia: Do you remember that? Joe smiled and nodded.

It seemed important to note that this changed the way they were relating and underlined the presence of more positive feelings between them.

CGR to TK: In talking about how they first met it seems that there are many positive feelings between Olivia and Joe, even though a few minutes ago we were hearing how overwhelmingly negative they had been feeling about their relationship.

In this interpretation, we were thus drawing the couple's attention to their splitting, but at the same time highlighting that there were resources in the relationship to work on.

As if to challenge our optimistic assessment of them, Olivia then said: Yes, but there is one thing we haven't told you about. Six months ago, I had an affair.

Joe looked quite surprised, as if he had not expected her to reveal this. Again, there was a rise in the tension level between them.

After a short period of silence, and in an attempt to make a containing interpretation, TK said: We appreciate that this is obviously a very sensitive issue for you both, but something important for us to understand. Can you let us know what happened?

Given that an affair can be thought of as a symptom of an underlying problem in a relationship, we found Olivia's next statement interesting.

Olivia: Well I am not sure the affair is the main problem, but I realise it didn't help things either.

She went on to say that she and Joe were not getting on well at the time and that she had to travel quite a bit with her job as a senior civil servant.

Olivia: I was finding myself getting close to a colleague with whom I had to travel. He was an older man I reported to. At the time, I was also in the midst of sorting out my father's unpaid tax issues.

She told us that her father had died from a long struggle with emphysema about a year earlier. The last days were especially stressful, seeing him in so much distress. She had been very troubled by the relationship with him, as he had been quite verbally abusive and unsupportive of her as a child. Her reaction to his death was not easy. We came to realise that she was letting us know that perhaps this couple were really presenting with the effects of a complex bereavement reaction and the impact of prolonged grief on their couple relationship.

She went on to say, in a way that had an unconscious continuity about it, that, unlike her father, she found her colleague to be very receptive to her. He had been able to help her out with the tax issue because of his legal training and it was in this context that she ended up becoming intimate with him during a demanding work assignment when they were both in China.

While she was saying this Joe seemed to be looking away. In response, TK asked Joe how he found out about the affair. He said that he had overheard a very intimate telephone conversation between the two of them. When he had challenged her about this, she had not wanted to talk about it very much. He also seemed to want to avoid talking about how he felt. CGR asked him how he felt when he found out. Initially, he said that he had been finding Olivia very touchy and that she seemed to find offence in just about everything he said to her. When he found out that she had had an affair on top of this, it made him wonder whether he could stay in the relationship.

Joe: It felt like it was all over.
TK: I am wondering how you managed your feelings about this.

He said he didn't really know, that he just somehow carried on.

Olivia then interrupted to say, in way that felt jarring, that from her point of view this was an example of what she meant when she said that he did not want to deal with things.

TK to CGR: Obviously, the affair has been a very significant event for both Joe and Olivia, but it feels like it hasn't really been discussed very much and it seems there are still a lot of strong feelings that are largely unexpressed about it in both of them.
CGR: Yes, and I was thinking that, given what Olivia said about things not going well before the affair, maybe the fact that it happened may have had something to do with unexpressed feelings in the relationship. I was thinking, for example, about what Olivia said about her relationship with her father.
TK: Yes. I agree. It seems important to understand issues that might be continuing to affect the relationship that may have been amplified by the affair.

In these interpretations, we were attempting to demonstrate our ability to work together in a way that conveyed a model of mind, but also to show that we could be a concerned "parental" couple for them. In this way, we were attempting both to develop further the container–contained relationship and also deepen, in this instance, the positive transference, which would be the crucible from which effective interpretations would arise.

Olivia then said in a distinctly more reflective tone: I think you might be right, but it feels in a way that it is already too late, especially given the affair and anyway . . . where do you start?

TK to Joe: I am wondering what your thought is?
Olivia: Well it's confusing really. I think we both probably had a lot of issues when we met each other, but we initially seemed

very compatible. I think it is also true though that we both experienced things as kids that have impacted on us, that we have never really dealt with. I know that is true for me, but given what I know about Joe's family, I think it is probably true for him as well.

She gave him a questioning look, but he did not respond.

Olivia: At the time of the affair I just felt swept away by someone who seemed to really care about me, even though it turned out I was not the first that he had done this sort of thing with. I think I was just very stressed and vulnerable at the time and we were not getting on. I was really confused by what was happening.

CGR noted Olivia's confusion and asked Joe what was happening to him at the time.

Joe: Well obviously, I didn't know about the affair, but I felt that Olivia was inconsolable after her father died and immersed herself in an overseas work project. I just had to help manage Jonathon and Zara because things had to go on. They were not easy to deal with either, as I think they knew things were not right between us and they seemed more unsettled and needy. Jonathon said more than once, "You are not going to leave us are you Daddy?" I was also pretty busy with projects at work and my sister was leaning heavily on me financially after a relationship break-up she had. I felt very much on my own; I felt Olivia was not interested in me and I felt very uncertain about our future, but I think I just withdrew really.

TK (while monitoring Olivia's reaction): I wonder if you also felt at some level quite hurt and pretty angry about the infidelity?

Joe: Maybe, but Olivia did apologise and in the end I accepted her apology. I think she was under a lot of stress. I don't know. I try not to think about it really.

Olivia: I think you are right. I think he is angry. I think he has been colder towards me.

TK to CGR: Maybe Joe decided to deal with his feelings by freezing Olivia out and that is part of what she cannot take anymore?

Joe smiled knowingly, as if to say, "You hit the nail on the head".

CGR to TK: I am just thinking that the circumstances around the affair have evoked a lot of confusing and overwhelming feelings in both Olivia and Joe. What they both say also seems to highlight how they each deal with their feelings very differently.

TK: Yes, I think it would be really good to try and make sense of how the affair came about (now looking at the couple), given you have both indicated that you want to try and work things out and stay together.

CGR (directly to the couple): Yes, but to do that I think we need to look at the bigger picture. I think we probably need to understand what each of you brought into the relationship that may have contributed to a situation where the affair happened.

TK then commented that Olivia looked very thoughtful as result of what had been said.

Olivia: Yeah, I was thinking about what you were saying. I have seen a lot of friends who had very difficult backgrounds, whose marriages have not gone well.

CGR: Can you relate to that?

Olivia: Yes, I can, actually.

TK to Joe: What about you?

Joe: I'm not sure, but I think it might be helpful to think about it.

Much of the first session involved discussing the circumstances and aftermath of the affair. In our second meeting, we heard more about their respective backgrounds.

The second assessment session

On returning a week later, they arrived together and were sitting talking to each other in a very animated way in the waiting room. They both greeted us with a warm smile and seemed more relaxed. We started by asking how things had been since we last saw them. Joe said that after they had left last week they both felt exhausted, but relieved just to be able to deal with the terrible tension that had been developing between them.

Joe: No matter how difficult it was, it was good just to get things on the table.

CGR to Olivia: How about for you?

Olivia: Well we have had a better week. We even took a walk together and talked about some of the things we discussed here.

She said that they had both acknowledged to each other that it had been good finally to really talk about things, but that Joe was surprised when she said she was still not sure if she wanted to stay in the relationship.

We later shared with one another that at this point we both had the interesting thought that maybe it might have been Joe who said this. We realised that this related to a pressure on us to view the infidelity from the perspective of splitting (and blaming).

TK then asked if Olivia could say something about why she felt that she was not sure she wanted to stay in the relationship.

She said that she had been thinking a lot about what we had said in the last session, about what they had both brought into the relationship, and that she was feeling that it was all too hard to fix. She added that she could not see Joe being able to change that much.

CGR acknowledged her uncertainty and said that perhaps if we could continue hearing about their backgrounds it might give us a chance to understand better what had happened to them over the course of their relationship, which might have resulted in the affair.

We heard that Joe's father had been away frequently, as an air force pilot when Joe was young, and that they had also moved cities a number of times. Joe's mother, a physiotherapist, was also busy socially and had little time for him and expected him to be rather self-sufficient and not trouble her with his problems. Joe was also left to take responsibility for his sister, who was three years younger than he. He had never really observed much of a close relationship between his parents, and described what sounded like a melancholic depression in his mother, when his father died from surgical complications when Joe was seventeen years old.

Olivia said that she had an alcoholic mother whom she could not trust and experienced as unpredictably abusive when she drank. Her mother had herself also suffered a lot with a cruel mother who was often verbally brutal to her. Her father had been a womaniser and interestingly she thought that was possibly because of his difficult wife. She said he was a man who was difficult to get close to and not a warm person and thus seemed to provide little compensation for her lack of mothering. Despite this, her three older siblings saw her as having had all the attention.

Having heard something about their history, CGR reflected to TK: I was thinking that it sounds like when Joe and Olivia got together, they may have sensed something of a hurt child in each other. I think they may have tried to respond to this, but somehow, after a promising start, their attempts to help each other went awry.

TK to CGR: Yes, it seems that something has happened in the relationship, especially since the affair, that has brought them both back to a lot of early hurts that have perhaps never been acknowledged, but which they both still feel very intensely.

CGR (looking to the couple): Does that resonate with you?

Joe said that it was certainly true that their relationship was initially good, but that, over time, something did change and they seem in a very different place now.

We asked Olivia if she agreed and what she thought had changed. She said that things certainly became different when she had her first child. We asked Joe whether he agreed.

Joe: It could have, but maybe we have just grown apart?

This seemed to be said with a sense of wanting to obliterate any way of linking things. We later came to realise that it was going to be necessary for him to first express his rage and narcissistic injury about the affair before he could allow himself to think about it. (This came several sessions later.)

His response, like Olivia's at other times, was typical of a series of forward movements that were met by resistance that we slowly worked our way through.

In a conversation we had with each other outside the session, we thought about the need to consider how the return of a repressed bad object in both of them had been projected into the other. This was an implicit interpretation, part of our psychodynamic formulation. The couple's capacity to receive and reflect on our individual and couple interpretations at this assessment stage indicated to us their suitability for analytic couple therapy.

At the end of our second session, the couple felt more hopeful about the potential for change in their relationship and readily accepted our recommendation to meet for weekly conjoint couple psychotherapy. Notwithstanding this, they each subsequently expressed resistance and ambivalence in the therapy as we touched on painful issues in each of them.

Discussion

Following subsequent work with the couple in our weekly meetings, we could see that our psychoanalytic assessment and formulation, especially that concerning the significance of unresolved loss, was extremely important. Over time, the implicit interpretations from our assessment that guided our work were confirmed by the couple's responses. The work of examining the meaning of the affair, in particular, exposed the impact of unresolved losses for each of them on their relationship. For example, we came to understand how Olivia was projecting into Joe the self-reproachful feelings provoked in her by the loss of her father, towards whom she had much ambivalence. Later in the work this was, in turn, reflected in unresolved losses for Joe. We also felt vindicated about our decision to offer conjoint couple therapy, especially for a couple who had such poor modelling of coupling in their families of origin.

In the two assessment sessions, we used a sequence of interpretations that enabled us, as a therapeutic couple, to deepen our relationship transference with them and begin to form a container–contained relationship from which transformative interpretations in the later stages of therapy could be made.

In doing so, we made use of reflective therapist couple interpretations. The connection with the couple and their subsequent engagement in the psychoanalytic couple work very much hinged on their experience of us being able to understand their individual experience and to think about this with them from the perspective of their ruptured coupledom. To do this required us to have a clear analytic stance and frame.

Very early on in our work, Joe and Olivia communicated their agreement with our implicit interpretation about loss, which allowed us to work with them on unpacking the meaning of the affair and indeed its antecedents in their relationship. This was ultimately able to be transformative and allowed them to construct a new, mature, and true psychological marriage with each other.

Moreover, the two initial sessions with Olivia and Joe demonstrate how the use of interpretation in the assessment phase of couple work helps to establish, not only the contract for the work to be undertaken, but also the blueprint for the co-constructed internal structure to be built in the course of the therapeutic work. This is the structure in which the couple will be contained and from whose secure base they will be able to manage together the constant external challenges that life will present.

References

Dicks, H. V. (1997). *Marital Tensions: Clinical Studies Towards a Psychological Theory of Interaction*. London: Karnac.

Keogh, T., & Enfield, S. (2013). From regression to recovery: Tracking developmental anxieties in couple therapy. *Couple and Family Psychoanalysis*, *3*: 28–46.

Keogh, T., & Gregory-Roberts, C. (2015). A valediction forbidding mourning: working with traumatic repetition in an older couple. Paper presented at the *First IPA/FEPAL Congress on Couple and Family Psychoanalysis*, Buenos Aires, 9–11 April, 2015.

Morgan, M. (2001). First contacts: the therapist's "couple state of mind" as a factor in the containment of couples seen for consultations. In: F. Grier (Ed.), *Brief Encounters with Couples: Some Analytic Perspectives* (pp. 17–32). London: Karnac.

Scharff, D. E. (2014). Working with affairs. In: D. E. Scharff & J. Savege Scharff (Eds.), *Psychoanalytic Couple Therapy: Foundations of Theory and Practice* (pp. 254–265). London: Karnac.

Strachey, J. (1934). The nature of the therapeutic action of psycho-analysis. *International Journal of Psycho-Analysis*, *15*: 127–159.

Wolf, E. S. (1993). The role of interpretation in therapeutic change. In: A. Goldberg (Ed.), *The Widening Scope of Psychoanalysis. Progress in Self Psychology*, *Vol. 9* (pp. 15–31). Hillsdale, NJ: The Analytic Press.

Note

1 This chapter, which was originally published in *Couple and Family Psychoanalysis* 7(2) 168–180 (2017), is reprinted with the permission of Phoenix Press and the Editor of the journal, Ms Molly Ludlam.

Editors' prologue to the discussant perspectives

The chapter by Keogh and Gregory-Roberts discusses the role of interpretation in the assessment phase of couple psychoanalysis and introduces the notion of iterative interpretations linked to a developing container–contained relationship. It also discusses the concepts of the reflective interpretation and the couple mutative interpretation. Damian McCann considers a number of issues arising from the ideas that the authors present, including when interpretation might arise from a selected fact rather than an over-valued idea and the use of history. Alicia Leisse de Lustgarten further discusses the chapter in terms of the value of co-therapy, especially (in terms of the unconscious parental situation it represents) with disturbed couples, and the value of the reflective interpretation as representing an important third position.

Discussant perspective

Damian McCann

By way of opening my response to Timothy Keogh and Cynthia Gregory-Roberts' chapter "The role of interpretation in the assessment phase of couple psychoanalysis", I feel the need to remind ourselves that the main body of thinking and development with regard to interpretation still comes from analytic work with individuals; we are therefore constantly faced with the challenge of translating that which is applicable to individuals to our work with couples. However, it is generally recognised that interpretations that resonate with patients are an essential part of most assessment interviews, since interpretations convey to patients the fact that they are understood. Interpretations also help in establishing rapport which, in turn, assists in the search for more meaningful information, a deepening of the transference and, of course, insight.

Part of the translation from individual to couple therapy lies in the therapist being able to hold what Morgan (2005) refers to as "a couple state of mind", since the couple therapist will inevitably be searching for some preliminary understanding of the area in which the couple's shared anxieties and unconscious phantasies lie. Indeed, the authors suggest that, ". . . interpretation was primarily used as a means of engaging them (the couple) in a transformative psychoanalytic process."

What is specific to psychoanalytic, and indeed all psychotherapeutic work, including that of first encounters, is how therapists listen and respond to the patient and, perhaps even more importantly, how he or she reflects on his or her mode of listening and responding.

With that in mind, I think it is worth considering the nature of the reflective function offered by the authors' co-therapy relationship and its particular contribution to the question of interpretation in the assessment of their couple's presenting problem, as a gateway to the ongoing therapy.

Steiner (1993) makes an important distinction between what he terms "patient-centred interpretations" and "analyst-centred interpretations", as well as a distinction between understanding and being understood. Although both approaches reflect the analyst's attempt to understand the patient's experience, analyst-centred interpretations are considered to be more likely to give the patient a sense of being understood. In Keogh and Gregory-Roberts' case example, we have two therapists not sitting side-by-side, but rather sitting diagonally opposite each other, so as to gain maximum access to each other's minds. Not only does this give the couple the sense of a "we" in terms of two therapists working and attuning their minds in the service of the couple's evolving narrative (and indeed in the chapter itself there are a lot of references to the

(continued)

(continued)

"we", even when only one of the therapists was actually speaking), but it also provides Joe and Olivia with direct access to the shared mind of the couple therapists as they wonder out loud about the nature of the couple's defences. Although the therapists, during the early stages of the work, were not technically adhering to analyst-centred interpretations in the sense that Steiner envisions, it does nevertheless allow for the development of this function as the work progresses, especially since the couple comes to know and accommodate a way of being in the therapeutic encounter that perhaps also models something developmental. For instance, the therapists in their presentation make particular reference to the couple's capacity to receive and reflect on "our individual and couple interpretations" as something vital to the process of knowing and developing. In addition, they also make great claim to the potential of shared reflective function to provide at least one of the building blocks that contribute towards the construction of a container–contained relationship. Moreover, they feel that a reflective interpretation between two therapists can be particularly helpful where splitting and projection have become entrenched parts of the couple's defensive bastion. In this regard, however, I think it would be interesting to learn more about how the co-therapy partners manage splits in their own thinking and moments when they are not of the same mind.

A further consideration, or indeed tension, in psychoanalytic consultations concerns the question of whether an interpretation offers containment through understanding, or whether it runs the risk of being unhelpful and intrusive (Crick, 2012). Indeed, this presentation also stirred for me questions about the nature and manner of the assessment and, to that end, I found myself returning to another distinction, this time that of Britton and Steiner's (1994) differentiation of a "selected fact" from "an overvalued idea". It seems to me that couple psychotherapists particularly organise their thinking and practice on the basis of the idea and search for the unconscious couple fit and notions of an internal parental couple. I notice in the case example how Gregory-Roberts, in particular, found herself, in response to the rise in the level of tension in the couple and as a means of containing affect, wondering aloud "if things have always felt like this" – a precursor to asking how they had first met. This seems to form a basic tenet of assessments in couple therapy since it, more often than not, reconnects the couple with softer and more romantic feelings, as well as providing clues to the early unconscious projections that pulled the couple together and accounted for their initial attraction. As with Joe and Olivia, this often leads to a softening of affect and usually results in a more contained couple dynamic. However, to complete the picture, couple therapists also actively search for the internal parental couple, mainly because this constitutes a key ingredient that helps make sense of the all-important links that explain not only why the couple got together in the first place, but also why they stay together and why they are now presenting for therapy. One might ask whether this endeavour is evidence of a selected fact or an overvalued idea. What is more, although I hold with the principle of the importance of early developmental history, I raise two questions concerning the practice of working with the history.

Firstly, it runs counter to Ogden's (2012) caution against the analyst interfering with the patient's efforts to consider the evolving meaning of his experience by introducing an agenda, as is done in collecting historical data. This is because activity such as this interferes with unconscious processes at work in the open exchange between the therapist and the individual or couple. In other words, it has a detrimental effect on the transference and countertransference relationships at work within the therapeutic encounter. I do, however, recognise that looking back may actually help the couple reconnect with their history and the unfolding nature of their lives and be instrumental in building the therapeutic alliance.

Secondly, it raises questions concerning the meaning of Gregory-Roberts' interventions during the assessment as she attempted to find the important links in this couple's early connection. Was she simply honouring the bedrock of couple psychoanalytic theory and practice in her efforts to shift the focus away from the immediate internal workings of the couple's dynamic in the here and now to the unconscious processes that give rise to the couple's disturbance? Or, was she unconsciously recruited, perhaps as a concerned "mother" of two vulnerable "children", to take the partners back to their childhood roots to help them rework early trauma and loss. Furthermore, we might also wonder what was happening to Keogh at moments when Gregory-Roberts was taking this more active role. I believe that their evolving co-therapy dynamic testifies to the importance of being alive and paying particular attention to transference and countertransference activity and material during the initial assessment phase.

The final matter I wish to consider is that of Joe and Olivia's response when their initial link failed to sustain their need of each other over time. Faced with this breakdown in shared psychic space, we find a couple in retreat, with Joe using his default position of withdrawing, and Olivia turning to an older man to meet her needs for a father, only to discover that, like her father, her lover was also a womaniser. I think it is worth reminding ourselves that Scharff (2014) speaks of an affair as a symptom of a breakdown in the couple relationship, suggesting that the strain that led to the breakdown has not remained within the bounds of the marriage. He believes that our job as therapists is therefore to

(continued)

(continued)

understand the meaning of the affair, or more precisely, to understand the unconscious meaning of the affair. Nathans (2012) adds another important ingredient into the mix with her focus on the difficulty one or both of the partners has with mourning past or impending loss, in which the infidelity acts as a manic attempt to replace anxiety or psychic pain with excitement, or, as in Olivia's case, a wish for comfort and understanding in the context of an actual father who had not met, and could not ever meet, this need.

In conclusion, I wish to acknowledge the important impact that the authors had in their early work with this couple and in the context of emphysema; it was as if they breathed new life into a couple who were gasping for breath. I am grateful to have been asked to provide this response and wish to thank Keogh and Gregory-Roberts for allowing us into the working of their co-therapy relationship and its significant impact on Joe and Olivia.

References

Britton, R., & Steiner, J. (1994). Interpretation: Selected fact or over valued idea? *The International Journal of Psycho-Analysis*, *75*(5/6): 1069–1078.

Crick, P. (2012). Consultation and referral: Introduction. In: B. Reith, S. Kagerlof, P. Crick, M. Moller & E. Skale (Eds.), *Initiating Psychoanalysis Perspectives* (pp. 42–47). London: Routledge.

Morgan, M. (2005). On being able to be a couple: the importance of a "creative couple" in psychic life. In: F. Grier (Ed.), *Oedipus and the Couple* (pp. 9–30). London: Karnac.

Nathans, S. (2012). Infidelity as manic defence. *Couple and Family Psychoanalysis*, *2*(2): 165–180.

Ogden, T. H. (2012). Comments on transference and countertransference in the initial analytic meeting. In: B. Reith, S. Kagerlof, P. Crick, M. Moller & E. Skale (Eds.), *Initiating Psychoanalysis Perspectives* (pp. 173–188). London: Routledge.

Scharff, D. E. (2014). Working with affairs. In: D.E. Scharff & J.S. Scharff (Eds.), *Psychoanalytic Couple Therapy: Foundations of Theory and Practice* (pp. 254–268). London: Karnac.

Steiner, J. (1993). Problems of psychoanalytic technique: patient-centred and analyst-centred interpretations. In: *Psychic Retreats: Pathological Organisations in Psychotic, Neurotic and Borderline Patients*. London: Routledge.

Discussant perspective

Alicia Leisse de Lustgarten

Interpretation is a fundamental tool in psychoanalytic practice. Along with transference and knowledge of the unconscious world, it constitutes a leading feature of the psychoanalytic scene. The chapter by Keogh and Gregory-Roberts proposes the use of interpretation as a technique to introduce the couple to awareness of a process that involves them both and in which they repeat unconscious, archaic, childhood patterns. I shall discuss three points that I consider essential:

1 Interpretation in the initial interviews, as part of the psychoanalytic assessment.
2 Co-therapy with couples.
3 Reflective interventions.

Interpretation in the initial interview of the psychoanalytic assessment process

Couples rarely consult us merely out of curiosity. Each person who comes to us is moved by some symptomatic urgency that expresses a range of painful experiences. With couples this is especially true; we receive requests for help when the difficulties have evolved into a serious crisis, or an imminent separation is at stake.

The question about what causes the conflicts that have come to rest in the relationship forms part of a contract that gathers the actors of the therapeutic scenario in a joint task; their task centres on a relationship and its history that has been built by more phenomena than can be attributed to a particular member (Leisse de Lustgarten, 2016).

The couple relationship has its own unconscious structure, with a network of agreements and unconscious pacts, and of mutual projections that re-enact childhood events. The inclusion of interpretation in the initial interviews suggests that we "evaluate" not only what pertains to the couple in its relational dynamics, but also that we appreciate the presence of conscious and unconscious states of mind so that we can find a way of working that is as immediate as is their suffering. In the words of the authors, it will point to "the couple's capacity to benefit from a psychoanalytic intervention and to determine their level of psychic functioning and the required level of interpretations". I see the analysts' formulation as an approach that explores the couple's potential for insight, their capacities for change, and the latent discourse in their presentation that has been woven into their relationship. In my clinical

(continued)

(continued)

experience, couples react more speedily; their insight, when found, may be more easily lost through defensive mechanisms, and support for it in the transference is more labile and volatile. So it would seem that the authors are proposing to create, from the outset, a psychoanalytic frame for the work with methods that are traditionally more typically found in individual analysis.

Co-therapy with couples

The proposal that we work in co-therapy is a welcome option as is illustrated in this case. It opens up possibilities when a couple resorts to massive projective identification. The therapist, who is the object of projections from both partners, can engage with alliances that resist intervention, such as when he or she is used as an ally against a partner, or seduced in favour of some positioning.

Co-therapy offers a place when dealing with more dysfunctional situations. The case material in Keogh and Gregory-Roberts' chapter reflects a discourse that is sustained in the complaint about the other, where the essential task is to establish what it is that each one of the partners brings. Olivia displays psychosomatic aspects that seem to be linked to more dissociative defences, but the tone of her dissatisfaction is quite consistent. Conjoint co-therapy with couples becomes more immediate, less analytical in the temporal sense, although in saying that I am not ignoring the unconscious commitment of each of the partners and the re-emergence of oedipal identifications and narcissistic injuries. To address this, the authors propose "mutative couple interpretation". Co-therapy is also highly suited to work with families and groups in which it favours intersecting transferences. By this, I mean counter-transferential reactions that occur in both co-therapists, as is shown in this case by Olivia and Joe, recreating an unconscious parental setting that facilitates a working through, and repair of, failed childhood experiences. This has long been my experience and I concur with the belief that psychoanalysis also cures through the creation of a new transferential experience. I find that interpretation seeks to put into words the relational meaning that both partners bring to the intersubjective, inter-linking schema that makes up their shared discourse. I should like to comment on the working alliance and positive transference. Although they go hand in hand, I think that interpretation in the initial meetings seeks more of a working alliance; however, the containment and the pertinence of the interventions of the analytical pair would favour positive transference. Interpretation would correspond more to approaches that are designed to probe, as is illustrated in the couple case under discussion or, from my perspective, when something in the dynamic taking place prevents the development of the session, such as with impenetrable silences, defensive closures and threats of interruption, to name but a few.

Reflective interventions

From the proposed approach of co-therapy, I want to emphasise the role of reflective interpretation as an intervention. We can connect it with what has been described as reflective function, which refers to the psychological process that underlies the capacity to mentalise a concept. I understand it as opening new psychic spaces, giving rise to repressed or dissociated representations and symbolic registers. By means of the exchange that they produce between them as a result of an emergent communication referred to as Olivia's affair, the authors try to open the circle of accusations and attend to the increase of tension that closes the discourse while working with childhood parental identifications. A reflective interpretation allows one to be rescued from the subjectivities that arise with couples because co-therapy introduces a "third" (person) who brings a symbolic intervention that is far from the imaginary world. It comes from the place in which everyone has their own thoughts. It opens a way of thinking from the perspective of the "other" who has something to say. It allows us to see the interaction between the co-therapist couple recreating a new parental pairing.

References

Leisse de Lustgarten, A. (2016). La pareja ¿una relación imposible? *Lúdica, Psychoanalytical Review*, *16*: 4–9. https://issuu.com/revista.ludica/docs/__dica_e0019

Losso, R. (2001). *Family Psychoanalysis*. Buenos Aires: Lumen.

Spivacow, M. (2005). *Psychoanalytical Clinic with Couples*. Buenos Aires: Lugar Editorial.

Chapter 4

Demand analysis

The treatment of a couple

Pedro Gil Corbacho and Carmen Monedero Mateo

Introduction

The therapist's capacity of containment with difficult patients and couples serves as a model for alternative identifications and helps to liberate them from pathological links. The treatment described below lasted about two and a half years.

The referral

The woman's voice on the phone was quick and anxious: My partner and I have been in a difficult situation for a year. We have many problems living together and I cannot stand it anymore. We cannot live together or apart.

She also commented that she was not able to pay for therapy, which was a disarming comment for the therapist. The therapist nonetheless made an appointment noting that the fees could be discussed in the first interview.

The first interview

Elena and Juan were a young couple with a mistrustful look about them. Elena was tall, thin, and expressive and seemed hyper-vigilant. She was the "expressive" one in the couple. She noted that she was unemployed. She had previously worked as a saleswoman in a department store and also as a waitress as well as other temporary jobs. She did not finish high school. She likes to read, write, and draw. She asked directly for our help. Juan was more measured and remained silent. He looked at Elena with surprise and admiration. Juan has a robust, less careful, less expressive physique and moves slowly or tiredly. He looks older than his age. He seems uncomfortable, but speaks more calmly than Elena.

When we asked about their financial situation, which had been alluded to by Elena, he lowered his head as if he was ashamed.

Juan said he works with his father noting that: He does not pay me much, although he does very well.

Elena asks him to confront his father and ask him for a raise: an issue about which they often argue.

Elena: The schedule is very long . . . he comes home very late and I feel very lonely . . . If you loved me you would come back much earlier and you would keep me company more.

She says that his father exploits him and Juan admits that this is the case. He clarifies that his salary is in the mid–low range of a skilled worker.

They are both the same age – 26 years old – and met in an alternative anti-establishment group. Their relationship is now quite fractured. They continue to accept the values and habits they shared at the time they met, such as sexual freedom or smoking joints, but life together has become confusing, especially in relation to where they were then and what they wanted to achieve together.

Elena's attitude, it seems, causes strong arguments and confrontations leading to physical aggression. Juan says that on one occasion when he was leaving for work she grabbed his neck and said, "*Do not go, do not go!*", scratching and screaming at him.

They tell the therapists that because of the precariousness of her finances, Elena's mother came every week to her parish district or to other places to get bags of basic products such as rice, beans, lentils and oil and then bring these to Elena. At first, we did not understand that this was part of a way of keeping Elena very dependent on her. They had also lived in a low rental apartment that had been arranged with a government agency by Elena's mother.

Related to this, from the first interview, phrases like "We do not have money", "we do not have enough", etc., were common expressions they both used. The therapists felt a great pressure to assume a parental role and an unusual sense of dependency with them.

Juan said that Elena sometimes returns to the bar where they met. Elena's old boyfriend also visits this bar. Juan has doubts about whether they still maintain a relationship or if it is blackmail to show him the consequences of not being with her. In response, Juan disappears from the house offended and angry, but the absence awakens in Elena a desperate need to win him back. This meant that Elena has sometimes ended up in an emergency room with a panic attack.

Juan confirms that she was admitted to the emergency room in the psychiatry unit for abuse of anxiolytics following a big argument. After the argument Juan had returned home and found her unconscious, on the ground, surrounded by the boxes of the pills.

Juan says that in addition Elena continues to maintain a friendship with a childhood friend and he is very worried about this relationship. They share an interest in art, the esoteric and the Gothic movement. He doubts if there had been anything else to their relationship. Creating an air of mystery Elena clarifies that the relationship is only a friendship, but told us that at one point in their friendship they played with the romantic idea of committing suicide together in order to become invisible and to be remembered forever by their beloved.

Juan says he feels a sword of Damocles hangs over him as a result of these relationships. She says this is not so. Juan also says he often does not know what kind of situation he will find when he returns home. He notes that he is subjected to ultimatums such as: "*Earn money, come earlier and join me and if not, watch out for the consequences*" which make him suffer from an unbearable tension.

In Elena's family history there had been several traumatic events. Her grandmother had suffered all kinds of hardships during the Spanish Civil War and later on as a result of mistreatment by an alcoholic husband who had himself been politically persecuted and imprisoned and who became ill in captivity. After his release, his illness prevented him from working and contributed to him becoming an alcoholic. In the post-war period, her grandmother barely managed to keep the family afloat. Elena's mother had to work as a housekeeper and obtain food and clothing from charitable institutions.

Elena's mother married when she was very young and had two daughters, but the marriage ended soon after. The father disappeared and the children were left in her care. Elena worked from a very young age in a large company as an administrative assistant. She never had any boyfriends. Elena spoke ambivalently about her mother, noting that although she had an ability to work, was sociable, and had the ability to get opportunities, she was not able to love.

We were told that Elena envied her older sister who is married and has two daughters, one of whom is an adolescent with anorexia and with whom Elena has a good relationship.

Juan has had a very different family comprising his parents, two older brothers who were rivalrous with him and two younger sisters who studied at university and still live at home.

They all worked in the father's business whose focus was housing reforms, although each one had a different occupation. Juan was the youngest of the three older brothers. He visits the family home the most, which is why – says Elena – he was his mother's favourite. This led to compensations such as gifts, take away food or protection from his father when he committed some transgression at work. Juan described his father as authoritarian. He was described as feared and the undisputed boss, both inside and outside the house. His mother took care of the housework and the two small daughters. During the interview the couple sat together and exchanged complicit smiles. Their non-verbal communication suggested that they were both attracted to, yet fed-up with, each other.

The session with the couple was 90 minutes in duration, with a pause at 70 minutes when the therapists left the consulting room for about 10 minutes to share their impressions of the process and the impact of the couple's projections, prior to ending the session.

In the first pause, the therapists agreed that dependence and exploitation were important dynamics for this couple, the dynamics in which they would like to include the therapists. The therapist noted their surprise that a couple which such backgrounds would present for a private consultation. The couple seemed to be continuing an unfinished adolescence. Elena seemed to manifest the anaclitic and fusional dimension of the relationship which Juan responded to repeatedly through risking his job by arriving late, leaving early and being unproductive. Juan valued Elena's support of independence towards his family. The projection of dependence onto the other, however, seemed to result in an exhausting game of love and hate from which they could not escape.

Their situation was becoming unmanageable. It had created an unhelpful scenario combining understanding, creativity, a sinister suicide game and unbearable guilt. They revealed a need to get out of this labyrinth of arrested development whereby Elena pushed Juan to a fight with his father, resulting in something between independence and marginality. This was a fight whereby she overcame the abandonment suffered in her childhood by her father, represented by what Bion (1962) calls "presence of absence", which seemed to have caused a generational transmission of void, abandonment and helplessness that affected women in her family. Her mother overprotected her in a way that resulted in deep fear, insecurity and helplessness. On the other hand, her object fragility and her insecure female identifications fuelled her hysterical resort to seduction and provocation. Juan also contributed to the couple his family structure centred on an Oedipal conflict. Notwithstanding this, there were valuable things about their relationship that could be saved or repaired: they were young, intelligent and had a lively attraction to each other. In many ways, they supported and supplemented each other.

The therapists agreed that their intervention could only be helpful if it rested on a clear and containing frame which reinstated the law, the limit, the castration and the weaning (Berenstein & Puget, 1988) along with better identifications and judgement of reality. The therapists thus agreed that they could lower their fees, but they were not prepared to provide free therapy. The frame had to start from a firm therapeutic contract that was clear and was accepted by both parties. This was particularly relevant given Elena's borderline features (Yeomans, Clarkin & Kernberg, 2002). The therapists also thought that as a therapeutic couple they could facilitate change in the couple's identifications, the conflict between them as a couple and between them and their parental figures. After the pause the therapists, therefore, proposed a rather definite therapeutic contract and specified how they worked, the structure of the sessions, their duration, frequency and fees (which were significantly reduced). The couple, when asked if they could afford the fee, looked at each other and agreed with the therapists that they could. The therapists asked the couple to think about it and let them know their decision in order to organise a schedule for the sessions. They called us five days later and once the frame was accepted the therapeutic work commenced.

The first phase of the work

At the beginning of the work, their unfinished adolescence was revealed through mutual disqualifications, challenges and fights during the sessions. They seemed to know everything and they looked at us from a sceptical, self-sufficient and challenging attitude based on the values of the original counterculture group in which they had met. To the extent that we did not react to these challenges but rather focused on their problems, this attitude faded away. Each member of the couple behaved dysfunctionally and whilst Elena's behaviour was more conspicuous than Juan's immaturity, linked to difficulties identifying with his father, it was no less worrying. Elena, highlighting this issue, said:

> Juan is a very intelligent man who has never been allowed to express himself at home. His father never recognised his value, as in their house the father's worth was all that mattered . . . nobody takes an opposite view . . . for me though it is his mother who gives me grief.

Juan characterised his mother as a martyr, which he saw as resulting from the impact of her father's character. Elena activated this archaic scenario by organising an unconscious mosaic which was shared by Juan, wherein she juxtaposed the psychic representations originally generated by her absent father and an abusive alcoholic grandfather with the loneliness and bitterness of his mother and grandmother. In this unconscious scenario, he had the task of saving all these martyred and unhappy women. Elena thus reinforced his Oedipal conflict encompassing the tyranny and cruelty of his father. The compassion towards Juan's mother by Elena, however, also involved a mixture of envy and rage because of the "special" relationship Juan's mother had with him. In this regard, Elena noted:

> You are your mother's favourite, the only one who defends her!

These associated conflicts with his father were the main reason that Juan could not progress professionally. Elena depended on Juan and he on her, but while he succumbed to Elena's dependence on him, he could not deal with the conflict with his family which had resulted in an inhibition of his development. He was a competent professional who could have found better-paid work.

Through the continuous work of clarification, confrontation and interpretation (Yeomans, Clarkin & Kernberg, 2002), the therapists were able to access less damaged internal objects. As a result Juan was able to come to see that neither his father was a monster nor his mother a martyr, as Elena saw them. This allowed an improvement of the relationship with his family and for Elena to confront the gaps and the deficiencies resulting from an absent father and the affective deficiencies in her relationship with her mother. She came to see her mother as neither cold nor distant, but a mother who had to be constantly working as a result of her concern for the welfare of her daughters.

The changes in dynamics produced in Juan an Oedipal appeasement that improved the relationship with his family. It became clear to Elena that she needed to confront her own family trauma and that the therapists were in fact there to help her.

The couple had been trapped in a turbulent late adolescence where they united, collided and could not separate. Pathological dynamics bound them whereby Elena could not be separated from Juan and in turn, he could not be separated from her, or adequately from his family. The intertwining of projective identifications generated an overwhelmingly closed atmosphere, with confrontations involving serious levels of verbal and physical violence. Their relationship was being destroyed. The feeling of dissatisfaction led them to consider a separation, yet this was not possible given the projective identifications that chained them together. Fighting together against tyrannical fathers and their joint values are what bonded them originally but were now not enough. In addition, there had developed a hatred and violence that had infiltrated their relationship that contributed to the end of their chimera of self-sufficiency, that is, an infernal circle based on fight – helplessness, guilt, failed repair – in which their dissatisfaction was being consolidated. They were united in fighting.

In many sessions, the therapists witnessed a real battle between the linking madness that threatened to consolidate this cycle and the work of therapeutic elaboration that deactivated it. Countertransferentially, the therapists agreed that the "inner pair" of our patients (Scharff & Scharff, 1994) could be understood by the "inner pair" of our therapeutic partnership. The therapeutic couple facilitated transformations and the inversion of the trend toward the psychic death of the link through containment and interpretations. Elena had lacked a sufficiently narcissistic mother to prop up her psychic apparatus and feminine identity and was preferentially addressing the female therapist in a quest for references and identification. In turn, the male therapist was facilitating Juan's identification with him, offering and opening spaces in which he could express his anxieties, fears and motivations because he was a much quieter person than she, and had not been heard in his family. This was acknowledged by Elena, who silently was ultimately able to better understand Juan's and her own emotions and to find in the male therapist the containing and limiting paternal figure she had lacked. The therapists were thus able to consolidate the presence of a law that included containment and respect, whilst promoting the presence of the "analytical third" (Ogden, 2008) constituted by the unconscious universe of the four participants in the analytical field, offering opportunities for understanding, identification and repair.

The analytic third and the game

At the end of the first year, the analytical field deepened and was enriched with the material arising from the transference–countertransference relationship that crossed over to the therapeutic couple and incorporated split aspects, produced surprises and changed each of the couple's point of view and calmed them. The therapists pointed out how the containment dimension of the work group formed by the four participants provided them with the soothing and restorative elements for the fear and psychic hunger they each carried.

During our work there were noisy, sometimes unbearably so, repair works taking place on the floor above us. Juan, as a professional, sometimes made a comic note about the hammering, metal saw, voices, radio, songs, silences, etc. At one moment when Elena was talking about something and she could not be heard well, the noise suddenly stopped. At that point Juan said:

> Take the chance to speak now. The man using the saw has gone to the bathroom!

This caused everyone to laugh and produced a relaxed atmosphere in the consulting room. Juan was coming to the session during working hours. He had spoken about this to his father who had no problem in replacing him. In addition, Elena had recently said that her mother had left food in a container for her. The therapists gave an interpretation:

> It seems that we have several companies working together: your reform company, your father's reform company, your mother's catering and the mental reform company or the "shrinks".

Shrinks, along with "magicians" or "sorcerers", were all words that had been used to describe the therapists. In a funny mood, Elena said she thought we had done some Harry Potter magic during the break because they left calmer and the feeling lasted for a while.

Spontaneous play and sense of humour were recovered and were good prognostic signs in the session as now when they met they were able to laugh together. Elena nonetheless recognised that when Juan left for work she could feel empty and could be filled with terror.

Elena: . . . I literally go crazy. I feel like a cockroach. I hate him. I think he's a bastard for leaving me like that and that he does not care about me. He takes advantage of me because he knows my weakness, that he has got me in his hands and then I want him to suffer because he is like his father, and I would like him to have horns this big!

Containment and repair

The therapists addressed the desire for revenge via Elena's infidelity towards Juan, based on her fantasy that he had his work, family and the favour of his mother and she just had her emptiness while waiting for him. They also addressed the impossible demands towards an idealised Juan that could never substitute for the father she never had. The therapists also acknowledged that they could not solve all the problems the couple had. They would have to do something for themselves. In this sense, the therapists rescued Juan from the guilt produced by Elena's hate towards the paternal figure engendered by his absence, with much relief and gratitude on his part.

It took us a long time to identify the area of their current chaos as a mixture of impulsivity, immaturity, sexual promiscuity, abandonment, alcohol and substance abuse, as the denial of hardness and the difficulty of maintaining a mutual commitment. The therapists were gradually getting them to see the futility of denial, of saying to themselves that nothing happens and that it does not matter.

Simultaneously, the therapist also recovered their positive capacities in order to be able to organise an alternative relationship, both what they originally saw in each other and those that appeared during the session. They were able to recover many things including Elena's attraction, good sexuality, creativity and dynamism, along with Juan's patience and solidity, his intelligence and resources and a sense of humour and play within which we were sometimes included.

Sometimes Elena cried bitterly when the depth and painful material of her helplessness and that of the women of her family, which she had attributed to Juan, were not going to be solved. When these outbursts occurred she became exhausted, but Juan took her by the hand whilst the therapists provided the necessary containment. This work of containment was arduous, as Elena would frequently stand to leave the session shouting: "I cannot stand this anymore!"

The couple tested the therapists' containment capacity and they were very worried at times when Juan said he could not stand it anymore and threatened to give up and leave, especially as Elena had threatened to commit suicide. The therapists convinced them that it was also important to take the prescribed pharmacological treatment seriously after her admission to the emergency room since her anxiety at times was overwhelming.

Although Elena sincerely believed in Juan's ability, this was not enough for him. Elena was at times the cheerful and funny girl who could allow herself to be what he couldn't and which represented their stolen adolescence. Her psychic conflicts, however, were intense and often overwhelming and prevented him from experiencing such moments. Exacerbating her conflicts, Juan could not avoid working outside the home because he was the one who brought money into the house.

On the other hand, certain attributes of their parental objects were rescued. These included Juan's entrepreneurial capacity (similar to his father's) and Elena's sociability (like her mother's). These were valid identifying elements that were within them and which could help them to grow another "psychic skin" (Anzieu, 2016). This would bring them closer to generating a different binding structure, a task to which we were all committed.

In one session, Juan said he had been making croquettes for the week. As we had not heard this before, we asked him further about it.

Juan: In the DNA of all Spanish there is an innate knowledge about making croquettes.

The couple and the therapist all laughed about this. He had learned this from his mother, who was an expert in recycling everything so that they ate croquettes at home almost daily. He had made calculations and claimed that he had eaten about 18,000 croquettes throughout his life.

Elena told him that maybe he looked the way he did because of this!

Therapist: Perhaps there are other innate abilities in your DNA and in Elena's that have not been developed until now, that you are developing with us and that we also reprocessing other things that you bring to the session?

The analytical field was integrating their different experiences into a joint record, a process wherein all the pathological circuits were also being deactivated. After the discussion breaks toward the end of the session, we returned to talk about what we had been able to understand. We perceived a certain "suspense" in them when we returned after our break. They looked at each other nervously but also with happy and expectant faces. In this way the therapists came to see that the couple's experience of them was that of a sublimated and detoxifying primary scene.

Therapist: You have a fantasy that as therapists we work our magic in between sessions, but the magic occurs during the sessions where we can all think together and get rid of the toxic elements that have appeared and also reprocess all the good elements that have hitherto gone unnoticed.

The therapists really needed breaks to detoxify and recover from their projections and to metabolise the innumerable verbal and non-verbal beta elements that appeared in the session, that generate not only links of thought (K) but also links of love (L) and hate (H) (Bion, 1962).

This transformation was the opposite of one into hatred (H-link), violence and aggression, and one that could appear unexpectedly. The magic of Harry Potter consisted of such a joint transformation, although sometimes in the pauses the therapists disagreed on our impressions and had to discuss them.

Elena ultimately started going to a city council writing workshop. She wrote stories that she shared with her classmates, which allowed her to fill in voids and no longer feel alone. Her creative side was emerging. The transitional space seemed to be recovering. This was reflected in a better mood which meant we could sometimes all laugh together at their ideas.

Conclusions

The understanding of links and individual dynamics in the couple produced an attenuation of the arguments and the violent actions and generated a greater stability and emergence of a creative potential. After a year and a half, Juan talked about the possibility of a business that required very little investment. The prospect of this project delighted both of them and they thought that they would be able to invest in it with Elena's funds, a loan from Juan's parents and the help of some friends. They discussed the details of it and five months later it became a reality. They are now both working on it, together with another partner. After some consolidation of their therapeutic gains and harmony living together, they also began to think about the possibility of having a child.

During this time Elena became pregnant, which caused her anxieties, fears and fantasies that she brought to the sessions. One day she reported the following dream:

> I was pregnant and had to go to a hospital. I'm wandering around the city, lost and lonely. . .I just remembered the anxiety of not finding the hospital.

Loneliness and helplessness were thus once again present as a result of the pregnancy, with the consequent fears and anxieties of not being able to reach the end. However, being able to recognise them, to name the terrors and to work in the sessions, considerably diminished this anxiety. The fantasies of death in childbirth, however, generated an amount of distress that was difficult to metabolise. There were several sessions in which there appeared an intense fear of losing the baby, which was linked to the women in her family and their helplessness. The therapist told her that in the dream she was not only the mother, but also the baby.

Therapist: There is a lot of fear that you will not be able to be a mother and that the child will die as a reactivation of your internal gaps and terrors so present in the women of your family, but we will continue to work here.

In this period the presence of the female therapist as a maternal, containment and identification figure was essential. During the pregnancy, Elena talked with her daughter and also wrote to her. Gradually, she felt that she could be a good mother when her daughter was born. When she talked about her baby and looking after her daughter, her face lit up. The couple knew that the baby was going to be a girl, which met Elena's expectations, and which she transmitted with an intense joy shared with her partner and with the therapists as the "therapeutic grandparents". The drive of life had succeeded in displacing the inertia of the chaos and the death drive that was being established between them at the beginning of the treatment. For the moment, the life drive had become stronger than the death drive and its destructiveness.

References

Anzieu, D. (2016). *The Skin Ego*. London: Karnac.

Berenstein, I., & Puget, J. (1988). *Psicoanálisis de la pareja matrimonial*. Buenos Aires: Paidos.

Bion, W. R. (1962). *Learning from Experience*. London: Heinemann.

Ogden, T. (2008). On holding and containing, being and dreaming. *International Journal of Psychoanalysis*, *85*: 1349–1364.

Scharff, J. S., & Scharff, D. E. (1994). *Objects Relations Couple Therapy*. Northvale, NJ: Jason Aronson.

Yeomans, F. E., Clarkin, J. F., & Kernberg, O. F. (2002). *A Primer of Transference-Focused Psychotherapy for the Borderline Patient*. Northvale, NJ: Jason Aronson.

Editors' prologue to the discussant perspective

The case of Elena and Juan presented by Pedro Gil Corbacho and Carmen Monedero Mateo highlights a modification of the clinical setting to include a 90-minute session wherein the therapists have discussion breaks in order to process the couple's projections. They note that this is experienced as a kind of magic by the couple. Their intervention enabled the couple to deal with unresolved issues from adolescence and more primitive issues which had resulted in a somewhat fused relationship that had led to intense arguments and violence. Rosa Jaitin discusses the chapter from the perspective of the paradoxical bonds in the couple relationship and from the perspective of their lack of separation and individuation, which had impacted on their ability to resolve satisfactorily their Oedipal complexes.

Discussant perspective

Rosa Jaitin

I will analyse this clinical material from a double perspective. The first concerns the paradoxical modality of the bonds between the spouses that enables us to define the problem of abandonment in their active and passive positions. This also includes the weight of the transgenerational issues impacting on their linking configuration.

The second perspective refers to the understanding of Oedipal complexes which have been studied in psychoanalysis, from Freud to his contemporaries (Freud, 1962; Klein, 1945), complexes which allow for an expansion of the meaning of the linking paradox. The therapeutic process of this couple illustrates a transformation incorporating such concepts.

The paradoxical link

The bond of the couple described is organised around the abandoning-abandoned paradox and the separation–non-separation testing of the symbolic value of exchange, which manifests itself in the relationship with the analysts and the arrangements concerning fees.

This "identity" paradox[1] (Racamier, 1992) corresponds to a narcissistic union, which aspires to be a unique body, dominated by a symbiotic nebula. The couple cannot mourn the illusion of a continuous, omnipotent relationship and uninterrupted belonging. The other does not constitute an object of desire but lives in an imprecise and unbounded atmosphere. Not being able to overcome the "original mourning", they settle in a relationship where "the magma" in which they are immersed becomes a kind of primitive psychic mass and indeed the reason why they come to the consultation. It forms an intense aggression between them, which does not allow them to separate. On the contrary, it becomes a paradox that binds them and confuses them even more.

It is the development of a capacity for disillusionment which allows the implementation of "original mourning". From early childhood, the ego, in order to emerge, must be able to renounce the total possession of the object by mourning the narcissistic union. The elaboration of this grief constitutes the condition prior to the discovery of the object, as well as the capacity to internalise it.

Original mourning is a process that never ends, and that is why the self finds itself in what it loses from the other. This constitutes an "identity paradox" because to find the object as different from oneself involves the acceptance of the loss of self in the other.

The passage between the generations is based on the mutual narcissistic support provided by family bonds. When these represent transgenerational failures, they produce a lack of basic security and a narcissistic withdrawal that further complicates the difference between the subjects. If families go through traumatic experiences, the work of psychic separation becomes complicated. Significant traces of the traumatic experiences from prior generations can remain inaccessible to subsequent generations. These remnant experiences can, however, emerge as ghosts in the subsequent generation and impact adversely on family bonds and a couple or family's capacity for transformation.

There is something happening in the life experience of the couple presented, Elena and Juan, that alludes to trans- and inter-generational narcissistic trauma in the maternal lineages. Both mothers are mourning because of the lack of support from the couple, which may have massively compromised their emotional investment with their children.

The premature disappointment in the parental bond has, as a result, the feeling of loss of parental love. Faced with the fragility of the family of origin, the child cannot express his aggressiveness and thus remains attached to the mother. As a result aggressiveness is substantially transferred to the couple's relationship in a displaced attempt to separate from the family of origin.

Both Juan and Elena identify with the ghost of a dying woman–mother, shattered by a father who does not support her. The linking structure of the families of origin of both spouses is similar; there is only one difference of degree. The masculine figures are not differentiated and therefore Elena and Juan do not manage to construct an internal triangular object, which takes the place of the negative. Consequently a denegative pact or unconscious alliance is founded as a type of common defensive psychic space, which both compromises the bond and at the same time consolidates it in this defensive way.

Together the couple attempts to help each other through family duels. This represents their attempt for the resolution of their difficulties such that each spouse is placed in a different stage of mourning connected to the family of origin of each member of the couple. The couple thus consults in a state of crisis in which the verbal dialogue is reduced and consequently their imaginary function and capacity for inter-fantasmatisation is impoverished. This situation encourages their use of projection, expressed by violent affective discharges, which exhaust the narcissistic reserve that gave birth to them as a couple. At the same time, the crisis produces an important modification to the economic and defensive aspect of their "conjugal self". As a consequence, a feeling of loss of their previous equilibrium emerges without knowing what the present and the future have in store for them.

(continued)

(continued)

The search for a subjective appropriation, in which the couple can take charge of their own history, opens up a way for a different future. It causes a transformation in the content and the affects of their psychic process. The therapeutic process with this couple is, however, very rich and highlights their original state of love–disaffection that sets in motion a conjugal bond which allows a double movement: On the one hand a regressive destructuring and on the other hand a progressive construction, as a rebirth of new and original elements which did not exist previously (Ruffiot, 1984).

Returning again to the clinical material, we can also think about this couple's Oedipal complexes in terms of their links. In general terms Oedipal complexes refer to triangular structures of fantasmatic family relationships that allow or hinder the construction of the identity of the subject (Kaës, 2008). Such structures are constituted by unconscious alliances, woven by bonds of love and hatred, of inclusion and exclusion, that inscribe the subject's family bonds. The pre-Oedipal complexes refer to the fantasmatic representation of inclusion and exclusion in undifferentiated triad relations. We could think that pre-Oedipal complexes, dominated by separation anxiety, organise the bond of this couple. Psychoanalysis has continued to develop the question. Klein (1945), for example, mentions the weaning and its relationship to the early Oedipus complex, whilst Lacan (1938) emphasises the presence of a maternal imago and the intrusion complex in the mirror stage. Pigott (1999) takes up the idea of Lacan from a group perspective, arguing that for the maternal imago to evolve and provide access to other complexes, the "original grief" must have been developed (Racamier, 1992) such that the self discovers that it must renounce the possession of the object before recognising itself.

Such triadic relationships are thus dominated by the anguish of separation, while the Oedipal complex supposes a self, more integrated and organised by castration anxiety. The therapeutic process is constructed by an intermediary space between the analysts and the couple. Creative resources emerge out of the work of the analysts in the transferential field that allow them to sustain themselves in a trusting link. This then allows the conjugal self to face the necessary developmental task, and provides methods of adaptation and survival to recover the autonomous self of each one (Jaitin, 2013).

During the therapeutic process, real or fantasied relationships with third parties, together with relationships with the families of origin, allow the couple to elaborate their anxiety of abandonment, since each member of the couple passes the tolerance test for exclusion. This opens the way to the elaboration of an Oedipal conjugal couple relationship that culminates with the birth of the parental couple.

To conclude, it is in the field of counter and inter-transference of the relationship between analysts that a negative hallucination emerges. The possibility arises for representing absence in order to get rid of the knotting of the conjugal relation. This representation of the unrepresentable allows a subjective appropriation of the family and social history of this couple.

References

Freud, S. (1962). *Three Essays on the Theory of Sexuality*, J. Strachey (Trans.). New York: Basic Books.

Jaitin, R. (2013). Construction identificatoire en psychanalyse familiale: complexes et imago (Identificatory construction in family psychoanalysis: complexes and imagos). In: J. C. Rouchy & P. Benghozi (Eds.), *Le thérapeute confronté à de nouvelles structures familiales* (pp. 35–46). Paris: Erès.

Kaës, R. (2008). *Le complexe fraternel* (The fraternal complex). Paris: Dunod.

Klein, M. (1945). The Oedipus complex in the light of early anxieties. *International Journal of Psychoanalysis*, *26*: 11–33.

Lacan, J. (1938). Les complexes familiaux dans la formation de l'individu: Essaie d'analyse d'une fonction en psychologie (The family complexes in the formation of an individual, an analysis essay of function on psychology). In: *Autres Ecrits* (pp. 23–84). Paris: Le Seuil, 2001.

Pigott, P. C. (1999). *Les imagos terribles* (Terribles imagos). Paris: Collège de Psychanalyse Groupale et Familiale.

Racamier, P. C. (1992). *Le deuil originaire* (The original mourning). Paris: Payot, 2016.

Ruffiot, A. (1984). *Le couple et l'amour: de l'originaire au groupal* (The couple and the love: from the original to the group). In: *la thérapie psychanalytique de couple* (pp. 1–83). Paris: Dunod.

Note

1 For Racamier (1992) the work of mourning is an arduous, living and durable work. It places mourning as a vital element, not related to death, but as a process of all discovery.

Chapter 5

Therapeutic intervention in psychoanalytical clinical work with couples

Miguel Alejo Spivacow

Introduction

Nowadays all sorts of couples seek out psychoanalytical intervention for their conflicts, yet most are probably unaware of the many theoretical and clinical challenges their presentations pose to our discipline. Although ours is "a discipline in search of a definition" (Clulow, 2011, p. 1), as psychoanalysts we have accepted the challenge and conduct the couple link treatments, albeit with variable success.

The purpose of this chapter is to discuss some of the many questions that we deal with once we have agreed to treat a couple and decide to intervene. In short, how does the clinical work with couples differ from that with individual patients? In what way does the analyst intervene in a couple's treatment? Which perspectives should be emphasised when constructing the intervention? What is the target of his/her interpretations? I note that a brief chapter such as the present one, with such a vast scope, must necessarily leave aside many important issues.

Intervention or interpretation?

At the outset I would like to state my preference for the term *intervention* rather than interpretation when referring to the analyst's main tool. The psychoanalytic tradition since Freud has used the term interpretation to designate the participation of the analyst, who aspires to make conscious the unconscious and to unravel the coordinates of the patient's desires. When treating couples, however, the purpose of the analyst's work is not exactly the same as that postulated by Freud with individual treatments, although it does include some similar features. Sometimes, the goal is to achieve a decrease in the level of violence so that partners can interact differently or to allow one of the partners to imagine what the other is feeling, or to be aware when one's partner's behaviour is far from the behaviour that is attributed to him/her. It also differs from the individual treatment approach in terms of what Freud referred to as *interpretation*. In our way of understanding psychoanalysis, interpretation is not exclusively constructed by the analyst, but jointly with his/her patients.

Allowing for these differences, the term *intervention* seems more appropriate when referring to this aspect of clinical work with couples.

The couple therapist therefore intervenes, choosing the content for the therapeutic project, a process that we will necessarily leave aside in this chapter. That said, apart from the content that his/her words transmit, he/she must mentally take on first what Morgan (2014) calls "the couple state of mind". The analyst should have this perspective present when intervening with a couple and, if the treatment progresses, it becomes internalised by them. From this perspective, the main focus for analysis is the relationship. There may be other foci, but the relationship is to be kept in sight and the therapist, from a neutral position, observes and ponders what type of "link" the partners are co-creating and what unconscious fantasies and beliefs support the link, which is understood as ". . . the bonds that unite, divide, and organise people in their intimate groups . . ." (Scharff & Palacios, 2017, p. 280).

In this way the couple is seen as a dynamic organisation in which each member carries aspects of the other in a permanent pendulum movement. Therefore, the therapist may address the functioning of one or the other member of the couple, or both, but always has the link in mind. Quite often, the intervention is centred on the exchange between both partners, the conscious and unconscious, the voluntary and involuntary, with its purpose being to clarify and address the way in which both partners contribute (unknowingly) to shape the psychic functioning. This contrasts markedly with interpretation as described by Freud, which fundamentally addresses the clarification and predominantly the modification of the manner in which a single subject privileges aspects of psychic functioning. It does not allow for attention to be paid to the relational context or the type of relationship established between the couple. That is, whereas the Freudian interpretation mainly targets the intra-subjective dynamics, the intervention with a couple focuses mainly on the inter-subjective dynamics.

Since it addresses two subjects, which are both present and usually in conflict, the intervention presents problems that do not exist in the Freudian style interpretation. The analysands are two persons with different defensive systems and resistances, uneven symbolisation possibilities and, in summary, different perceptions and capabilities. Consider the following vignette in order to consider these differences in approach.

Orlando (in a very aggressive tone):	When you talk to her, the first thing you need to consider is her pride, that the lady won't be offended. I´m tired of having to always consider her first, Daddy's girl, the Jewish Princess.
Rita:	You are so bitter (while she looks at the horizon, offended and vengeful). You always see the glass half empty!
Therapist:	This is difficult, isn't it?

While saying this, the analyst considers why they are saying these things to each other. He wonders how to speak for both of them; no matter what he says, he will be included in one or the other side of the war. Orlando will think that the analyst is colluding with the Jewish Princess and her vanity, while Rita will think that he is Orlando's accomplice for not exposing more emphatically his depression.

There is a relatively long silence and the analyst senses from the atmosphere and the faces of Rita and Orlando that there may be a chance of dropping these relentless recriminations. He decides, although hesitantly, to intervene again.

Therapist: I believe there may be a point in what each of you says of the other, but I don't think a festival of attacks and retaliations will help. You are both enhancing the worst in each other. You offend each other, but can't think of what the other is saying.

Addressing two subjects with different positions like these poses countless problems of timing and strategy, mainly in constructing interventions whose formulations will not trigger an unmanageable rejection or resistance in one of the partners, since one may feel supported while the other may feel exactly the opposite. This problem can't be resolved with artificially pacifist and equidistant interventions, but instead requires a comprehensive assessment of the therapeutic project and tactics, the strategy and policy of the intervention.

As Kaës (1994) explains, "all the difficulty and the stakes of the process undertaken in a group analytical situation depend on the others 'responding', while that 'other' who is the psychoanalyst does not respond, or does not respond in the same way" (p. 43). It isn't easy to speak in a battlefield, and the partner does not function like the analyst in the Freudian individual analytic framework, as he/she is a very particular interlocutor, governed by the rule of abstinence.

In couple therapy, the focus to work on is how both partners co-construct the suffering that brings them to consultation, how what one of them does feeds back on what the other does. In this exchange, the protagonist that is probably essential is *bi-directionality* or *inter-determination* (Spivacow, 2011). The therapist focuses on the different ways of relating with the other, metabolising and symbolising what comes from him/her, their link and the subject him/herself. The analysis is biased and focuses on inter-influences and the ways in which both partners signify, resonate, disagree, receive, contain, reject, bind, enrich or expel either what comes from the other or what is produced in the relationship. The focus of observation is whether the members of a dyad are attuned (Spivacow, 2011) or ignore each other's contributions, that is, whether they can put themselves in the other's place and either attack, confirm, disconfirm or manipulate what the other feels, and how much of each other's proposals they understand, and whether or not they validate them (Spivacow, 2011).

Interpretation, according to most of Freud's descriptions of neurotic disorders, centres on infantile neurosis and repetition compulsion whereas the intervention in couple psychotherapy centres on the intersubjective dynamics; these are two supplementary, albeit different perspectives. Analysis of such couple exchanges goes through different phases according to the singularity of each link. Generally, the first phase is centred on the conscious aspect of bi-directionality and is later followed by more latent processes. To grasp the idea of what happens in a subject's psyche, Freud used free association as a technique, which functions as a map representing a means of accessing the elusive geography of the mind. The map representing this elusive geography in a couple session is the *joint discourse*.

Moreover, the dynamics of a link are expressed in the session as a *joint discourse*, a concept that designates the plot of words, gestures and facts, associations and interactions produced by a couple during a session. Whilst free association results in a single order of determinants – i.e., the intra-subjective production of a single subject, with the least interference of others so as to better reflect his/her inner world – the joint discourse in contrast results from two main orders of determinants: those that respond to unique functioning of each partner (one could say his/her inner world), and those that derive from the interaction and the link that joins them. It forms a pattern in which at times, what one of the partners says and does gives a sense to the other partner's expression, resignifying his/her behaviours and words, whereas at other times individual participations seem to be independent from the interaction and come close to a *free* association. The other's interferences and disruptive presence make up the matter of the joint discourse itself and the expression of the inter-subjective during the session.

In the joint discourse, we pay attention to both the verbal and non-verbal. Firstly, we pay attention to what is said as in free association, but also to that which results from the inter-subjective encounter, in particular, misunderstandings, interruptions, manipulations, significant repetitions, and similar thought contents in the words of both partners in the dyad, polarisations, distribution of roles, inductions, arguments that are unacceptable for the other, contradictions between saying and doing, as well as various fantasmatic inter-influences. In sum, attention is paid to the multiple manifestations resulting from the conscious and unconscious interaction between partners and with the analyst. Regarding the non-verbal aspect, "the silent film" of the session or the gestures say as much or more about the encounter than words, and in many sessions it may be that the only thing that one of the members of the couple *says* is, for example, looking at the floor or grinding their teeth.

Working with links, the specific "lever" of the intervention with couples

The interventions of the analyst, as in all types of psychotherapy, may refer to any of the infinite and interesting issues of life, but if a treatment of links has been implemented, most probably the analyst will be principally concerned with the inter-subjective conflicts that cause the couple's particular distress. Generally then, we focus on conflict between both partners arising from their more or less complex link but occasionally focusing on some of their intra-subjective aspects.

The most frequent intervention therefore consists of demonstrating, with the appropriate timing, the various perceptions and foci of each of the partners, and the effort both make to impose their own way of giving meaning to the conflict and its eventual solutions. The most common therapeutic project is working through with the couple ways of metabolising which are different from the dysfunctional solutions that they themselves propose (such as manipulation, expulsion, submission, isolations, splitting, denial, etc.), that is, to volunteer to be a facilitator of a way of relating that takes a new direction and in doing so aiming to remove obstacles and stereotyped interactions. The goal is to reformulate their inter-subjective conflicts, reformulating negativities (Kaës, 1999); this is what the partners exclude from the conscious exchange, and its dysfunctional effects. By working on these tasks we expect to achieve the greatest potential for psychic change.

Generally one does not seek – although it may be useful to do so – to communicate a better or more appropriate criterion than that proposed by the partners with regards to the conflict. Nor does the approach consist of interpreting the meanings that arise, as Freud did, for example, with the symbolic elements of a dream. The goal is rather to target some aspect arising from the inter-subjective matrix, i.e., some aspect of *the work with links or inter-subjective work*.

In fact, rather than focusing on the multiple and various tasks of the psychic life, we focus on *working with the link* (*travail de l'intersubjectivité, trabajo vincular*), which is seen as the mode of functioning that bonds two subjects together. Working with the link means working on how one subject attempts to impose or relate their reality onto the other and vice versa (Spivacow, 2011). Put another way the link is determined by what one subject does with the reality the other presents (Pichon-Rivière, 1956–1957; Spivacow, 2011).

The type of work with the link that the analyst will try to promote will be unique for every link, but in general it entails a metabolisation or way of thinking about the couple's conflicts which has the greatest chance of producing a new awareness, allowing for the best possible distinction between internal and external objects without excessive violence (Aulagnier, 1975). All this presumes the possibility to negotiate the narcissism and related agendas of each partner, by promoting a capability in each partner of putting themselves in the other's place and their tendency to dominate and to submit. In this regard, our concepts of attunement and validation (Spivacow, 2011) reflect our idea of what may be for both partners the most acceptable form of working with the link, remembering that adjustment and pleasure include maladjustments and conflicts, and that working with the link does not only involve the inter-subjective, but that the inter-subjective and intra-subjective both influence and mobilise each other.

Like Archimedes, the therapist positions him/herself using the work with the link as a point of support. As the sage of Syracuse said, "Give me a point of support and I shall move the world," perhaps overestimating his discoveries about the power of levers and pulleys, we might say that the point of support on which most of the therapeutic levers pivot in couple treatments is the work with the link. The analyst's activity focuses on the psychic work that each subject imposes on the other and/or that the other arouses in him/her, in the manner of a facilitator or analyser of the exchange. The great lever from which therapy seeks to make effective psychic change is the dynamics of the link at its conscious and unconscious levels. Since what Freud emphasised for the *intra-psychic* functioning applies as well for the *inter-psychic* functioning, the psyche acquires its determinant forms in the unconscious strata. Hence, although stereotypes in the psyche and the exchange are anchored in a variety of psychic functions, primarily the intra-psychic, couple therapy is a treatment that achieves its best results when the focus is on the couple's bidirectional conscious and unconscious exchanges. If our intention is to work simply on the intra-subjective, then individual treatment would be more appropriate.

In the following clinical vignette the analyst illustrates such an approach by asking a couple to provide an example of their difficulties.

Alicia: Well . . . I believe Coco limits himself to what is concrete; he doesn't look at things in depth. I see that I function more often as a mother than a wife. I want to change this, but he believes that I want him to quarrel with his parents, and it isn't that, his mother intrudes and he doesn't understand. The other day his mother called to tell me that Coquito had trouble with something and I had to solve it. She said, "you have to do it". And when I told Coco, he did not react. On the contrary, he said "what do you want me to do if she calls you?" He doesn't assume an active role. He doesn't plan to have a house for the two of us, a project together, a financial project. I found out that his parents knew some of our intimate secrets as a couple and I feel that he has a complicity with his parents that is lacking between us. I feel that he doesn't defend me from his parents.

At this point, there is a long and heavy silence.

Coco: Well, I don't see things this way, but . . . Alicia is extremely sensitive, obsessive, she has excellent sight and perception, nothing escapes her. I am just the opposite. My mother is a ball breaker, that's for sure, but I don't pay attention to her. She wants to meddle and give her opinion, and Alicia expects me to be drastic with them, she makes faces and frowns at me about it. She's always jumpy, everything rubs her up the wrong way, and in the end I prefer not to tell her anything. Whenever I tell her something, the issue comes up of whether someone knew about it before her. I prefer to keep quiet because if I tell her something, there's always a fuss about why someone else knew it before she did.

Alicia: I feel that there are concealments and deceits. He says don't tell Alicia . . . he says it to the children, about silly things . . . it's like a fraternity from which I am excluded. Suddenly, he goes out with the children to shop for clothes with the instruction "don't tell Alicia", I'm the bad guy in the movie.

Coco: What happens is that we have a big set of demands to support.

Alicia: In the past what happened was that I was a millionaire and I used to pay for everything. Back then it was easier.

Here they explained how when they met and got married, both of them were coming from difficult divorces of previous marriages. Alicia was making a lot of money; she would cover all the financial gaps, and helped Coco very much. Now that is no longer the case, and, conversely, at times she needs his help. But everything is very complicated, since it seems that Coco doesn't like helping her.

This vignette of the dialogue between Coco and Alicia can help us to understand the positioning of the therapist. Coco is a passive and childish man; Alicia is a woman who wants a husband and didn't realise that a husband who was bought with money has such problems. Now, the lack of money and other issues have triggered a crisis of their unconscious alliances (Kaës, 1999) and assignment of roles. While Coco had never had or requested psychological treatment, Alicia has had several episodes of treatment throughout her life. The analyst must assume that the couple feel that their conflict can't be resolved because, if it were, it would mean that one of the partners would dictate how their relationship must work. In contrast the goal in working with the link is to allow them to find and construct a new balance that can be somewhat more satisfactory for both. The vignette of Orlando and Rita exemplifies another way of intervening when working with links. The case of Coco and Alicia highlights an important question in couple consultations: What possibilities do both have of benefiting from link treatment?

The intervention and the working alliance

Treatment of couples, whether analytical or otherwise, does not help with all the disagreements of a couple. What leads two subjects in conflict to attend a consultation? What keeps them in a "therapeutic process" aimed at changing their mode of being and relating? How do they construct a "working alliance" with a professional, i.e., a relationship focused on their conflicts that is "rational and relatively non neurotic" (Greenson, 1967, p. 193)? How do we conceive the working alliance in the process of psychic change?

> With these questions in mind consider Gustavo and Marcelo who consulted as a result of Marcelo's extramarital relationship being discovered. Marcelo, facing the situation, proposed couple therapy and Gustavo agreed to come to a few interviews, but right at the beginning, he frankly said: "Doctor, I do not believe in psychology; I don't think you can help us. I doubt that psychology can be useful for this type of thing."

If we start some type of therapy, we must not lose sight of Gustavo's conscious mistrust/indifference towards psychology and, moreover, his (valid) affirmation that psychology doesn't work in all cases. He is brought in, one could say dragged in, by his partner and his attitude towards therapy caused an obstacle from the outset. However, the possible therapeutic work is not an academic discussion about what a couple therapy may contribute. The task is to begin working with the couple and, according to the therapist's good judgement, to demonstrate some psychic dynamism while dwelling especially on analysing the resistances of the partner who is the "enemy" of psychology. Along this path we will see how Gustavo's objections and resistances and the treatment overall evolve. Coming back to Coco and Alicia, Coco turns up with a passive attitude which is not predisposed to benefiting with a treatment focused on the link. The analyst will have to work mainly on addressing Coco's subjective position. Hence, just as a "psychologically minded" subject is likely to benefit from an individual treatment, to benefit from couple therapy a view of the world that is not circumscribed to a persistent individualism is more likely to produce a positive outcome.

Beliefs, ideologies, values and world views: Their role in the intervention

The sufferings and joys of a couple relationship depends greatly on the beliefs that one or both partners have regarding the relationship, and what they think should happen within it. Such beliefs are often unconscious and conform true world views. Often strongly invested in, they are usually partially autonomous of the life experiences from which they originate, and they are sustained independently from their biographical anchorage.

In the case of Coco and Alicia, as well as in a great number of couples, the main question is up to which point the couple can see their conflicts including the involvement of their partner (and others) as a protagonist from the perspective of the link. Many people are driven by our current culture and sometimes as a result of poorly conducted psychological treatments, to see their sufferings from a strictly individualistic perspective, and hence cannot benefit from a treatment of the link, e.g., "*I take care* of my *problems and you take care of yours. If you are hypersensitive, unstable, whatever, it is your problem.*"

Other examples of the importance of beliefs may be found in the conviction that "*love is eternal*" or that "*there can't be any arguments when there is true love*" or that "*if a couple gets along well, they must agree about the ideas conveyed to their children*" or "*we have to tell each other everything*". These types of ideas make up dysfunctional beliefs and need to be worked on intensively to counteract the damage that they might cause. These are usually ego-syntonic postulates, with an intensity that is comparable to that of religious and fanatical beliefs, and similarly to the latter, must be related to the culture in which the analysands live and to the internalisations and transformations they have made of the social mandates, occasionally quite arbitrary and far from the original cultural precept. It should also be said that such beliefs clearly have an important role in cognitive therapy, but in the psychoanalytic field – until now – they have not been given priority. Dysfunctional beliefs play the role of the protagonist in many couples' problems. Couples often recruit ways of thinking that perpetuate sufferings, and therefore these must be addressed in the therapeutic intervention and often prioritised over other productions.

> Jorge and Liliana sought treatment because of the disagreements that they had been having since the birth of their first child. A great part of the work during their sessions was centred on the fact that both feel that their differences indicate severe disturbances. They both felt that they should get along well and be very happy with their recently arrived child, but instead they quarrel frequently and are irritable with each other. This is worse on days when they don't sleep well at night, since the baby, who is four months old, wakes up and cries.
>
> For the therapist, a main factor in their suffering is the belief they both share, that if they love each other and the baby, there shouldn't be any ambivalence between them or with the child in their new life situation.

As can be inferred from the vignettes presented, any intervention by the couple analyst should first of all consider how much countertransference and the culture are influencing his/her perspective. This is a huge problem which is beyond the scope of the current chapter but it can be considered in the following vignette.

Culture and countertransference

> Cecilia belongs to a micro-culture about which the therapist has very little information, and she hates her husband. Their link is full of all sorts of abuse and emotional harassment. It has always been. Within that atmosphere, one day after many years of humiliation and abuse, he stops seeking sex with her.
>
> Cecilia attributes this to the "choleric" nature of her husband, and to the surprise of the therapist (an analyst of French origin) her bitter reproach to her husband is focused on the fact that he doesn't have intercourse with her. She says, "I'm not a woman"; "he doesn't make me a woman".

> For the therapist, Cecilia's behaviour is not attributable to essentially masochistic dynamics. When she first heard her narrative, she imagined that Cecilia would be relieved by the lack of sex with a man she hates. But she is not. For Cecilia, due to the internalisation that she has made of beliefs that prevail in her culture, the lack of sexual relations is just one more vexation. As usual, the values of the culture in which Cecilia was raised do not coincide exactly with the internalisation that she has made of them.

This example illustrates the marked influence of culture and countertransference and how much they sometimes become reciprocally intricate.

The perception of the other, intra-couple transference

A fundamental perspective to adopt in the treatment of couples is to consider how the other is perceived. A usual finding is that he/she is perceived in an arbitrary manner, more akin to the pleasure principle than to that of reality. What frequently happens is that one member of the couple, regardless of what he/she does, "*is like that*", because a pre-fabricated object is projected into the other. Such an object belongs to the psychic reality and is quite far from the principle of reality. The notion of transference may help to understand and work on these clinical situations, to work on a particular modality of the transference, which we have called *intra-couple transference* (Spivacow, 2011), where the bi-directionality confirms and feeds back the transference projections. If we take Orlando and Rita's dialogue as an example, we may add that one of the problems with which the analyst dealt constantly was that Orlando transferred to Rita a manic, frivolous and disconnected object, close to characters of his childhood story, and Rita transferred to Orlando a devitalised object, that could be related to a family with many psychiatric disorders.

The therapeutic project and the ethical compass

In conclusion, it becomes obvious that the subject matter of this chapter cannot be addressed in full in just a few pages. The appropriate intervention, in psychoanalytical clinical work with couples, results from the intersection of numerous perspectives, and their hierarchical order stems from the way the therapeutic project is conceived. To achieve psychic changes, we rely on self-knowledge, an understanding of each of the partner's psychic functioning and their link, as well as other resources such as the analyst–patient relationship and the work on beliefs, the "*via di porre*". Regarding the issues addressed in a session, as in any psychotherapy, they are extremely varied, but if a couple setting has been chosen this is probably due to the fact that the goal is to work specifically on the relationship's problems, or to use the couple link as a pivot because one or several previous individual treatments have failed to resolve certain relationship conflicts. That is, when implementing couple psychotherapy, we aim at making the couple link a protagonist of the therapeutic work.

The spirit of our practice is essentially non-directive and aims more at a freer development of the subjects in the relationship. This may not be possible, however, when destructiveness prevails or where direction is required such as in cases involving the legal system or a police mandate. These are cases where there has been physical violence or other forms of potentially lethal destructiveness. In many such cases, the psychoanalytical approach may not be appropriate.

Another essential characteristic of psychoanalytical couple therapy is that it incorporates Freud's ethical and clinical attitude with individual treatments, and as such promotes the capacity to love and work. The most harmonic and satisfactory parts of the relationship can begin to flow solely if the intervention is based on these objectives. The proposal is, however, not to encourage the couple to adapt to any model of functioning of the social and cultural establishment or to "save" the couple, say from a divorce. As such, in many cases the best result might be the dissolution of a disastrous relationship. Also, following the Freudian tradition, we embrace tools from other psychotherapeutic schools. The same applies to couple therapy as with psychoanalysis in general: we must incorporate many contributions from other disciplines that can fill in the gaps of psychoanalytic theory. Undoubtedly, we should include contributions from the systemic theory, cognitive psychology, neuroscience, psychiatry and many other fields of study. We know that to achieve the best outcome with psychoanalysis we should not lock ourselves in a glass box.

References

Aulagnier, P. (1975). *La violencia de la interpretación*. Buenos Aires: Amorrortu, 1977.

Clulow, C. (2011). Couple psychoanalysis and couple therapy: Context and challenge. *International Journal of Couple and Family Psychoanalysis*, 1(1): 1–19.

Greenson, R. (1967). *Técnica y práctica del psicoanálisis*. Buenos Aires: Siglo XXI Editores, 1976.

Kaës, R. (1994). *La palabra y el vínculo*. Buenos Aires: Amorrortu, 2005.

Kaës, R. (1999). *Las teorías psicoanalíticas del grupo*. Buenos Aires: Amorrortu, 2000.

Morgan, M. (2014). The couple state of mind and some aspects of the setting in couple psychotherapy. In: D. Scharff & J. Scharff (Eds.), *Psychoanalytic Couple Therapy* (pp. 125–130). London: Karnac.

Pichon-Rivière, E. (1956–1957). *Teoría del vínculo*. Buenos Aires: Ediciones Nueva Visión, 1979.

Scharff, D., & Palacios, E. (2017). *Family and Couple Psychoanalysis. A Global Perspective*. London: Karnac.

Spivacow, M. (2011). *La pareja en conflicto. Aportes psicoanalíticos*. Buenos Aires: Paidós.

Part III

Interpretation in family psychoanalysis

Chapter 6

Interpretation in family analysis

Anna Maria Nicolò and Diana Norsa

Introduction

The family and the couple are at the crossroads between individual functioning and group functioning, between the individual, the family and the couple of which it is a part and between the inner world of the individual and the world of the relations that it contributes to the construction of and from which it has been generated. Psychoanalytic therapeutic work in these contexts must, therefore, focus on the continuous interrelationship between the individual and the family and between the inner family of each one, and the external and the real family. This is why the family assessment needs to address the individual unconscious phantasies as well as the unconscious phantasies of the family group, as the latter often represents the coagulation of numerous phantasies, some of which are trans-generational (Nicolò, 2002, p. 113).

Given the "economic policy" (Tabak de Bianchedi et al., 1988) inherent in the functioning of the family at the phantasy level, we can investigate the mental life of the family group in terms of the inter-exchange and distribution of emotional suffering, with particular emphasis on its goals, methods and consequences, by "focusing attention on the strategies it adopts" (Nicolò, 2002, p. 114) as well as "the bonds that the family members co-construct together" (Norsa & Zavattini, 1997, p. 75; Nicolò, 2014; Norsa, 2014).

We therefore not only have to take into account individual defences, like repression or negation, but also defences the family employ such as malicious fusions with the other, that can intrude and colonise the mind of the other, along with his existence or identity, from birth. Interpersonal and transpersonal defences are thus ways in which the bond that unites the members can be made explicit. It is precisely because they are constructed in such a circular way that they elude the causal explanation for the symptom, but instead highlight the needs of each member of the family group, involved in their relationships in a circular network.

As Kaës (2008) notes, the human being is characterised by mental functioning which always requires psychic work in relation to others. As such the purpose of psychoanalytic work with families, as with individual analysis, is to reactivate this capacity for psychic work, in the absence of which real events are otherwise rendered meaningless.

In particular, families have the task of doing the internal psychic work which transmits an affective sense to past events and promotes in the new generations feelings of hope (Meltzer & Harris, 1976). This very important task, however, can be interrupted and hindered by a psychic suffering such that it cannot be worked through and instead generates a vicious circle of interpersonal defences which then creates a strong pressure on the capacity of the individual to do this psychic work. We see such dynamics in families who consult us as a result of their adolescent or child experiencing a breakdown, but also with families with trans-generational traumas who are struggling with parenthood.

For this reason, offering a family consultation can itself represent an implicit interpretation, suggesting that the suffering of the individual not only has an intrapsychic dimension but is also linked to the relationships in the family group. The analyst, supported by his/her analytic training, must, above all, have an internal structure that allows him/her to recompose in his/her own psyche the different, confused or split aspects of the processes in the family, to allow them to gradually acquire a meaning; that is, he/she must function as a container of the undifferentiated (Winnicott, 1965) and un-integrated aspects of each of the family members, which together form the psychic family.

The result of this internal psychic work can then be translated into various interventions of which the interpretation is only one, yet often the most evolved. With families, listening to the account that each member gives of him/herself and of their family, as well as the transference and countertransference dynamics of each member and of the family as a whole and towards the analyst, are equally important. Whilst confrontations between members of the family and their delineation are important (Shapiro, 1967, 1968; Shapiro & Zinner, 1989), the multiple associations activated by the analyst, which in certain families are blocked, made concrete or acted out due to the difficulties of containing the mental suffering linked to growth and change, are essential. One tool, which is particularly important in cases of more serious and primitive pathology, is the use of metaphor and the process of metaphorisation.

Some specifications on interpretation, however, are useful. As noted in "The Italian approach to family and couple therapy" (Scharff & Palacios, 2017):

> Interpretation in the family and couple setting in general concerns the content communicated by an individual member, as well as the link between the members which, being a third element, draws out from each version of themselves complementary to the version that the other member actualises. Interpretation will also highlight the relational configurations immobilising the members of the family or couple; it will be an interpretation of the transpersonal defences that the members have built together, in the course of time, to cope with the shared anxieties that are re-enacted in the here-and-now of the session.
>
> (Nicolò & Norsa, 2017, p. 32)

We refer here to the concept of the link as expressed by Kaës when he notes:

> I have defined link as the specific unconscious psychic reality built up by the encounter of two or more subjects. This definition, which refers to the content, accentuates the unconscious psychic reality that is the constitutive object of psychoanalysis. It is specified by an approach in terms of process: the link is the, more or less, stable movement of investments, representations, and actions that associate two or more subjects to fulfil some of their desires.
>
> (Kaës, 2008, p. 770)

Taking account of unconscious psychic reality brings with it many interesting implications for us as analysts such as the identification of psychic suffering, the different forms of representation and communication, and above all acknowledging the phantasy dimension. Understanding the function that psychic pain plays and how family links distribute it, and how each one "interprets" it, is a crucial understanding for the analyst in order for him/her to define an interpretive intervention suitable for the emotional context of a particular family.

Moreover, we need to understand that the

> study of mental pain requires not the only definition of its quality and reference, but also of its distribution and source. Because mental pain can be distributed in both the external world and the internal world, it is necessary in the clinical situation to ask: "whose pain is this?" Pains may be passed serially within any social grouping and modifications of quality and intensity, consequent to this serial passage must be clarified.
>
> (Meltzer & Harris, 1976, p. 389)

That is, mental pain, which is:

> The central phenomenon in all psycho-analytical conceptions, may generally be divided into three categories: persecutory, confusional and depressive. The first refers to pains involving a threat to the self, the second implies a threat to the capacity to think and function and the third indicates a threat to love objects.
>
> (Meltzer & Harris, 1976, p. 389)

There are families who do not have the capacity to mentalise their experiences and function according to a concrete operating model. Words are equivalent to actions which touch, strike, injure and in parallel, the concreteness of reality is full of meanings, mostly persecutory; there is consequently a lack of the capacity to communicate emotions because there is no capacity to listen to and differentiate not only those of others but also one's own (Norsa, 2017).

The words of the interpreting analyst will also be received more for their sensory impact than for the meaning they communicate (Aulagnier, 1975;

André Fustier, 2009). If this state of affairs is not taken into account, the classic interpretation which addresses defences will be experienced as a violence at the level of the implied relations (Aulagnier, 1975). At every moment in the life of a family, and consequently in every family session, a process is underway whereby the interpretation needs to be situated inside that process. The reference to the link as a movement of investments, representations and desires reminds us that without psychic movement there is no emotional life. Therefore, an interpretation must be first of all a psychic movement by the analyst capable of understanding those prompts embedded in the material of the session that can restart a transformative process. The mental structure of the analyst, in particular his/her capacity for contact and comprehension of the patient's experiences, fantasies and desires, will be fundamental. This capacity develops as a result of the analyst's training and above all from his/her personal analysis.

The work of interpretation is not only for the analyst, but also for each member of the family, as each can perform an interpreting function, that is, a function that reactivates the co-construction of an affective meaning. At times this could be a dream; at other times it could derive from the way children play during the session, or from a memory with a potential mythopoeic power, helping to recover an affective sense that was known unconsciously to all, but with which they were not familiar.

Clinical vignette I

The capacity for working through by a family member

The material is provided by a psychotherapist who is presenting case material for supervision.

The family consists of two parents, one older handicapped (quadriplegic) daughter, aged 12, and a son, aged 6. The issue the family brings is that the parents are afraid that the handicap of their first-born daughter might adversely impact on their younger child.

Session material[1]

The day the psychotherapist meets the family she is somewhat anxious since the parents have described their daughter as a violent and destructive child.

The parents have told the therapist: You will see how she will turn your office inside out!

Dania, their elder child, is a 12-year-old girl with spastic quadriplegia who walks into the consulting room with some difficulty. She makes dystonic movements with her limbs, has thick glasses and a hearing device. As soon as she sees the psychotherapist, however, she smiles and shows her joy to be in her office. The psychotherapist immediately likes her. Giodi is a 6-year-old with glasses; he has an inquiring and intellectual look. He makes the analyst think of a child who has become an adult too early.

As soon as he comes in, Giodi says that he had a dream he wants to recount. He describes the dream through a drawing. There is a big house with many rooms for each family member, several playing rooms with toys and rooms for relaxation, as well as an attic with a heating source and a treasure chest, where Giodi's baby souvenirs are stored. Near the chest, Giodi draws a little spider that he would later call the Spider–Therapist.

Giodi's dream/drawing paves the way to associations and/or drawings by the rest of the family where each one expresses a wish to have his/her own place and space. Dania sketches a black and white house with a closed plan without any door or window. Upon ending the family sessions, Dania's house would become a coloured one and she would even write the date she has made it.

From this clinical vignette, we can observe some important aspects of interpretation.

The children's contributions in the session

Children or adolescents bring a different language to that of words. It is an immediate way of communicating, as it is closer to affects, sensations, needs; it is expressed through images.

Giodi's dream/drawing clearly conveys a wish for himself, yet concerning the other family members too – the house that has to contain everyone is to give welfare as well as delimited, differentiating spaces between adults and children, males and females, etc.

The analyst's function of listening and paying attention to the unconscious contents

Here the psychotherapist tells us that she grasped the meaning of Giodi's drawing/dream, with which a similar communication to that of his handicapped sister – despite her lower representational skills – resonated, and gradually all the family members were encouraged to participate at this level. The small detail of the spider in the drawing allowed interpretive work that connected it associatively with the therapist's name, suggesting a positive transference has been activated by the therapeutic project.

The countertransference

The psychotherapist indicated she was concerned about the description the parents gave of their daughter Dania as a violent and destructive girl, a description consistent with their paranoid experience about her handicap also damaging their healthy son. The psychotherapist's countertransference experience, that enabled her to tune in with the girl's smile, became a very important element of interpretation and transformation. It was part of an interpretative process initially formulated within herself. She next had to work to make this potential interpretive line also available to the family and be able to understand where such a negative fantasy came from.

Our emphasis in this commentary is captured by Meltzer and Harris when they note:

> The family acts on the psychoanalyst trying to lure him/her into its defensive system or trying to push him/her to act rather than to understand. A psychoanalyst without adequate training is in fact easily exposed to the risk of acting to get rid of the emotional pressure. The main effort of the psychoanalyst should instead be to rebuild the scattered, confused or cleaved aspects of the thinking processes of the patient in their own psyche to allow them to gradually acquire meaning. The psychoanalyst must be a sort of container of unsorted and non-integrated aspects of the self.
>
> (Meltzer & Harris, 1976, p. 409)

As referred to in the introduction there are families that have not developed an adequate representational system of emotions; for such parents, Dania's body, offended by an incident at birth, carries a violence that produces destruction in the others (her brother, the therapist's office). In this pathological picture, Giodi seems to be the most capable of a pictographic representation, the mouthpiece of the capacity to represent the sensory experience as a foundation on which emotions can be acknowledged and distinguished. He is also the one who anticipates, by drawing the spider in the wished-for home, the possibility to have positive transference in this family.

As far as psychic pain is concerned, we may identify in Giodi the beginning of depressive pain that also takes into account the object and not only the self. Here we see the possibility to start off therapeutic work that has to access the family links. The parents' concern for their second-born child experiencing some developmental misadventure becomes a persecutory anxiety that marks a chasm within the family between those who are healthy and those who are ill, attacking the link between the siblings. What we might call "bewildering pain" is based on the assumption that there is an ominous destiny which has already struck the family so many times and will continue to haunt them. Here the impossibility for the parental couple to carry out a reparative function is clear, and the request of the children to the therapist is to be helped to find this lost ability: Giodi with the spider in the home, Dania with her smile.

What type of psychic process does one find in this family consultation? We can define it as an "involutive process", with a persecutory level of anxiety, characterised by the belief that a negative destiny will sweep everything away. This picture, however, although serious, cannot be defined as psychotic functioning, whereas the clinical situation that follows is.

Metaphor and process of metaphorisation

The characteristic nature of family functioning opens up a unique therapeutic potential not available in the individual analytic situation. Precisely thanks to its multidimensional functioning, the family introduces the analyst to primitive levels of functioning where the mental and the somatic merge and where the boundaries of the self are fragile; it introduces us to those primitive states of the individual mind and of the family unconscious, where traumas that are not able to be thought about or mentalised have been deposited. In these settings, material that is accessible only through paths other than verbalisation, is often presented to the analyst capable of decoding it. The family acts so as to make its members, as well as the analyst, experience emotions, sensations and somatic pains that arise from mental states where repression is operating and there is a possibility of remembering more inaccessible mental states wherein the capacity for thought has never evolved. These are the levels that Bion (1974) defines as inaccessible mental states, which in our opinion are not part of the conscious or the unconscious. In "Mind and its relation to the psyche-soma", Winnicott (1949) differentiates two types of memories: memories that can be thought about because the child has not undergone excessive interference from the environment, and another type, memories that cannot. The latter are seen to be due to traumatic impingements arising in the environment at a point in development when the child is unable or not yet ready to face them. They form an interference to the sense of a continuity of being and are "catalogued" or frozen until the hope of a transformation opens up.

These unthinkable memories can then be deposited in the soma, in acting out, in sensations and, in our view, in the links that each member builds up with the other. The role of the other is crucial as a depository of the psychotic levels of functioning or primitive states. Green (1993) describes an implication of this phenomenon in his conception of the *The Work of the Negative*, where he focuses on the role of the other as the depository of that part of the story of the subject which occurred without having been lived, because "the child was unable or was not yet ready to face those experiences" (Winnicott, 1949, p. 184).

That is, here is a member of the family who holds the story, the functioning of which has been given expression through lives of the people, without ever having been thought about or remembered. Moreover "the other, or better their absence, is that from which everything started, the place of stolen existence, of the non-formed, synonymous with a loss but also the vehicle of a potential new beginning" (Nicolò & Accetti, 2015, p. 15). How can we foster "the integration of weakly inscribed psychic elements?" (Levine, 2013, p. 49). How can we think something that has never been thought?

We are convinced that the family setting can allow effective work on these levels, because of the "presence" of the other and of the group as the carrier of these contents. Although worthy, a greater exploration of this issue is beyond the scope of this chapter.

Starting from these ideas, however, we want to illustrate an "expressive method" that analysts can use and which allows them to mobilise these frozen or primitive states more easily such that they can provide an intermediate link, leading the family towards being able to think about them. To illustrate this aspect, we will describe a short clinical case.

Clinical case

The session of a family with an 18-year-old patient, Elena, is exemplary of the usefulness of the metaphor. Elena had a developmental breakdown with the onset of menarche at the age of 13. Depression and apathy emerged with a disorder of socialisation at that age. Her elder sister, Maria, was diagnosed at 16 years of age with severe ulcerative colitis.

When she came to therapy, she was pursued by an irrational idea. She felt possessed by a demonic man she met casually, who wanted to push her to have sexual intercourse with strangers. She tried to resist this, but was afraid of losing control and therefore often played truant from school.

The father was very peripheral and busy with work or his studies. The daughters had always been the possessions of the mother. The mother stayed at home, always in an agitated state which led her to be controlling.

Family therapy was commenced with once-weekly meetings for about a year. At the initial session attended by all the members of the family, Maria, the sister, said that the evening before she had seen *Gomorra*, a film about the Neapolitan Camorra. She was struck by how the women were treated. She remained awake and her mother also said that she could not sleep either and did some work in the house, not knowing what else to do.

Elena related a dream she had that night:

> She was followed by a man with grey hair like her father's. The man was very powerful because he was in the Mafia. At the beginning, someone put him in prison, but he was able to escape.

The members of the family offered a few associations with the dream. The atmosphere felt suspicious and thus the therapeutic work was blocked. The analyst attempts an interpretation of the dream, which links to *Gomorra* and Elena's problem of hearing a demoniac voice inside her, but it does not seem to have any effect. She then decides to play with an image, the one that is present in the film *Gomorra*, which the analyst has seen, and decides to circulate it as a metaphorical image of a Mafia member in the family and each of its members. The analyst asks each of them to think of the advantages or disadvantages there are in being in the Mafia. The father says, "becoming rich easily"; Elena, "they can afford to have a lot of lovely things"; Maria says, "they are violent"; and the mother says, "they go unpunished, they do what they want."

The atmosphere becomes a little less tense and so the analyst suggests: There is a Mafioso in each of us. She asks each of them what they think of that.

Mother opposes the idea and the daughters laugh, saying that their father certainly cannot be one. They do not see him as being so macho towards women. The father says that he certainly is not, but all the men in his wife's family seemed slightly violent. Elena speaks about the mistress of her grandfather's brother. Nobody had met her, but everyone said she was a whore. The session ends here.

A few sessions later, the mother and Maria relate a very serious piece of news. The mother had told Maria after the *Gomorra* session that the uncle they had talked about in the session had raped her when she reached puberty and had continued afterward as well, and her parents did not seem to have realised. It was something that the mother had also hidden from her husband and from her daughters, and that she had decided to confess after the work we had done in the session.

Comment

The secret of the rape that had been well concealed for years had in actual fact been communicated in a silent family lexicon, which had been expressed in Maria's body and in Elena's irrational idea. The family had a secret about an event that had taken place but which could not be remembered. This secret had been translated into significant patterns that had influenced the feminine identity of the two daughters who had both shown an illness, one somatic and the other psychic, in adolescence during their sexual maturation.

We know that trans-generational secrets are often manifested this way. After the dream and the association concerning *Gomorra*, the family became blocked, as often occurred. The use of the metaphor to which they were all linked, however, had allowed the change in atmosphere, enabling each one to associate freely. The metaphor had also made explicit, by denying it, the problem that was at the basis of the symptoms. In Greek, metaforà means transport. The symptom or the dream is a metaphor of mental functioning or conflicts. The analyst can also use metaphors in the session and start a process of metaphorisation (Nicolò, 1980).

The characteristic of the metaphor is that it condenses many symbolic meanings. In this sense, it does not have only one meaning, but multiple ones can be derived from it, as we have seen in the clinical example, where the circulation of the metaphor between the members of the family was enriched by new meanings and images that were generated. It is precisely this that allows otherwise inaccessible mental states to find a possible representation. The non-thought in the folds of the family interaction and in the body of some of its members can then be encouraged to manifest and be enacted. This is a result of the process of metaphorisation generated by the analyst who, listening to their countertransference experience, can identify the significant points of association. The content of the metaphor, therefore, belongs to the family, but its development and its transport towards symbolic functioning belong to the new relations co-constructed between the family and the analyst.

Conclusion

This phenomenon finds clinical confirmation in all those situations where the problem is not so much that of "remembering", solving the symptom through work on repression but, on the contrary, not having enough space for thought, or due to the incapacity, perhaps even temporarily, of suspending thought.

In this regard César Botella (2001), whose classic contribution to the topic of figurability has been re-published, notes that the mental state or instrument which, starting from a "regredient" movement which is similar to the dream of the analyst, allows the latter to exceed the limit of the mnestic images to open up to the sensory and transitory elements that reflect what patients cannot remember, but carry within them due to early trauma.

The profound functioning that is established in the analytic couple and the capacity of the analyst to dream the dreams that the patient has never dreamed (Ferro, 2011) is consequently the answer in this new frontier of clinical psychoanalysis, showing a psychoanalysis that is alive, capable of changing always by questioning itself, but always keeping its own identity and continuity.

References

André Fustier, F. (2009). La sensorialité en thétapie Familiale. *Le Divan familial*, *1*(22): 127–147.

Aulagnier, P. (1975). *The Violence of Interpretation*. East Sussex: Brunner-Routledge (The New Library of Psychoanalysis), 2001.

Bion, W. R. (1974). *Two Papers: 'The Grid' and 'Caesura'*. London: Karnac.

Botella, C. (2001). Figurabilité et régrédience. *Revue française de psychanalyse*, *LXV*(4): 1149–1239.

Ferro, A. (2011). *Avoiding Emotions, Living Emotions*. London: Routledge.

Green, A. (1993). *The Work of the Negative*. London: Free Association Books, 1999.

Kaës, R. (2008). Definitions et approches du concept de lien. L'ésprit du temp. *Adolescence*, *3*(65): 763–780.

Levine, H. B. (2013). The colourless canvas: representation, therapeutic action, and the creation of mind. In: H. B. Levine, G. S. Reed & D. Scarfone (Eds.), *Unrepresented States and the Construction of Meaning* (pp. 42–71). London: Karnac.

Meltzer, D., & Harris, M. (1976). A psychoanalytic model of the child-in-the-family-in-the-community. In: A. Hahn (Ed.), *Sincerity and Other Works* (pp. 387–454). London: Karnac, 2013.

Nicolò, A. M. (1980). L'emploi de la métaphore en thérapie familiale. *Thérapie Familiale*, *1*(4): 301–324.

Nicolò, A. M. (2002). La tecnica nella psicoterapia psicoanalitica con la famiglia. In: A. M. Nicolò & A. F. Zampino (Eds.), *Lavorare con la famiglia* (pp. 113–121). Roma: Carocci.

Nicolò, A. M. (2014). Where is the unconscious located? Reflections on links in families and couples. In: A. M. Nicolò, P. Benghozi & D. Lucarelli (Eds.), *Families in Transformation* (pp. 65–84). London: Karnac.
Nicolò, A. M., & Accetti, L. (2015). Introduction to the Italian edition. In: H. B. Levine, G. S. Reed & D. Scarfone (Eds.), *Unrepresented States and the Construction of Meaning*. Milano: Franco Angeli, 2013.
Nicolò, A. M., & Norsa D. (2017). The Italian approach to family and couple therapy. In: D. E. Scharff & E. Palacios (Eds.), *Family and Couple Psychoanalysis. A Global Perspective* (pp. 27–33). London: Karnac.
Norsa, D. (2014). Transformations through repetitions of female and male representations in reconstructed families. In: A. M. Nicolò, P. Benghozi & D. Lucarelli (Eds.), *Families in Transformation* (pp. 109–125). London: Karnac.
Norsa, D. (2017). Dora and Carlo. In: D. Scharff & E. Palacios (Eds.), *Family and Couple Psychoanalysis*. London: Karnac.
Norsa, D., & Zavattini, G. C. (1997). *Intimità e Collusione*. Milano: Raffaello Cortina Editore.
Scharff, D. E., & Palacios, E. (Eds.) (2017). *Family and Couple Psychoanalysis. A Global Perspective*. London: Karnac.
Shapiro, R. L. (1967). The origin of adolescent disturbances in the family: some considerations in theory and implications for therapy. In: G. H. Zuk & I. Boszormenyi-Nagy (Eds.), *Family Therapy and Disturbed Families* (pp. 221–238). Palo Alto: Science and Behavior Books, Inc.
Shapiro, R. L. (1968). Action and family interaction in adolescence. In: J. Marmor (Ed.), *Modern Psychoanalysis* (pp. 454–475). New York: Basic Books.
Shapiro, R. L. & Zinner, J. (1989). Family organization and adolescent development. In: J. S. Scharff (Ed.), *Foundations of Object Relations Family Therapy* (pp. 79–87). Lanham, MD: Jason Aronson.
Tabak de Bianchedi, E. T., Scalozub de Boschan, L., De Cortiñas, L. P., & De Piccolo, E. G. (1988). Theories on anxiety in Freud and Melanie Klein. Their metapsychological status. *International Journal of Psycho-Analysis*, *69*(1): 359–368.
Winnicott, D. W. (1949). Mind and its relation to the psyche-soma. *Through Paediatrics to Psycho-Analysis*. London: Tavistock.
Winnicott, D. W. (1965). *The Maturational Process and the Facilitating Environment*. London: Hogarth Press.

Note

1 I thank Dr Ragno [in Italian, spider], the psychotherapist who presented this case material.

Editors' prologue to the discussant perspectives

The chapter by Anna Maria Nicolò and Diana Norsa highlights the value of being able to understand and work with the bonds created in a family, which they suggest are revealed in the interpersonal and transpersonal defences that a family use. They also importantly draw our attention to dream interpretation and children's play in the family context. Carl Bagnini, in his discussion, highlights the value of dream interpretation in family psychoanalysis as well as underlining the importance of the children's play in the communication of the family's difficulties. Janine Puget takes up the case material from her particular understanding of the family-group, suggesting that it is the link, as it is experienced, which facilitates the expression of something previously unheard of in the family that is stimulated by the foreignness of the other (the analyst) to the family.

Discussant perspective

Carl Bagnini

In their chapter the authors contribute theoretical ideas and two dream analyses to illustrate the value of interpretation in family psychoanalysis. In this regard let us firstly consider the individual treatment context. In this situation the patient shares a dream with the analyst, who needs to be open to receiving it. Either the analyst has solicited dream material as part of the frame, or there is a development in which the patient needs to use a dream to capture the analyst's imagination for treatment to move forward. Under favourable conditions, the analyst may have a countertransference dream about the patient. The analyst's dream may be a result of resistance to or from the patient, or a need for the analyst to provide a containment function. Dreaming about one's patient, along with receptivity to the patient's dreams, can expand the unconscious field. We thus view dream analysis as an indication of hope, valuing dreaming, the dream-content, and what the dreamer can reveal in the inter–intrapsychic field of the clinical situation.

The current work addresses dream material from a family and represents a new frontier in working with such material. Dream work with couples and families has been the accomplishment of a passionate and dedicated, though relatively small, group of internationally renowned clinicians. In the work they have presented they have expanded the utility of dream interpretation, which provides clinical access to a family's unconscious life across cultures and contexts.

In their 2003 article Nicolò, Norsa and Carratelli extended the classic intrapsychic notion of the function of dreams to an interpsychic one by linking dreams to the impact of the presence of a third party into the transference dynamic of the couple. The authors pointed out that dreams are an elaboration of self and other object relations, which can include those representing the psyche-soma and those that include traumatic forms of unmetabolised elements. Bion (1992) has noted that the "work of the dream" incorporates a continuous re-elaboration of internalised experiences which can yield much useful clinical material.

I published an article in the Italian journal *Interazioni*: "Clinica e ricerca psicoanalitica su individuo-coppia-famiglia" (2006). It accompanied a number of excellent articles concerning dream analysis written by my Italian colleagues, including the authors whose work I am discussing. Their current chapter adds to this much needed literature on the usefulness of dream-work with couples, families and groups.

Earlier, David Scharff (1992) in his book entitled *Refinding the Object and Reclaiming the Self*, also made the important and simple comment

(continued)

(continued)

that a dream is an unconscious family communication. That is, that internal object relationships are interpersonally activated, and during the sharing of dreams, the introjective and projective identifications become manifest for use in the family treatment. I believe that Scharff's discussion of dream analysis, written 25 years ago, was a forerunner of contemporary developments in dream analysis in family treatment. One implication of his and the current author's work is to underline that dreams can reveal the otherwise inaccessible unconscious material in couples and families.

From my frame of reference, I see clinical work with families and dreams as an encounter with ordinary tragedy, whereby the psychoanalytic instruments of free association, interpretation and reverie serve to reduce painful edges of the undigested trauma, and thereby open it up to transformation. Psychoanalytic theory informs us that the mind manages threatening truth with particular defences, which guard the individual and family against breakdown. The individual and family mind from this perspective is divided into the ingested (emotional exposures) and the evacuation of the indigestible (unmetabolised behavioural symptoms, role stagnation, and rigid beliefs) (Meltzer, 1983).

I found myself in familiar territory in terms of theory and practice at the beginning of the current chapter, especially the idea that family psychoanalysis and interpretation involve containment of a group that includes different generations and developmental challenges. The authors emphasise that the analyst encounters unseen, but felt, ghost-like representatives of previous generation's legacies and burdens, which affect the current and potentially future generations. It thus involves the need to contain three generations.

When children are present in a session the affective elements of the psyche, including dreams, can leap out, due to children's often heroic investment in the analyst on the family's behalf. A child's dream, however, requires analyst reverie. As such I think of Bion's notion of reverie as an essential quality of environmental mothering, and openness to what emerges. In this regard, I also prefer the term "dream work" to dream-analysis as analysis can sometimes be viewed narrowly as a cerebral activity aimed mainly at constructing a new emotional experience through insight. The analyst must be able to function as a listener, to do this openly, and to pay attention to the unconscious communications in a couple or family. That is the important action of reverie. Working from a position of emotional resonance in analysis also requires a focus on the importance *of the analyst's capacity for thinking* which in turn links to the analyst's containment function.

Moreover, as couple anxieties often increase when discussing parenting issues with their young children, we can experience affective disturbances in our search for buried psychic treasure. The psychic treasure needed to effect change is often located in the children; therefore family therapists must be able to operate as child therapists. Child work in the family context, however, teaches us that insight is not the direct means for a transformative experience. Colours, shapes, geographic locations, human and ghost-like figures may populate the experience the child offers through their play. This can then allow elaboration of psychic material, a point well illustrated in the current author's sensitive work.

I also fully embraced the co-author's use of individual dreams to capture significant aspects of the unconscious aspects of the family tragedy and to potentially detoxify historically determined events and relationships that have been compromised by it. In their current clinical example, we see that the family who sought help was not fully aware that one generation's un-metabolised horror and grief was attacking the next generation in malicious and frightening ways. The co-authors named these trans-generational inheritances "the vicious circle". In responding to the family of Giodi with its acute persecutory and paranoid anxieties, I also experienced this "vicious circle" and found it shaped my countertransference to this family. My responses to the family situation involved more dread than hope, and I considered such feelings might have influenced the initial family consultation, especially when the 6-year-old child's dream was enthusiastically offered. I did not experience a positive transference and will explain this more fully.

Families at various levels of regression appear to allow, even embrace, dream work. Dream-work resembles children's art and play. As I suggested above, offering a dream can represent a member's desire to collaborate with the analyst. In this situation members of a family are usually at least neutral about children's productions in family sessions and are pleased to receive them. In such a context the usual verbal and behavioural clashes and competitions give way and there is a reduction in judging creative or spontaneous material as "good" or "bad" or right or wrong, real or unreal. That is, there is a temporary relaxation of tensions about being judged or having to judge. In such a context, the effect of a severe super-ego is reduced and the family may free-associate for the first time, opening a potential space of relaxed interaction.

Following on from this comment on child's play and dreams, I now want to enlarge on the place of reverie in a family treatment. The dream that emerges from a family is not taken as a fact, or as an essential truth about the individual or family. The clinical situation involves the dream content, the dreamer's presentation and memory after dreaming the dream, and the various interpretations offered by the family and by the analyst. The author's honesty about the work they have presented suggests an integrity and open-mindedness in learning from experience.

(continued)

(continued)

Rather than intellectually seeking a unitary or causal meaning, the analysts offer their mental representations of the experience of the dreamer. They imply that the dreamer's experience is more important than arriving at a consensus of meaning as in a specific truth of a dream. I suggest the analyst here is dreaming up her emotionally inspired clinical version of the dream in reverie with the dreamer's affective experience at the time. This enlarged version of a dream is discovered in the transference–countertransference experience in the analyst's working mind. Influenced by the dreamer's communication, the analyst or the members of the family can thus talk about unspeakable memories within the group, and the child may become freed from the "negative destiny" of blind adherence to unconscious fantasies in the family.

The reference to sensory images in the current chapter also evoked in me a playful engagement with language which helped me find meaning in the family material. In this regard, the analyst's contribution in the session often derives from their ability to imagine which is linked to their personality, history and tool kit. It represents a type of artistic embellishment (Sharpe, 1931). In this way I played with the words "Dream" (unconscious experience during sleep) and "Drama" (the treatment setting as a theatre for the family expressions). The result was the term "Dreama", an amalgam or fusion of interrelated parts. In the reverie of analyst (mother) with the child or family distress and neglect, we have an "investment and desire" for co-constructing a new emotional comfort.

I have mentioned how the mind defends itself against more pain and how the treatment stimulates defences being brought into play when interpreting dreams. What is revealed in one creative moment will simultaneously conceal what is unfelt, or felt but unsaid in another member. The oscillation of hopeful expression and woeful repression occurs in every interpretive endeavour. We may be blinded by our hope, fearing for family fragility or taking one side of the dream's value, such that our countertransference may interfere with our ability to recognise multiple meanings held by other family members.

The authors observe that classical defence interpretation is experienced by the family as "violence". They caution to be careful when raising awareness. Moving from reverie associated with early infancy and childhood we can also make use of alternative techniques with more regressed families, including conflict interpretation and anxiety interpretation. In this regard a family can subtly suggest through their responses to the analyst how best to intervene with them.

Defensive manoeuvres manage anxiety stirred by the analyst's probing. The analyst therefore graciously welcomes a positive transference reflecting the offering of the buried psychic treasure reflected in a family dream.

A comment on the analyst's choice of material to interpret

Analysts make choices about what family material to work with. My comment on the choice of material to interpret relates to the analyst's countertransference and their personality qualities.

Out of my reverie with the clinical vignettes the authors provide, I would like to offer some additional meanings. My impressions of course arise from listening to a description of the family, not from a direct contact with them. I was therefore at a distance from the dream, the dreamer, and the setting.

One of the family vignettes featured 6 year old Giodi's dream and play. It also presented Dania's (the 12 year old with spastic quadriplegia) black and white house with no doors or windows from which to leave or enter (cannot escape a claustrophobia). There is also a reference to the "spider"–therapist, which I thought might be a frightening, as well as welcome, addition to the family setting. The analyst's reference was to a positive transference. I thought of the contrast between Dania's production and Giodi's. I speculated that each child seemed to carry parts of a split in the family. When the analyst observed the positive transference, expressing hope for the family in treatment from Giodi, I shifted my attention and observed a different transference element from Dania. I felt her anxiety, a frightening or terrible closed-in family "web". I associated that the spider was extremely agile in its own silky web, a web the spider constructs as a safe home for the spider and a waiting snare. Those who enter the web become trapped and are eaten for dinner. I thus felt that Dania carried the family's worry that she would be violent; I assume this was on the analyst's mind as well. I was absorbed into the role prescribed for Dania.

A closed-in room offered her and the family, and perhaps the analyst, protection. The young girl's smile was not reassuring to me, as it seemed too soon for a containment to be established, even if the family might imagine the setting offered them a different experience than at home. My fantasy was the family was safe if Dania was in solitary confinement, and therefore the family's aggression, and Dania's aggression, was contained. However, we can see that while in the black and white house she would not be in the outer world, unable to breathe fresh air or learn to be with others.

I thought that the cocoon image intermingled with the spider web (analyst) had interpretive value. In particular, I thought the analyst might represent despair *and* hope. Ambivalent tendencies that each child might carry were aspects of the situation. As the analyst wanting to help, would I have missed the split or ambivalent aspects in the two

(continued)

(continued)

children? The one with the "bad" reputation, and the other Giodi in the role of the "good" but threatened child? I might have wished to hold *my* hope firmly in place under the pressures of a collapse of thought. For example, the countertransference was described before the session as a parental conviction, "she will tear your office inside out". That was not experienced or received as metaphorical, but as *real*. The fear of further breakdown in the group could have limited my interpretation.

The authors tell us the dream can provide a new interpersonal space, for hearing and eliciting new affects, perspectives and longings for solitude and healing. In the family space alpha and beta elements of individual and family internal strife may at first present one member as the index patient. The two case reports dramatically reveal how dreams are converted into psychic representations in the group, releasing the index patient from possible scapegoating.

In the other vignette we have an example of *dreaming up* a member's dream. In the initial effort the analyst does not get far with individualising her interpretation with Elena. The Mafia metaphor emerges from the working mind of the analyst. The film *Gomorra* and a series of questions for the group led to an horrific discovery. The mother and daughter return a few sessions later having shared the shocking realisation that mother was raped by the uncle. Where were the other family members?

The secret society, the Mafia, was no longer in the shadows. In this example unconscious pain is multiplied, the generations are locked into rigid survival roles. Repressed memories become unstuck, and the generations become freed to re-work relationships. The sisters, Elena and Maria, may now become more whole, no longer haunted by mother's ghost, which has received a proper name and context. Interpretation unfreezes the frozen and guides the new discoveries through the use of *metaphorisation*.

Conclusion

As I reveal in my discussion of this chapter I am devoted to dream work, yet I am aware that we may at times idealise this aspect of analytic work and neglect its challenges and consequences. When re-directing the family group's mental digestive system to its excess of mental pain, we may become zealous, and over interpret. Anxieties and defences against "knowing" are usual. The authors acknowledge and illustrate how we need to utilise transferences and countertransference to guide the analytic process so that it evolves at a tolerable pace.

In the current chapter we have learned how the analyst helps a family who are missing their alpha function. When the analyst's alpha function detects the family unconscious dimensions she establishes a therapeutic space in which the dream is never merely a dream. To establish this important moment of comprehension, the analyst may suffer the collapse of her own psychic space – like the claustrophobic house that the child Dania puts forward, and as I interpreted it, the dual transference possibilities about the spider web that Giodi employed. The "security device" of a second look in the throes of sensory overload (Baranger & Baranger, 2008) is warranted when the two siblings, for example, may have held different transferences.

I have appreciated the opportunity to discuss the author's impressive chapter concerning interpretive dream work with families and note that: "*There are dreams*" as Emily Bronte reminds us "*which go through one's life like water through wine*".

I conclude with Meltzer's (1983) apposite comment that:

> Dreams are an enrichment of one's vision of the world with an intoxication of emotional colouring as never before. Or is it a heady vision that once was apprehended and lost, awaiting a dream to reinstate its dominion in the aesthetic relation to the world? When such a dream has visited our sleeping soul, how can we ever again doubt that dreams are "events" in our lives? In the dream world there is determined the great option between an optimistic and pessimistic view, not only of our own lives, but of Life.
>
> (pp. 94–95)

References

Bagnini, C. (2006). Accedere al labirinto dell'inconscio delle coppia attraverso i sogni (pp. 45–56). In: G. Tavazza (Ed.), *Interazioni:* Clinica e ricerca psicoanalitica su individuo-coppia-famiglia. Italy: Franco Angeli.

Baranger, M., & Baranger, W. (2008). The analytic situation as a dynamic field. *International Journal of Psycho-Analysis*, *89*(4): 795–826.

Bion, W. R. (1992). *Cogitations*. London: Karnac.

Meltzer, D. (1983). Dream-life. In: *A Re-examination of the Psycho-Analytic Theory and Technique* (pp. 86–95). London: Karnac.

Nicolò, A. M., Norsa, D., & Carratelli, T. (2003). Playing with dreams: The introduction of a third party into the transference dynamic of the couple. *Journal of Applied Psychoanalytic Studies*, *5*(3): 283–296.

Scharff, D. (1992). *Refinding the Object and Reclaiming the Self.* Northvale, NJ: Jason Aronson.

Sharpe, E. F. (1931). The technique of psycho-analysis. *International Journal of Psycho-Analysis*, *12*: 24–60.

Discussant perspective

Janine Puget

The idea that the analyst's training is what facilitates a better understanding of what takes place in family and couple devices should be carefully considered. I do not think that such training is enough; analysts must have experience in link analysis. Otherwise, they will only be able to apply and expand their understanding of the individual psyche to the link device. When we think in terms of couple, family, or group relationships, manifold paths open up.

We could engage in a polemic, creative debate on the different approaches to this link or linking device. In my view such an approach facilitates the development of missing parental functions. Moreover, the presence of others throws individuals off centre by virtue of their inaccessible foreignness. Only on occasion is it useful to think of them as potential depositaries of psychotic or primitive anxieties. Sometimes the recourse to identificatory mechanisms constitutes an attempt to reduce otherness to sameness.

For the authors, in contrast, family therapy is an intervention that lies at the crossroads of group and individual therapy. In this sense, their theoretical framework is clear and in keeping with the vocabulary they use. In their framework, unconscious fantasies, the primitive levels of the mind, the un-thought, and what they call the "malicious fusions with the other, intrusion and colonisation of his mind, existence or his identity ever since birth" have their place. Their approach leads them to seek causal explanations and to try to render thinkable what hitherto could not be thought. They point to families' difficulties in thinking together and listening to interventions beyond their purely rational effect. We can thus see why the authors focus on metaphor. My discussion of the material will be guided by my way of understanding the family group.

The first family session

The analyst is first struck by Dania's smile and by the unexpected ease with which Giodi, a very intellectual child, establishes a relationship. The presenting problem was the parents' concern about the effect of one child's physical defect on the mind of the other. What should be done with this problem? Would one focus on the present and look at the parents' discourse, which imposes meaning? Would it be possible for a physical defect not to have an effect? How do we make room for difference when it may be negatively viewed by society?

There is an assumption shared by the parents and the authors that this defect generates violence or leads to the emergence of negative primary representations. If this were the case, we could think that analysing the family's primitive prejudices would reduce the impact of the defect. Yet if we want to know what to do with the effects that are produced in each situation, the problem becomes more complicated. How can we make room for the other components that affect the constitution of a link?

One possibility is to focus the session on other difficulties arising in the link. Dania's physical defect may require extra work because it challenges traditional models of a perfect family. In this sense, we should dwell on the dream that Giodi relates/draws. There is a big house that could lodge everyone, but it entails some danger. There is a spider, and a treasure that must be safeguarded. There is something to build and protect. Is it each family member's internal world that must be protected, and will a space have to be built that respects singularities that contain riches and dangers?

Dania draws a house that has a closed, inaccessible room. This house is black and white. The two drawings are called houses, but one contains a treasure and a spider, and the other, only a private world. Still, the analyst wants everyone to participate. Why? Wouldn't it be better to wait and see if they actually want to do so? Does the dream belong to everyone? Many will agree that this is the case. I think it does not, but perhaps all the family members will be able to appropriate it. There are two closed spaces. Could there be a family secret that has not come to light yet? Could this be a very intrusive family, and the dream, a request to protect someone's privacy?

Second session

In this session a problematic daughter is described. The daughter recounts a dream, and mentions having seen *Gomorra* . . . the Mafia . . . . She did not sleep well, and neither did the mother. The analyst tries to turn this material into the entire family's material. Why? Instead, waiting to see what parents and children do would give the analyst an excellent opportunity to see how they interact, since each has a different life experience, and it is not easy to do something together when they assume that they have to share a way of thinking. There is something Mafia-like in this family; it has clear rules of behaviour, like the Mafia. The discussion of the movie serves as a precedent for the confession that appears a few sessions later. Elena and the mother talk about the grandfather's brother's lover, who is a whore.

The conversation about *Gomorra* also unlocked something; the mother tells her daughter about her experiences of abuse. So how should we understand this development? The authors explain it causally. I would suggest that the link experience opened a space to talk about what had

(continued)

(continued)

remained unspoken, which is associated with the Mafia. Here the analysts relate to the primitive levels of the mind. Is this actually the case? When Maria and her mother talk, do they talk as mother and daughter or as two subjects who are sharing something?

An analytic space has been created whereby talking and remembering become possible. Are we dealing here with the Mafia aspects of each family member, or with a different way of speaking? They may be talking about the difficulties and risks inherent in living together. Each sees advantages in belonging to the Mafia, but there is a danger expressed in the dream, and it is the danger of being caught.

In conclusion, I would suggest that we can interpret causally and deterministically, or we can intervene in the present. Interruptions–interferences constitute a necessary condition of a link.

Chapter 7

Links to the past and to wider social issues in a family assessment

David E. Scharff and Jill Savege Scharff

Introduction

The case material presented in this chapter is designed to demonstrate our way of "working through" with a family and in particular how we use interpretation. We present a family who sought help from us, as co-therapists, about the conflict in handling their toddler daughter. The couple had been married for eight years. Mrs Wall, a teacher, is now at home with her daughters, Margaret, 16 months old, and Lizzie, four years. Captain Wall is in the military service. As parents the Walls found the pregnancy and raising the first child quite easy, but are reeling from the second pregnancy and care of their difficult-to-soothe toddler Margaret.

We see an assessment, as a tiny sample of a family's life, which gives in-depth access to family links and social unconscious, a fractal of the whole structure of the family's personality and its members. The patterns seen in clinical assessment have a similarity to the family's daily patterns at home. We do not expect much change in these few sessions, but we do see a sample of the therapeutic relationship that could develop over time if we establish conditions for growth. In conjoint family therapy, we rely on our therapeutic personalities, honed by training and personal therapy, to be an effective force to produce a change in the couple and family and in the psychic structure of individual family members (Scharff & Scharff, 1987, 2011).

Our clinical work uses natural language to communicate, not theory, but we can see how the flow of speech and the interactive behaviours of talking and playing all communicate both consciously and unconsciously, in direct verbal ways and more thoroughly through non-verbal vehicles. We can get to know something about the links into which this family unit and each of its members were born, the effect that their past and current links had on family attachment patterns, and the family's ways of entering into and warding off unconscious fears. What follows is a transcription of a video family session, which provides the actual words spoken as the couple interacts with their playing children and the co-therapists.

Clinical case material

First segment

The parents, Captain and Mrs Wall, introduce the children to the therapists, David and Jill. The children next begin to play with toys on the floor. The parents describe 16-month-old Margaret as extremely clingy with her mother, as well as extremely irritable and difficult to soothe. Mother feels her toddler never leaves her alone and whines or cries easily. Captain Wall says Margaret never gives him difficulty when he is caretaking. He is better at limit-setting, conveying the feeling that his wife is weak and at fault for allowing Margaret's crying to persist and get to her. Mother's first pregnancy was easy and that child, Lizzie, is easy. The trouble began with Mrs Wall's unrelenting migraine headaches in the last trimester with Margaret, for which she was medicated with Tylenol with codeine. Consequently, Margaret was born addicted. It was revealed that both mother and baby had to go through withdrawal, leading to Margaret's irritable inability to be soothed.

While we are talking, Margaret scribbled on Lizzie's picture. David asks Lizzie if that happens often, and Lizzie says, "Not so much." It's OK to have a sister, but she's not convincing.

Mother tells how Margaret pushed Lizzie aside the other night during story time in order to claim her mother's lap. Margaret says something and goes to David.

David: What's she saying?

Mom: Doll.

David (directing his comments to baby Margaret who is holding a tiny doll baby): Oh, you want the baby? Thank you.

Mom: See, I'd say she doesn't usually go to people like you? Would you, honey?

Dad: I don't know. I'm not around. Probably not.

Jill: You're not around her as much as your wife.

Dad: Well, no. I work all day long. I think my wife overreacts to crying so I'll turn her off (meaning his daughter), because sometimes she'll push me to my limits. I just leave her in the room and let her cry for a couple of minutes. When she notices that I'm not paying any attention, she stops.

Jill: Is that difficult?

Dad: It's difficult for my wife when either of my kids cry other than if they fall down and hit their head or they're hungry or something.

Mom: But wouldn't you say that she cries more for me than for you?
Dad: Yeah, she (meaning his wife) can leave for a couple of hours and she (meaning his toddler) won't say boo. She walks in the door; she runs to the gate and starts crying.
David: You agree?
Mom: Yeah.
David: So, you don't find it a problem. If she whines, you just put her in her room.
Dad: No, I just ignore her, and she stops.
Mom: I've tried that. If I'm cooking dinner or something, she's clinging to my leg the whole time, and I just go on. But it doesn't work. So I have to sit down and pick her up, because after ten minutes it gets on my nerves. She's still not sleeping through the night; she gets up about five times. She was up five times last night.
Dad: Well, two or three maybe. Maybe she's teething.

In this material, we already see signs of the unconscious transmission of distress as the baby's crying during the session gives voice to, and reflects, a level of tension in the couple that must exist at home. Mother and foetus were joined in an intolerable cycle of physical distress for a month before the birth, and after delivery when mother still had headaches and the baby was in narcotic withdrawal. So the body bore aspects of the link that could not be tolerated mentally, and that has carried over the ensuing two years. We see clues about the family members' attachment styles, hints of a history that has fuelled the infant's irritability, and painful couple conflict.

Parental tensions over housework and child care

Father now says his wife does things more slowly than he does because he doesn't allow the kids to distract him the way they do his wife. He does not mention her by name. Then he tells us that she insists on ironing his uniform shirts imperfectly rather than taking them to the cleaners. She wants to do this, and besides, taking them to the cleaners takes time too. He feels she is not organised, while she protests that she is. His disparagement is clearly painful to her. Now we hear suddenly from the four-year-old.

Lizzie (complaining about Margaret's disruption of her play): She just knocked it down!
David: That's funny, Lizzie, that's just what your mom's saying your dad did, and your dad's saying your mom did.
Dad: OK, Lizzie.

Jill: Disappointing isn't it? She thought she was just playing. Lizzie! Was that a house you were making (that Margaret knocked down)?

Lizzie: Yeah.

David (to father): So you feel your wife lets you down.

Dad: Yes.

David (to mother): And what did you feel?

Mom: I felt mad and upset because I didn't know he wanted it to be done that day. I thought it was no big thing. So . . .

David: What were you mad about?

Mom: That he was upset with me because I thought that it was something that we were just talking about. (To Lizzie): What sweetheart?

Lizzie: Keep Margaret away.

Dad (to his wife): It bothers you when you think the kids are fighting . . . I won't step in until there is blood.

Mom: There's not actual blood.

Dad: Margaret's a very active kid.

Lizzie (to her sister): Don't you dare touch this!

David: Now Lizzie is having considerable trouble with Margaret.

Dad: Lizzie will sit there for hours and draw or play with blocks – where Margaret's span of attention is not long. If you don't keep your eye on her, it could be dangerous. She'll stand on the kitchen table, so we have to move all the chairs or put them upside down because in a minute she'll go into a drawer. All the drawers have kid latches.

David (to father): It seems that generally, you feel your wife hasn't done as good a job as she should?

Mom: Or I don't get enough accomplished. It's irritating to hear "God! I can do this in a weekend and get everything done. Why do you have a problem?" That's irritating when you're trying to do it. He said that I've improved. I think he's improved a lot, these seven years too, as far as having to be neat. He's loosened up some.

So far in this session, we have seen that Captain and Mrs Wall are disappointed in each other. We wonder what links in the parents' childhoods led to their expectations. We also see that the children's play interacts with the parents' arguments, echoing their distress.

Links to family cultures

We asked the couple about their family backgrounds.

Dad: I grew up in an old German type family. Every Saturday you got up and cleaned the house from top to bottom.

David: The whole family?

Dad: Yeah, when we were old enough. My parents, myself, my sister, we'd vacuum and clean the toilets. (As he talks, Lizzie whines that Margaret has scribbled a line right through her picture. David sympathises with her.)

Mom: I never cleaned toilets until I got married, because my mother and my father were both working. So weekends Mom refused to spend time cleaning because she had worked all week. So on weekends, she'd have a cleaning lady, and we'd go off to the mountains and have fun. So I never really did chores or . . . toilets. So, when I got married, I thought, "I'm making a big adjustment because I'm doing a lot of things I've never done before, and I'm really trying to do a good job at it."

The link between the children's play and the parents

Now that the parents have described their domestic life growing up, Captain Wall having to help keep house and Mrs Wall's mother having household help, we can understand that Captain Wall feels Mrs Wall messes up his system and Mrs Wall feels that he is unwilling to have fun. In resonance with this dynamic, the baby messes up her sister's drawing. Throughout the interview, through unconscious transmission, the children pick up the emotional atmosphere of their parents' interaction. Their play forms in continuing resonance with their parents' relationship. In this segment, their play also expresses the conflict in links that *each* parent brings. The father is from a compulsive family that required conformity to set patterns; the mother is from a family that valued differentiation, flexibility and fun. In her play, Lizzie tries to get her work done. Margaret disrupts it, echoing the way that father feels mother disrupts his workman-like perfection.

At this point, we have now heard about three generations of links. In the next section, we hear about the link to wider social issues. All of this helps to prepare us for interpretations we will make later in the interview, centred on the links each parent has brought, the link between them that is also the link in which the children are growing up.

The social link

Dad: My wife has improved. When I was in graduate school I was also commander of a reserve unit. I had to be organised because of limited time. Everything had to be boom, boom, boom. It's hard to break those habits.

David: What's so concerning about the habits is the feeling between you that she has a long way to go.

Dad: Not a long way, but I think she doesn't know how to prioritise. Sometimes she allows what I consider trivial to occupy her time.

Mom: See, I feel the same about him. (To David): If I leave a bottle out or something, that's not so critical. You've got to have room in your life to be able to goof up.

David: Not *goof off*, but *goofing up* is ok.

Mom: To make a mistake. And I'm not saying on purpose.

David: You're saying he doesn't give you the room to goof up.

Mom: Sometimes he doesn't. He thinks I do it on purpose.

David: Do you think she does it deliberately?

Dad: Not deliberately. Careless! I find something goofed up and she'll say, "I tried." I've been in situations where – trying is fine but sometimes making a mistake costs you a lot. Whether it's "you goofed up a bill" or forget to do something, it may cost you. She'll say, "I tried," and I'll say, "That's fine, but now we've got this big problem." I'm always concerned: If the military sent me away, would my wife be able to take care of business at home? She's getting better. When we were first married, she didn't know how to balance a cheque book and wasn't quite sure how to take care of things. If there were problems, I more or less coerced her to do it, because the issue may come up where I'm not around.

Mom: If he's really pressured at work, then it comes home.

David (to Lizzie who is upset with Margaret): What happened there?

Lizzie: She knocked the blocks. I was making a barn for these animals. Margaret knocked it down. (To Margaret): There's nothing else you can play with (Margaret cries).

Mom: Margaret, why don't you play with these things over here?

David: Did you notice that they went at it just when you started to talk about this difficulty between you two?

Mom: Well, she just does that a lot, just when we're trying to talk.

Here we were reminded that Captain Wall works for the military with the possibility of mobilisation. This is the wider social context into which the baby was born, including that the family was actually moving from his previous posting. Now we realise that beneath the pressure he puts on Mrs Wall to perform perfectly, lies his anxiety to ensure that the family could function without him in the event of emergency deployment. He protects against this death threat through perfection. As they talk about this defence against unpredictable separation and danger, Lizzie pushes Margaret away for spoiling the safe home she is trying to make for her animals. Margaret cries, and they fight in identification with, and distraction from, the parents' argument and the anxiety about the uncertainties and risk of military assignments. We can now see that the insecure attachment seen between the parents, between the parents and the military world, and between Margaret and her mother, relates to the risk of separation and death. We conjecture that Mrs Wall's somatic symptoms (the violent headaches) in her pregnancy conveyed these issues and that Captain Wall's compulsive orderliness and his pressuring her is an ineffective defence against his own fears about being an abandoning parental figure and represents their shared identification with persecuting and demanding internal objects.

Competition for love splits the parental couple

As the session continues, the children squabble. David refers back to how the toddler's cry interrupted her parents. Mother explains that since Margaret's birth, they try to make Lizzie feel special, yet Mother is frustrated because Lizzie accuses her mother, saying Margaret gets all the attention.

David, attending to Lizzie: What's Oscar doing with the horsey?
Lizzie: He's living in the barn. He's opening the cages. The animals come out.
David: Why's Oscar doing that?
Lizzie: He wants to play with someone, so he's letting all the animals out to play with him.
David: Is Oscar lonely?
Lizzie: Uhh-humm.
David: No one to play with?
Lizzie: Yeah, he left Sesame Street.
David: And he's all alone?
Lizzie: Yes. All the animals were locked up, so he can't play with them.
David: Why did Oscar leave Sesame Street?
Lizzie: 'Cause he wanted to play with some animals.
David (to Mom): Oscar was lonely. That's what we're talking about. And you're saying Lizzie's a bit grouchy about it.

Mom: We give her a lot of one-to-one. We've even hired babysitters, so we can do things as a couple just with Lizzie.

Jill: But what you can't do is to make her be the baby again like she was before Margaret was born.

Mom: So she's jealous that she's not the baby. Sometimes she'll say, "Waa, Waa. Hold me!" like a baby.

Jill: Something about Margaret's cry is troubling – I don't know if it's because you're in the studio and you don't want to make the noise in the microphones. You feel she has to be quiet right away.

Mom: I admit feeling that! He tells me I do. And I do!

Jill: Something about her cry is urgent. She looks so distressed.

Mom: Her cry is always like that.

Jill: She gets you to zero in on her anytime she cries. She even feels herself that she needs to stop crying. She'll put her pacifier in her mouth to try to stop – while reaching for you.

Mom now says she's frequently in an impossible position. She can never do enough for either girl. When she tries to set limits on Lizzie, Lizzie announces "I'm a bad girl!" and refuses solace, leaving Mom feeling like a bad mother. Then Lizzie turns on her, saying, "I hate you." Mom doesn't know what to do next. At these times Lizzie feels Mom's disapproval seems to be inevitable, but it produces real pain between Lizzie and mother, moments that seem to express Lizzie's deep resentment. We ask for examples.

Mom: For instance, she'll come in and take Margaret's bottle and whack her on the head.

Jill: You're annoyed with her.

Mom: I am!

Jill: You don't hate her, but you're mad.

Mom: Right, but I don't hate her.

Jill: You don't hate her because you know that you can be mad and still love her. But she doesn't know that. I'd say if Lizzie's mad then she hates at that moment. An hour later she might love again.

Mom: One thing Tom's good about – If we correct her, we always follow with affection. If I correct her, we always hug her and tell her we love her. So she doesn't leave feeling, "They don't love me." I don't want her to feel bad. Because she's a child I feel like I need to follow that with affection too . . . .

David: Now, I want to cut under this a bit. You follow with affection right away if you correct her?

Dad: Not right away. Unless I really blow my top and think I overreacted. I generally wait until I see the behaviour. I want to let her know that after she's behaved herself that . . . .

In this section, we see how the parents, as a pair and individually, relate to the children as they play and how they do so at home. The insecure attachment links that organise these patterns, between the parents and between the children and their parents, reassert themselves at moments of distress and pull the couple to a repetitive pattern. We also note that Mrs Wall's speech became repetitive in these periods. She went over and over the same point as if we would not get it otherwise.

In the session, sibling rivalry is magnified during the parental upset, and, playing on parental guilt and over-concern, it produces excessively excited object relating. One of our interpretive comments points that out to the family. Father, in his own way fairly immune, leaves the mother to absorb Lizzie's attacks at home that have an Oedipal colouring. She splits her parents so that she can hope to hate mother and get more love from her father in compensation – leaving Mother feeling that she is a bad mother.

When Margaret is upset, the parents feel they can't do anything right. This pattern produces an increase in the anxious/ambivalent attachment that characterises the family link in a repetitive way, made more difficult by the baby's crying since she has such a limited repertoire in her moments of distress. The girls' squabbling and the baby's cry feed back into the family system to add an increment of anger and frustration throughout the family and between the parents.

We also learned that Lizzie, the apparently contained child, has hateful temper tantrums when not given her way or when she feels criticised. As therapists, it was a relief to hear the range in Lizzie's affective expression, but we also know that she is feeling judged by her mother and that without modification of this link she is at risk for developing a pattern of hatred and self-attack. In this session of evaluation, we do not explicitly comment on that possibility.

Now we return to a segment that expands the intergenerational link in this pattern.

Intergenerational transmission of attachment: Mr Wall

Dad: I don't carry a grudge, because of how my own mother dealt with me.

David: Tell me more about that.

Dad: Two weeks after something, she would bring up an incident I thought was buried. I try to think, "OK you goofed up!" (Baby cries.) And I want to make sure that after the situation is over, that she understands that she's behaving herself. Now the issue is over. Let's not drag it out.

David: When your mom did that to you, she'd bring up a grudge. How?

Dad: Just about any way you could think of. You know, "You didn't do this in school; you didn't hang your clothes up," or whatever.

David: What didn't you do?

Dad: Oh, I didn't do as well as she expected, even though you really gave it your best. It's not good enough.

David: When she carried this grudge, how would you feel? (Baby cries.)

Dad: Frustrated.

David: Frustrated? That sounds like an understatement.

Dad: Angry, PO'd.

Mom: Remember, Tom? She would even bring up things maybe a year later, wouldn't she, Honey?

Dad: She still does that now?

Mom: She still does that now. She'll bring up something that happened a year ago and say . . . I don't know if you want me to say anything?

Dad: Sure, go ahead.

Mom: Well, like when his dad died, it was an emergency. It wasn't like we knew he was dying of cancer. He went in for knee surgery and everything was fine. Then a week later he took a turn for the worse and was moved to ICU. The day we got a call, his mom said, "They said he may not make it." I called the airlines for the earliest reservations, but it takes five hours to fly and three hours to drive to his parents. So by the time we got to the hospital, he missed his dad being conscious by two hours. But he stayed with him in the hospital until he died. But his mom still says things like, "You didn't get there in time before he lapsed into the coma. Why couldn't you have gotten there the night before?" We did the best we could, being 3000 miles away.

David: How did you feel about this?

Dad: I just think: "That's her!" I don't let it bother me anymore. I just sort of tune it out.

David: But there are other feelings?

Dad: Frustrated, sort of like no matter what you do, it's not enough.

David: The words that you're avoiding are about how hurt you feel at being accused of doing less than your best.

Dad: What makes me more sensitive to it, is sometimes I feel that I do the same thing to my wife. (Margaret cries.) What's the matter? Your sister is picking on you, huh?

The family origins of personality are now coming into focus. Captain Wall hated his mother's nagging, grudge-holding behaviour, and is upset to see that he is behaving similarly towards his wife. The organising of the house to prevent a collapse in case of death has its antecedent in the family link which includes a sudden death of a father, made traumatic by distance imposed because of having moved across the country, and magnified greatly by his mother's continuing pressure on his already harsh judgement about himself. His mother is a persecutory object with which he has identified. Here we might have made the interpretation linking his pattern to his mother's, but he made the link himself, which we consider a much better thing.

We also learned that the family's last move happened eight months earlier when Mrs Wall was eight months pregnant with Margaret. That took her away from the area of the country that is her home. She had been very close to her mother and sister; they had supported her during her pregnancies. She was distressed during the pregnancy, leaving home and losing their support. The move exacerbated her stress, requiring medication that effectively medicated the foetus too. Then after the birth, both mother and child had to be withdrawn from codeine dependency. Mrs Wall still worries guiltily that her baby's brain was permanently damaged.

Mrs Wall's family

Mom: I have one older sister. We did a lot together, travelled together. See, I wouldn't have gone to Hawaii without my sister. My mom and I got along real well. I could tell her the things I felt. We still have a good relationship. She never put me down, always supportive and let me find things out for myself. I loved my father, but I didn't feel close to him like my mother. I did more with my mom. He was a perfectionist. Every weekend he would spend time in the yard until it was perfect. About once a year he would say, "You should keep the inside as neat as I keep the outside." But we didn't. He didn't mind if we went off for fun on the weekend. He'd just stay home and work in the yard.

Dad: My feeling is that when her father died, when she was about 20 or 21 . . .

Mom: 19.

Dad: 19 . . . her mother assumed both of the roles. She was a little protective, perhaps that's why maybe Roberta relied so much on her mom or her sister when problems came up.

Mom: Because she would try to do it all for you. I mean if you said you didn't want to go exchange something, she'd do it for you. My dad's perfectionism bothered me. He missed out on things although he had the most perfect yard on the block.

David: So this is kind of the debate between the two now – perfectionism as protection or as death.

Mom: I mean he died! The doctor told him, "If you don't give up a perfect yard, you'll die. Hire somebody to do this yard work." So my mother hired someone, but after the guy did the work, Dad would go out and do it over because it wasn't perfect. And in less than a year he died. So I felt, "Was it worth the price he paid?"

David is taken with Lizzie's animal play and does not notice Margaret playing quietly by herself. Now Margaret lies down in the doll bed, which does not quite fit her. It looks like a grave.

David: Lizzie, who's over here with these animals?
Lizzie: The horse.
David: The horse is all alone. Is the horse lonely?
Lizzie: Uh huh.
David: How about the two sheep?
Lizzie: They're not lonely at all.
David: 'Cause they've got each other.
Lizzie: Yeah, yeah.
Jill (to Mrs Wall): Were you mad at him for not taking better care of himself that last year?
Mom: In some ways I guess I was. He could've still been here today if he would have just had that attitude. He died in his sleep, his heart just stopped.
Lizzie: The cow is going into the horse's place because the horse is all alone.
David: So the cows are going to keep the horse company.
Lizzie: And then in a few days they're going to go back to their house.
David (to Mom): Lizzie's horse was pretty lonely, but the animals that had each other did fine.
Jill (to Mrs Wall): You, your Mom and your sister had fun while your Dad was perfecting his garden. It became important for you to *not* do things perfectly because that is what took him away and then it killed him.

Attachment relationships

In this section, Captain Wall uses his wife's first name for the first time as he becomes sympathetic to her plight, after admitting fearfully that he may treat his wife the way his mother painfully treated him. Lizzie's play picks up the theme of a lonely singleton compared to a happy couple. Margaret plays out the deaths by lying still in the crib as if it were a grave. Their play is not disruptive because now the parents are dealing with their mourning about broken family links. As the parents begin to talk about their losses and disappointments in a straightforward way, their relationship calms and becomes tangibly more secure and mutually supportive. As we now see their relationship as softer, more directly loving and supportive, the children become able to play calmly. As Mrs Wall describes her father's obsessive behaviour in the garden, we hear it echoed in her obsessive form of speech, which presents thoughts repeatedly as if to get it right. This fractured speech pattern contrasts with the narrative about her family. Her emotionally coherent flow of memory presents a secure picture, but the rhythm of the words is not cohesive. She seemed to have, overall, a secure attachment within her family, but we have seen how her vulnerability can push her towards an anxious–ambivalent state. Now we were able to make the summarising interpretations about their criticisms of each other about perfection – to protect against death from her side, and to prepare for the possibility of his death from his side. And we could show them that the children's upset mirrored their own.

Based on these assessment interviews, we can see how this couple's stress illustrates how a couple relationship is a link at the cross hairs of the generations and of their connection to the wider society. Then the children's personalities are built both on the couple's relationship and on relationships to each parent individually.

Conclusions

A fussy baby, having been addicted to codeine in utero, is born into a family link filled with her parents' guilt and irritation at her crying, sadness and resentment at loss of family support. Both parents carry grief and guilt in relation to deaths of parents. The parents' link is full of the anxiety of relocation and military mobilisation. The parents, caught in cycles of projective identification, disagreement and blame, induce guilt and inferiority in the wife in relation to a standard of perfection. The husband uses perfection to avoid death anxiety; his wife believes perfection could cause early death. Their shared unconscious organises around fear of death.

In family consultation, the parents work with therapists towards undoing destructive patterns and move towards the possibility of adaptive reintegration. Working interpretively from the baby's symptomatology to the family's relationships, attachments, inter-generational transmission, and unconscious links to wider society, the therapists help them reach a more empathic position and give the limitations in the family unconscious system the possibility of arriving at a more mature and adaptive organisation.

References

Scharff, D. E., & Scharff, J. S. (1987). *Object Relations Family Therapy*. Northvale, NJ: Jason Aronson.

Scharff, D. E., & Scharff, J. S. (2011). *The Interpersonal Unconscious*. Lanham, MD: Jason Aronson.

Editors' prologue to the discussant perspective

In their presentation of a family assessment, David and Jill Scharff work with both the intra-psychic and the inter-personal defences and illustrate the impact of the links into which the Wall family children were born. They highlight in this by demonstrating the way the intergenerational links can impact on the functioning of a family and how they can be worked with. Anastasia Tsamparli, in her discussant article, highlights the manner in which David and Jill Scharff's work with their countertransference acts as a platform for effective interpretations concerning the intra-psychic and inter-personal difficulties that are impacting on the family, which are now voiced by the symptom bearer for the family, their daughter.

Discussant perspective

Anastasia Tsamparli

Introduction

To comment on other therapists' session material is most rewarding, as one is able to witness the way in which "minds meet" in the session, the readiness of the therapists to "dream" the family's world and, having processed their experience, to feed it back to the family through their interpretations. This "feeding back" can be seen as analogous to a mother bird feeding her babies; they chew food to turn it into a digestible form and then regurgitate it for the babies. That is, the therapist's main function is her readiness to take in the family's psychic material and in this "state of mind" (Morgan, 2005), mentalise it through her *reverie* and deliver it in the form of interpretation for the family to use. This is what we witness Drs David and Jill Scharff accomplishing in the present session. They establish conditions for growth by adopting what Bion (1961) refers to as "binocular vision", i.e., they differentially focus on the reciprocal interweaving between the intra-psychic, inter-personal and the social ramifications of links.

The vivid images presented by the assessment sessions provide material for reflection on various aspects. I will comment specifically on the therapists' function depicted in interpretation. We are informed that the Walls were a happy family until the birth of their second child. What brought about their *impasse*, expressed in the designated patient's symptoms, was their difficulty to contain new input in their existing links: The somatic link (migraines), loss of family networks of support, the mobility imposed by the husband's military profession, all coinciding with the birth of a second child. This case demonstrates beautifully the inter-subjective assumption that a family, just like an individual, has no permanent state as they move on their life circle. Experiencing the new givens, the Walls are faced with a mobility/morbidity dilemma: They either mobilise their containing function to articulate painful experience or they fall into the morbidity of links fuelled by the awakening of inter-generationally-transmitted trauma. The Wall family feels inconsolable, a state of mind particularly evident in Margaret's whining. According to the therapists, the Wall family organises their links with each other around a defence against a fear of death. As a result, the family's links acquire a survival quality. Mother does not risk her husband's criticism and loss of family support; father risks the family's survival if his work sends him away; Lizzie's play does not survive Margaret's disruption and the family's containing function does not survive Margaret's whining.

(continued)

(continued)

Establishing conditions for growth

Interpretation functions as "a tuning force and leads to a workable here and now" (Scharff & Scharff, 2011, p. 116). It calls for the therapist's capacity to decode the quality of interactions in the session and, above all, to contain within her mind conflicting feelings, thoughts and beliefs (Fisher, 2008). In the setting of family therapy this is a very difficult task, as therapists have to track simultaneously different dimensions of the unconscious (intra-psychic and inter-personal) as well as its expressions in time (past, present).

The therapists present us with a family assessment. I assume that one of their main concerns is to create a safe context, a *sine qua non* precondition to delivering an interpretation. With this in mind, I will comment on the ways in which the therapists address interpretation in the session.

The therapist's "state of mind"

The therapists *acknowledge* the family's emotional world (children's play, parental interaction) and how they have constructed this, their fantasmatic family edifice. For instance, David, following Lizzie's play, asks her: "Is Oscar lonely?" or when Lizzie protests that Margaret has disrupted her play, David says: "Now Lizzie is having considerable trouble with Margaret." I associate this comment with the quality of the family links and how these generate feelings of "having trouble with" each other, for example, the problems between father and mother about dealing with the children's fighting, mother's problem dealing with father's rejection, Margaret's feelings not being contained, and Lizzie having her play disrupted by Margaret.

At other moments in the session one member's feelings towards another are acknowledged to empathise with how this other member feels. By acknowledging these feelings, the therapists provide an emotional environment of acceptance and therefore safety. This is a necessary precondition if they are to function as responsive parental objects so transformational experience may unfold. For instance, David Scharff says to father: "It seems that generally you feel your wife hasn't done as good a job as she should." By articulating the husband's disappointment, Dr Scharff makes it easier for the father to re-own this issue and at the same time empathises with how his wife feels (being judged).

Safeguarding the family's shared space

The therapists take charge of the creation of the shared space of the session by assuring the participation of all the family members. At the same time, and by inviting members to comment on what others say, the therapists reveal the narrative of individual stories that can gradually be linked to the shared story of the family. For instance, after father acknowledges his disappointment, Dr Scharff asks his wife: "And what did you feel?"

Encompassing the intra-psychic and the inter-subjective

Interpretations address the here-and-now of the couple relationship with the internal working models of each partner. Consider, for instance, when the husband refers to his habits saying, "When I was in graduate school, I was also commander of a reserve unit. I had to be organised because of limited time. Everything had to be boom, boom, and boom. It's hard to break those habits." Dr Scharff responds: "What's so concerning about the habits is the feeling between you that she (wife) has a long way to go."

Underscoring what "has not been appreciated"

In their use of interpretations the therapists aim at underscoring the difference of meaning ascribed to the same fact by each of the parents. Jill and David Scharff comment on mother's feelings that she has ". . . got to have room in (her) life to *goof up*." David Scharff comments: "Not *goof off*." The difference of meanings corresponds to the way husband and wife allot meaning to the wife's "making mistakes". It highlights the husband's judgemental stance towards his wife and echoes the husband's experience of his judgemental mother (with whom he identifies). In underscoring their difference David Scharff sheds light on the quality of their link, the power relationships that it entails and the rejection/anger quality it contains.

Linking different locations of the unconscious

The therapists' focus is on the family's *interpersonal unconscious* (Scharff & Scharff, 2011) and how it is expressed. For instance, they deal with the children's play as a free association that resonates with the parental discourse. In fact, it is like witnessing intergenerational transmission *in vivo*. In particular, they underline the manner in which the children's play is consonant with the parental anxieties and link this to the shared phantasies of the family. Equally, the therapists use their interpretation of the play as a means to foster an elaboration of emotions that infuse the family's links. For instance, David Scharff says to the parents: "Did you notice that they went at it just when you started to talk about this difficulty between you two?" By focusing on the resonance of the children's

(continued)

(continued)

play to the parents' irritation, the therapists establish links between conscious and unconscious material. That is, they provide a way for the parents to see what their children do in their play and its connection to what the parents do: They co-construct a relationship where power relations predominate. On another occasion Lizzie is complaining about Margaret's disruption of her play by saying: "She just knocked it down!" David Scharff comments: "That's funny, Lizzie. That's just what your Mom's saying your Dad did, and your Dad's saying your Mom did."

So, through interpretation, the therapists link two apparently disparate events and give them a new meaning. Later on in the session David Scharff links Lizzie's complaint about her play being "*knocked down*" by her sister Margaret to interpret what her father feels about his wife. David Scharff says to father: "So you feel your wife "*let you down*".

Intra-psychic/reconstructive

The therapists also equally focus on the intra-psychic dynamics. For example, David Scharff explores the father's feelings and interprets his trauma as being linked to maternal rejection. He asks: "But there are other feelings (about mother)?" Father responds: "Frustrated, sort of like no matter what you do, it's not enough." David Scharff: "The words that you're avoiding are about how hurt you feel at being accused of doing less than your best."

Joint interpretation

Having constructed hypotheses concerning the unconscious assumptions that trigger their conscious behaviours, the therapists proceed to a joint interpretation highlighting the couple's transpersonal defence. David Scharff says to the couple: "So this is kind of the debate between the two now – perfectionism as protection or as death."

Finally, in this session we can observe how the therapists gradually co-construct the family's unconscious world in their minds and pick an appropriate time to deliver the different levels of interpretations. For instance, Jill Scharff, registering mother's feelings in her countertransference, reflects to mother: "Something about Margaret's cry is troubling. I don't know if it's because you're in the studio and you don't want to make the noise in the microphones. You do feel she has to be quiet right away." Later on, she advances a step further delivering to mother, in the form of a "because" statement, the outcome of her reverie: "You, your Mom and your sister had fun, while your Dad was perfecting his garden. It became important for you to *not* do things perfectly because that is what took him away and then it killed him."

References

Bion, W. R. (1961). *Experiences in Groups*. London: Routledge.

Fisher, J. (2008). The role of imagination in the apprehension of difference. *Fort da*, *14*(1): 17–35.

Morgan, M. (2005). First contacts: the therapists 'couple state of mind' as a factor in the containment of couples seen for consultations. In: F. Grier (Ed.), *Oedipus and the Couple* (pp. 17–32). London: Karnac.

Scharff, D. E., & Scharff, J. S. (2011). *The Interpersonal Unconscious*. Lanham, MD: Jason Aronson.

Chapter 8

Interpretation and family psychoanalysis

Mónica Vorchheimer

Introduction

Bion drew our attention to interpretation in a most simple and deep way when he noted, "Worse than being right or wrong is the failure of an interpretation to be significant, though to be significant is not enough; it merely ensures that it exists. It must be also true" (Bion, 1970, p. 79). This is our challenge, to make an interpretation significant and at the same time true. When working with a family, we are presented with what at times can be a bewildering range of choices about how to respond. We are all aware that choices depend on numerous factors, but undoubtedly it stems from the analyst's explicit and implicit theories about psychoanalysis as a general theory of psychic functioning, and families as a specific psychoanalytic object. My assumption is that when seeing families, the presence of the members allows conjecturing about how meaning is borne out of what they do in the presence of the other and *with* the presence of the other. How this *presence* impacts on the members of a family group, and how this effect results from being part of specific relationship, something that the participants of the link cannot view, means that interpretation can only aim to describe and infer its meaning. There always exists a tension between the individual internal representation of the family and the effects of being in the family in the real presence of the others. Hence, I consider that an important task of interpretations is to describe what can be named as the atmosphere, the climate in the session which includes all the members (and sometimes the analyst as well). I try to grasp it through what they say, what they do not say, what they are trying to do with what they say, and of course, through the scrutiny of the impact that all of these have on the analyst's mind (countertransference), as can be illustrated in what follows.

Background to the clinical case

Described below are two sessions of the third year of a family analysis with Carlos and Veronica (both aged 50), Sergio (19) and Lorenzo (17). They requested a consultation as a result of their difficulties in dealing with the younger son, Lorenzo, who mobilised the family when his phobia progressively restricted his movements such that he was not able to leave the house. They described him as a tyrant.

The parents argued a lot, not about differences in how to manage the family as a couple, but because father reproached mother about leaving him alone "playing the role of the evil one" when he set limits. In her own defence she said that she "did not know what to do" and needed to find refuge at work where she disappeared for long periods from the house. Their arguments about Lorenzo were characterised by "proving who was wearing the trousers" at home and rules were set with this in mind. As a result frequent confrontations occurred. The couple's conflicts were often displaced onto conflicts between the siblings. Their elder son was described as "a guy who never raised troubles" and usually backed up "father's authority". This "upped the anti", leading to power struggles and arguments that depicted the challenge of establishing or overthrowing authority. By the time these sessions took place, Lorenzo "had declared his rebelliousness" and was not coming to the sessions.

Initial session with the family

When the first session took place the socio-political context in the country (Argentina) could be depicted by the image of a crack, alluding to an ideological split which divided people in two opposite sides according to their support or opposition to the incumbent regime. *The square*, alluded to in the session, is the emblematic scenario of political demonstrations.

Carlos: Lorenzo was almost coming.
Veronica: We are just coming from the square.

The analyst feels very surprised with this assertion. In the previous session Veronica had brought in her fears about what was going on in the country on the eve of elections and her panic reactions and will to flee; the political instability due to her childhood history – her parents' involvement, deaths and living clandestinely – made her feel terrified and she felt something similar was drawing close if the government – which they had supported in the square – would not change. (In the previous session, as well as in this one, the family had assumed that I would share their same ideological perspectives.)

Carlos: We were there the four of us, but Lorenzo did not want to come to the session.
Veronica: It was really very moving. The full square . . . all of us.
Carlos: Yes, it really was . . . I am ignorant regarding what motivation Lorenzo had for his participation. Well each one had his own and that was clear but Lorenzo . . . maybe it was because the four of us went there, all of us together, it was wonderful. We came directly

from the square in order not to be late. It was so nice being there together, the four of us, supporting institutionalism rather than this regime. I felt like in other times, something I know so well, we know (including Veronica). It was a long time since I last went to a protest.

Carlos: The guys (an ironic reference to the regime supporters).

Veronica: We did not find X among the crowd.

Carlos: Sergio also liked being there. Didn't you?

Sergio: Yes. It was my first time participating in a demonstration of this kind.

Veronica: Despite my fears, being there the four of us, with all these people behind, 100,000 people all together, helped to face instability. I sang the hymn; we all sang it. It was beautiful, very, very beautiful . . .

Analyst: There is a climate today at the square and here, a very *family-like climate*, so to speak, something very familiar, so you should imagine that we are all in the same track even if Lorenzo is not here.

Carlos: Hmm (ironically and being complicit with Sergio) she seemed to like it, the leaps, the singing, she was very involved.

Veronica: Yes, the march, I had not sung it for a long time. It was exciting; the faces I recognised, soothing.

Analyst: And being together, feeling you belong to the same is soothing, it facilitates facing the instability, the family instability (said as though completing the sentence).

Carlos: It was good to be there though I am not a "*peronist*" . . . I am very "gorilla[1]", every day more.

Veronica: When I met you, you were *gorilla* but then you were inclined towards *peronism*.

Carlos: I know them well, but every day I am more a *gorilla*.

Analyst: I can see that being part of that crowd, of that homogenous set, bears more weight than the personal ideas do, like the gorilla ones.

There is a brief silence.

Carlos: Sergio did well on his exams. Today during lunchtime, before we went to the square, I wonder how the topic came out.

Veronica: We were recalling what was happening a year ago today; I was on a trip, you were dealing with your uncle and business problems, Sergio's exams and you were recalling something . . . .

Carlos: I said something and Sergio, kidding, yet serious, said: "you have me too much in mind." They always criticise. If I remember, it is "you have me too present" and if I do not remember, it is that I neglect them.

Sergio (defending himself from the accusation): It was a joke Dad; I do not believe you neglect me at all. I have said nice things about you many times here; I understand that you can take it as criticism, but it was not my intention; it was just a joke.

Carlos: Yes, yes, it was a joke; but deep down you were questioning me. You always attack me and I am tired. (Carlos sounds discouraged and the initial fun atmosphere is diminished; Carlos and Sergio discuss this fact and Sergio tries to calm his father down. He adds, softly, that his father is very susceptible and Carlos once again stresses that he is tired. Veronica keeps silent.)

Analyst: Carlos says that he feels that his government is always questioned and I understand that it must be very tiring to feel he needs to defend his power all the time. Instead, Sergio seems to be saying that this is due to father's susceptibility, whose authority and government he recognises, in spite of its differences and Carlos' doubts. How can one know if the government is strong or not if differences exist?

Carlos: I don't know. What I do know is that the square was nice, and quiet. I can see Vero's fears and I also share them. When you know the characters, the unionists, the guys, and you know the codes, you can see the threat of a *coup* . . . that is why although I do not belong to that group, one has to defend institutionalism because a coup is worse. We know that. What do you think?

Analyst: When you feel together, belonging to the same regime in a cohesive climate as in the square, you can face instability and feel fine. But you fear a *coup* might make one destitute and question the government which is felt as threatening – as Carlos seems to feel with Sergio's joke which he does not feel to be such a joke – you need to look for political and family support. Veronica does not seem to join the *coup* atmosphere; perhaps this is why Carlos addresses me, to find support, feeling lonely, without alliances that back him up?

Carlos: Maybe . . . a good extrapolation. (This sounds disqualifying but looks like a flimsy response.)

Carlos: The anti-system *coup* perpetrator is at home and it is Lorenzo. He is always in an anti-system position, opposing.

Veronica: Law exists, he recognises it but does not want to obey (minimising how Lorenzo speaks).

Analyst: Interesting to think: opposing and being a *coup* perpetrator. Are they the same? Different? How does one know?

Veronica and Carlos join in a kind of long diatribe on adolescence and the law and "normal rebellion", but Carlos insists that Lorenzo is more than normally rebellious.

Carlos: I remember once Sergio said something important here: "I will obey you, though I do not agree." This is the true adolescent attitude; it doesn't represent transgression. The system has to be questioned from inside. Lorenzo wants to violate it. As we said last session, when he ended up breaking the computer. I am still waiting for him to take responsibility for the screw-up. (It feels as if he is bragging about his authority as the father; he speaks up as if addressing a speech at the square, showing his strength and how important keeping his strong annoyance is.)

Analyst: Keeping your annoyance makes you feel that you govern?

Carlos: Yes. Now I tell Lorenzo "no", without explanation as I used to before. The analyst notes a smile on Sergio's face and ask what's in his mind.

Sergio says tenderly: I was recalling the absurd things my brother does to repair the damage; I believe he is sorry. But he does not want to pay for it. He even wanted to fix it with glue (they laugh). He is much more communicative with me; he's changed.

Carlos and Veronica agree and say that Lorenzo is on better terms with everybody.

Carlos: However, we should keep firm.

Analyst: Sergio introduces a tender perspective, like when he said it was a joke before. Perhaps he remarks that if one remains only suspicious, only seeing defects, feeling critical, one can miss new things, changes. It is like when a government always has to be defended from threats.

Carlos: Yes but still, one should be alert. I see the changes but protect myself from "being soft". I need to give support to what annoys me.

Veronica: It's true that things are better. The other day it was Sergio's birthday and we went biking with Lorenzo. It was the first time in months that he had gone out.

Carlos: But be careful, remember he wanted to decide the route and I did not allow him to do so.

They then discuss whether or not things are changing or everything is the same or if things are different, in that they are improving. Carlos includes himself agreeing though adding a "yes, but still" clause.

Analyst: I can see that discussing whether or not there are changes and differences seems important. If one does not see differences the risk is that one will be participating in a useless atmosphere of conflicts that might not actually be present. Is it like having a need to see *coup* threats to mark a government with the stamp of resistance? The problem is that this might create a weak authority or a government, always at risk of being removed.

Veronica: The other day Lorenzo agreed to come and work at the office. So the two are coming.

Sergio: No. If he comes, I won't.

Veronica: Why?

Sergio: I don't want to! I've told you, mum, and you ignore it.

Veronica: I didn't understand it was important.

Sergio: I told you, but you don't pay attention. (the little boys together, scornfully) No.

Veronica: Time is over, isn't it?

Session two: Several months afterwards

Carlos and Veronica tell me that Lorenzo is not coming since he is delayed doing paperwork they had asked him to do.

Carlos: It was unimaginable some time ago that Lorenzo would go out as he does now. Strange things are happening in the family . . . .

Veronica: We asked him to go and pick up something and he accepted. And he went to a football game too.

Carlos: Sergio is doing sports too.

Veronica: Lorenzo phoned saying he would not come; apparently he intended to come.

Carlos: That's surprising. He goes out, he is learning to drive and went pretty far.

Veronica: He looked at the map and went!

Carlos: Perhaps one should let things happen?

Analyst: Let things happen?

Carlos: Yes. Apparently . . . I guess now that he is going out we will be facing things we already know and we have to react differently than when they were younger. They are not the same. We cannot measure the same quantity of water in the glass because they might have different thirsts. When Lorenzo starts driving the car, perhaps one will have the car three days and the other four; or one will have four days and the other three. We'll see . . . but I can glimpse problems . . . .

Analyst: On the one hand you say new things are happening, surprising strange things; however, at the same time, you say you know what you'll be facing, as if it was more of the same, as if you imagine that there are still two kids arguing for the car as they might for a glass of water.

Carlos: It's not the same because we'll be reacting differently. Anyway, it's difficult. Lorenzo missed many things over these three years and they are unrecoverable. He won't be able to study at Harvard and I have to accept it. I have to see what he is achieving in relation to his capacities and not according to my expectations. But it's complicated. When I see he is doing nothing . . . I permit or not accordingly.

Veronica: By the way, he asked me to buy new sport shoes. Remember the issue, when you said you would not buy him another pair of shoes because you felt that if he was remaining at home it was enough to have one pair. But now it's different.

Carlos: I gave him the money the other day!

Veronica: Yes, but he wants another pair, a more expensive pair.

Carlos: He should buy them with the money I gave to him!

Veronica: But he wants a more expensive pair.

Carlos: He needs to manage what we gave to him. That's it. Don't undermine me!

Veronica: I told him "If you want to spend more, go and get a job and earn your own money."

Analyst: Because you agree with Carlos?

Veronica: Mmmmm.

Analyst: So. How do you stipulate how much can be spent on sport shoes?

Carlos: I don't know. No criteria (as if being caught red-handed).

Analyst: I was asking because I have the sense that you try and do your best to see something new and to agree; however, when you get to want to create some limits, let's say on spending money, there does not seem to be any criterion for how much they might cost. It seems that the spending money given for the shoes should not be higher because Lorenzo does not deserve more or because he won't be studying at Harvard. This feels like a punishment.

Carlos: Maybe.

Veronica: It is. Isn't it Carlos?

Analyst: So money is like a protest? I won't be giving more because painfully you are not as I would have liked you to be?

Carlos: It is difficult to accept that he has been locked inside the house for three years while life has gone on outside . . . difficult to accept that he won't be a Harvard student. We had always saved our money for that. It's the best place for them to study. And Lorenzo won't. But it's our problem, not his. Each one will be doing his own life. We'll see how this ends up . . . .

Veronica: And we'll see what happens with us too, what we'll do with our lives.

Sergio is silent and the analyst notes this.

Sergio: I have nothing to say about Lorenzo. We do not talk to each other. He is angry with me.
Veronica: And you with him.
Sergio: I'm not angry; he is the angry one.
Veronica: Since the computer issue.
Sergio goes on to insist that he is not the angry one.
Analyst: I tell Sergio that he says he is not angry but he looks affected by something.
Sergio: Yes, I was impressed by what happened the other day, somebody throwing a cup.

Carlos smiles.

Sergio (sounding irritated): What are you laughing about?
Carlos: I'm not laughing.
Sergio: It's not funny.
Carlos: Sergio, you are also angry, you both don't talk to each other!
Sergio: I don't talk to him because he had a knife and said: "if you touch my plate I'll kill you."
Carlos: You were both hopping mad!

Sergio then gets more and more annoyed insisting that it was his brother, not he. Carlos describes how Sergio provoked him: "You told him, come on crazy, come and knock me down, you ill, mad man."

Sergio: It's not the same.
Carlos: It is!
Sergio: Only crazy people do that.
Carlos: Crazy people provoke in such a way, though I am not justifying what he did.
Sergio (he shouts): It's not the same and don't laugh. (He then cries.)
Carlos: I'm not laughing. I'm eating a candy. It's my muscles moving.
You haven't seen the whole scene. I was in the midst of a battle trying to stop you both. You both went mad.
Sergio: He was crazy.
Carlos: You don't own a *normalmeter*.
Analyst: Each one has a *normalmeter* and it seems important to have one so as to be able to know where to place madness. And apparently diminishing the relevance of feelings contributes to create madness or painful annoyance, incomprehension, when something is felt as very dramatic and is not seen as such.

Veronica (almost inaudibly):	Nobody is mad in the family.
Analyst (I am aware that I cannot get rid of my concern about Sergio's pain and crying to which his parents do not respond):	For Sergio, it is mad to throw a cup. You think that provoking might be equally mad.
Carlos:	Provoking where it hurts more.

Carlos goes on to give examples of when they were young. He said that Sergio argued with his brother. Sergio threatened him saying he would kill him and Lorenzo was terrified. Once they found Lorenzo in the street too scared to come into the house because Sergio was mad and said he would kill him. Also, once, the maid phoned saying she could not separate them and that Sergio would hang Lorenzo.

Sergio says that was not true, but Carlos remarked that he does not have a total view of the facts and cannot remember everything. They confront and Sergio's anxiety – and mine – increases.

Analyst (wanting to say something trying to cool the atmosphere as if trying to separate two siblings):	Maybe I cannot totally understand what is going on right now. Sometimes it's not possible to get a picture of the total scene when one is part of it; however, my impression is that now I am watching a scene of two siblings quarrelling and a parent watching without knowing how to include herself. (At this moment I realise that although I thought I was referring to myself, perhaps I have also grasped Veronica's contribution to this configuration.) I add: It seems that there are different ways of feeling angry; some are acceptable and reasonable while others are described as "insane", "crazy", "unreasonable". Who defines this in the family, therefore, does not seem irrelevant.
Carlos:	Veronica has also thrown up plates and stuff (laughing); she threw them and I tried to catch them. (He dramatises the scene.)
Analyst:	You mean this is also crazy?
Sergio:	To throw them up in the air is not the same as aiming with the intention to harm another.
Veronica:	True, mine were explosions.

Carlos: We were having difficult times, fighting to survive. It's understandable. We fought hard, we were poor and starving; instead, you two fight over stupid things.

Analyst: So there are understandable explosions and others which are not, depending on whether a fight justifies them? A fight, which does not have the same connotation, as a fight for stupid things.

Sergio: When father laughs I feel he doesn't take me seriously. It's not funny. Nor is it when mother starts crying and she disappears. They think we are the only crazy ones. If I don't keep silent and say what I think, I am seen as crazy. Am I? That's not fair.

Conclusions

When adolescence arrives in this family and creates emotional turmoil it questions and suspends the identifying references that offered certainties in the past. The family scenario is filled with uncertainties, such that previous meanings in the field of knowledge, authority, sexuality and generational differences are seen to have expired. But if families resist novelties these can be experienced not as such, but as a threat of dissolution of the family, a threat of no more being.

With this in mind, while the analyst is sitting in the consulting room he is in some way like journalists are; sometimes he can keep adequate distance to describe the complexity of the pictures that shape the psychic surface. He can infer that there are forces in the depth that draw up these lines and is aware that he can get only asymptotically close to the object of observation. On other occasions, unconscious forces drag him to the battlefield, as journalists who cover war events, and he needs to recover an appropriate angle to maintain observation without losing perspective.

Interpretation is a privileged tool, which not only provides understanding to patients, but allows the analyst to place himself at the best point in terms of therapeutic temperature and distance.

Reference

Bion, W. R. D. (1970). *Attention and Interpretation*. London: Tavistock.

Note

1 Gorilla is an epithet coming from Argentine political jargon; it is used to name somebody extremely anti-peronist and is also used contemptuously to refer to a reactionary right-wing person, a militarist, an anti-communist or a non-democratic person.

Editors' prologue to the discussant perspectives

Mónica Vorchheimer presents a family at the centre of a revolution concerning the family government. The analyst shows us how she approaches their difficulties by interpreting the links in the family, especially those pertaining to Sergio and Lorenzo, which contain the projected elements of the parents (especially the father). Pilar Puertas Tejedor notes that that it is the interactive dynamic of the drive in the here and now which needs to be the main focus of the intervention. He suggests that such an approach requires an adaption of the traditional method, especially in relation to interpretation. Jeanne Magagna argues that in this family the main issue is that there is a protest, an anger and hostility regarding unmet needs for nurturance and understanding. In a close examination of the interpretive work of the author she suggests some additional interpretations that could be considered. These relate to her view that the predominant family problem – its need for wealth and achievement – supersedes some of the requirements for emotional satisfaction of needs within the family.

Discussant perspective

Pilar Puertas Tejedor

In providing this interesting clinical case material, the author has virtually synthesised in two sessions a family diagnosis, its evolution and the path of interpretation followed by the analyst. Before beginning my discussion of the case, I would like to explain my approach to interpretation in couple and family psychoanalysis. In such a case, the focus of my interpretation gravitates to a focus on the inter-subjective, rather than on the intra-psychic. In other words, I see the interactive dynamic of the drive as the main focus. One also occasionally explores the intra-psychic aspects of the couple, which might also be currently impacting on the couple relationship. The present family are alienated in subordination to the dramatised enactment of the unconscious experiences of the family members. The main goal in such cases is to drive the clinical attention onto a real focus on the "here and now".

The family case presented by the author illustrates these issues. The manner in which the family introduce themselves immediately provides some indication of the underlying problem in the family represented by Lorenzo's symptom. The ultimate diagnosis substantiates this. The intervention of the analyst is centred around underlining the poor transmission of a protective and supportive super-ego in his parents. By her intervention, the analyst suggests the couple may have failed as a symbolic matrix of generational and sexual difference: a reference matrix useful in building a protective super-ego.

The rivalry between the couple exposes that they are organised in an anal mode, with an organisation which is based on the dominant and submissive roles in their relationship. The complementarity in the union of different sexualities is also disabled, causing the absence of an adequate Oedipal function. The second generation takes over this position through Sergio due to the absence of this function in the father–mother dyad. The role of Lorenzo is to denounce this lack via his symptom and to expose this problem in the family. That is, his phobic defence protects him and, at the same time, denounces this fault in the family. It is thus a symptom that forces the family to look for a treatment, to help them overcome this organisational deficit from which they suffer.

Mourning the loss of his childhood has, for Lorenzo, been interrupted by the lack of a parental function which could have sheltered and sustained his identity configuration. The parental objects thus fail as limit establishers. The assumption of the parental function by Sergio is insufficient to protect his brother from chaos.

I would now like to comment on the family session material.

(continued)

(continued)

The first family session

During the first part of the session, the analyst points out that the blurring of differences between parents and children is being defended against, especially underlining the "all for one" attitude. All differences, in particular the generational ones, are wiped out, which makes the whole family operate at the same level. Consequently, the authority position is denied; if there isn't such a position within the family, there is no possible conflict. Therefore, conflict arises when the father isn't able to function in establishing limits. Carlos, the father, acts as he did when he was an adolescent himself, wanting no commitments. His wife follows his lead and both try to make their analyst join them, manically seducing her as they attack her transmission function, as well as the authority position she assumes.

In such a context, the analyst makes the family's defence obvious, a defence which they use to try to neutralise the distress caused by the helplessness aroused when confronting the conflict they are suffering. The analyst notes: "Being together, feeling they belong to the same, makes them feel better, which enables them to face the instability of the family."

In the next part of the session, Carlos shows his distrust of his son Sergio, as he feels his authority is being questioned, when it really isn't. Here, I see a very interesting emerging symptom which could be treated, which is the blame Carlos feels due to failing in his role as a father. He tries to manage such blame masochistically. This self-blame which is not yet elaborated involves his son retaliating. He experiences his blame in a persecutory way, and attributes to Sergio this demand of an authority which isn't functioning in this family.

Carlos tries to sustain this function in an anal manner through violence, raising his voice, but lacking an orientating super-ego. In doing so, he changes from being like them, another son, to being a tyrant.

The analyst points out the fragility of this imposed position of authority.

The second session

The second session starts with the painful feeling evoked by the view that Lorenzo will never be the son who sustains the phallic project of his father through his academic merits. The analyst points out his difficulty in establishing a protective limit, a "no" which doesn't emerge from vengeance. Sergio denounces the violent anger of his brother which is trivialised by their parents. Both defend themselves against the castration Lorenzo imposes on them by his denial to study. The parents revert to the context of their childhood, as if time had not passed and opportunities were not lost. They re-deny the fact that time has passed in order to heal the narcissistic wound of the son's failure. Sergio is unattended by his parents who deny the passage of time and leave him unsheltered in a crazy present; his parents return to a time when Harvard was yet possible.

Sergio is the porter of emotions, emotions which haven't yet been elaborated in a depressive mode, such as helplessness, sadness and loneliness. This is why his parents, who are supporting Lorenzo, are defaming him. Their joint defence is based on a manic strategy. The analyst tries to rescue Sergio from this psychic orphanage where his parents have placed him – the orphanage where the father/mother function is unable to guard him.

Process

The work done by the analyst with the family process has proceeded with delicacy and profound knowledge. The result of such work is the capacity of Lorenzo to overcome his social phobia, as well as Sergio's denunciation of his parents' "craziness". In my opinion, this assertion confirms what has been experienced: "When my dad laughs, I feel he isn't taking me seriously; he is not being funny. When Mom starts crying and disappears, it isn't funny either, but for them the only crazy ones are us . . . ."

In addition to what I have mentioned previously, there is something I would like to point out about clinical work. It is advisable to consider the combination of interventions at an interactive level, with specific incursions at the intra-psychic level, as I have already commented on.

In the current case, I support the approach taken by the analyst with Sergio. Moreover, I wonder if sustained by the analyst he will be able to confront what his father is projecting into him and how this is interfering with his identity construction.

I consider that an important focus of the interpretation in this case would be to intervene more closely on the elements projected by Carlos into his son and the blame that is affecting the whole relationship with him. It may then also be necessary to intervene specifically in the father's intra-psychic issues. Is the interactive level sufficient? Moreover, one might ask, is it the unresolved mourning in both parents about their childhood which emerged during adolescence? What undermined the bonding with Lorenzo and inhibits the ability to destroy the authority Sergio represents?

In these types of situations, the difficulty lies in the capacity for deactivating the abducted core areas that are being kidnapped by the individual psychic economy. These act in the evolution of the family process in a resisting way. In my opinion, contemporary psychoanalysis should adapt its technique to these new areas, which are to be addressed. This requires our knowledge to be adapted to applied contexts, such as family psychoanalysis, which require a non-traditional approach, especially to interpretation.

Discussant perspective

Jeanne Magagna

Mónica Vorchheimer presented family therapy sessions with a family composed of a father, Carlos (aged 50); a mother, Veronica (also aged 50); and their children Sergio (19), and Lorenzo (17), who have been in individual therapy for three years. I am grateful for this opportunity to open the discussion with you regarding the interpretations made in these various family therapy sessions.

One fundamental issue for the family seems to be that there is a protest, an anger and hostility regarding unmet needs for nurturance and understanding. The family all talk about supporting the current government but wanting it to change. I would suggest that this represents the basic position they all hold regarding the family. They want to keep the family intact, but they want something to change within it. Before interpreting this issue, however, I might do some exploratory work, looking at what it is that the family members want to change within the institution of the government, using the government as a potential symbol for the nurturing and rule-making functions of the family. I then would be tempted, as the analyst was, to talk about the wish for support which all of them share in their protest and indicate how the family appreciates her, the familiar face, joining in their quest to create a supportive, contained family environment.

In the course of family therapy, sessions presented also seem to be various additional places in the conversation where a comment could be made. For example the father, Carlos, says: "I must protect myself from being soft." I wonder what soft means? Does it simply mean relaxing the authority role in the family, or is Carlos describing how he feels about being at this point in his life. Is he is afraid of "being soft" and acknowledging his needs, needs which he would like his wife and the family members to meet?

I might take his personal comment and talk about how each family member has "a soft, vulnerable self" that is perhaps in protest about needs which they would like to have met within the family. They might want to say more so that the analyst and the other family members understand just what they are expecting?

Carlos also says: "Sergio says, 'I will obey you, but I don't agree' but Lorenzo wants to violate the rules of the family." At this point, I might suggest that each family member shares disagreements and protests regarding the way the family meets each other's emotional needs. Locating the violent protest in Lorenzo who doesn't come to the family meeting and breaks the computer seems a way of holding the anger in one place. I would again want to elicit more from Carlos and the other family members about their feelings concerning the unmet needs about which they are protesting.

Their son Sergio, 19, suggests that Lorenzo isn't so hostile as before. The analyst indicates that he is describing how there have been some changes in the hostile atmosphere in the family, located in Lorenzo. In this way, she works on the splitting and projection into Lorenzo who is holding the family's hostility about unmet needs. Veronica, the mother, says she is inviting 17-year-old Lorenzo, to join Sergio, in working in her office. Sergio responds, "If he comes, I won't. I told you. But you don't pay attention." The boys together say "No!"

The session is coming to a close as mother, Veronica, states "Yes!" I think the central issue is now being alluded to. Each boy requires a separate, individuated meeting of his individual needs.

Sergio complains about how each of the boys can have separate and individuated spaces in the parents' hearts, but he is also alluding to the fact that somehow there is a difficulty in hearing and understanding his needs too. I think this requires another interpretation such as: "It is the end of the session. We are not going to hear and understand more of your protest, Sergio, but it is clear that you, not just Lorenzo, are protesting about some unmet needs to be understood by me, by the family." In this way, one begins to unravel the splitting-off of hostility and projection into Lorenzo, which has occurred by both Father and his son, Sergio.

I also think about the developmental stages of these two boys. At their age, part of their support base should be their peer group. I feel the family is perhaps "sticking together" by incorporating them into mother's work and that there is some difficulty in thinking about how this institution of the family is going to be undergoing a radical change as the boys leave home and find their lives outside the family. I also sensed that perhaps mother and father's work and the family's focus on achievement seems to perhaps dampen the needed focus on the changing emotional needs of each member in the family. "The absent parents" replaced by the nanny or nursery is a common cultural phenomenon. We see, however, that the violent quarrelling between the boys, with Sergio trying to strangle Lorenzo when they are left alone with the nanny, suggests that he has not yet received and developed the capacity to bear "sharing the emotional space" with his parents.

This seems to me to be a reflection of the predominant family problem: The family's need for wealth and achievement supersedes some of the requirement for emotional satisfaction of needs within the family. This, I feel, is the central issue which also requires discussion and interpretation.

(continued)

(continued)

Session two: Several months later

There seems to be a change within the family system. With the discussion regarding the need to earn money and both boys driving, there is an acknowledgement of changes in the life of the family. I shall focus on several comments in this session which I feel are central issues requiring interpretation.

Carlos speaks, with reference to Lorenzo going out and learning to drive and sharing a car with his older brother Sergio: "I guess now that he is going out we will be facing things we already know . . . I can glimpse problems." Then Carlos says, "Each one will be doing his own life. We shall see how this ends up." And Veronica, adds: "And we'll see what happens with us too, what we'll do with our lives."

Sergio, in response to the analyst's question, then says: "I have nothing to say about Lorenzo. We do not talk to each other. He is angry with me." A description of provocation of Lorenzo and threat by Sergio with a knife ensues. I cannot help feeling that the parents' wish for "Harvard boys", for achieving boys, creates a bitterness rather than a sense of goodwill between parents and children. I think the issue here to be interpreted is that there is a wish for the boys to grow up, take financial responsibility for their own lives, but at the same time there is a difficulty in accepting that they are who they are and need to find their own goals and fulfil them, rather than meet the wishes and expectations you have.

"Harvard sons" fulfilling your own dreams – I think the analyst alluded to this when she talks about the money to be earned or given for the shoes. I also repeatedly felt there was a diversion of focus by Carlos and Sergio onto Lorenzo. This was part of projecting their own hostility into him and preventing a focus on what was inherent in Veronica's statement, "We'll see what happens to us," i.e., the couple relationship.

I therefore might interpret: "Family life is changing as the boys grow up. Perhaps the two of you, Carlos and Veronica, would like some time in private, to think about how that affects each of you and what you would like for your own lives without the children. You see, I think Sergio was noticing, when father smiled, how father finds some relief in seeing fighting between the boys rather than locating his own hostility about something, perhaps how his own needs are met within the family. I think mother shares that feeling as well. The family is now clear that mother also has rages and throws plates and goes away crying." I feel that such an interpretation is really about unmet emotional needs which need to be brought to light within the couple and between the couple and the children. There needs to be clarity about "the fight" which is continually located between the siblings rather than owned as a family phenomenon between parents and children, and the husband and wife. I sense that there has been a scarcity of emotional nurturance and understanding in the previous generations and, as Selma Fraiberg describes in her account of "Ghosts in the nursery" (Fraiberg, Adelson & Shapiro, 1975), it is hard to help the parents keep owning their own needs and hostilities in order stop the projections into the boys and to help some of the boys' quarrels between each other to redirect themselves to the therapist/analyst in the transference and to the parents.

Reference

Fraiberg, S., Adelson, E., & Shapiro, V. (1975). Ghosts in the nursery: A psychoanalytic approach to the problems of impaired infant-mother relationships. *Journal of American Academy of Child Psychiatry*, *14*(3): 387–421.

Chapter 9

Crossroads in contemporary family clinical practice

Alicia Monserrat Femenía and Elizabeth Palacios

Introduction

In considering families, which include same-sex parents, McDougall (1993) notes:

> What is most important is not homoparentality, but the capacity of being a parent. This is what really counts, the possibility of loving your child, and bringing him up in order to make him become a subject. Making that subject feel full of life, active, dynamic, make him capable of loving his freedom and developing his sexuality. Parents who can identify his children in his desires and needs, allowing them to be open to the world and its expectations, make us think that being homo or hetero has no importance at all.
>
> (p. 93)

The clinical material in this chapter is part of a group of such materials that we have been investigating in Madrid's Psychoanalytical Association since we started our work in its Child and Adolescent Department, learning about contemporary cases and the links between parents and children.

In our investigations we are interested in examining what we think and what we do with families in psychoanalysis nowadays (Monserrat, 2005). We are also interested in studying the type of contemporary presentations of families that come to see us asking for help. When we work with families using psychoanalysis as a means of understanding links, we suppose that the suffering that triggers the consultation is essentially inspired by the manner in which these links play out among the subjectivities of the members of that family (Palacios & Monserrat, 2017). The psychic change proposed by means of our clinical actions intercedes in the conflict and suffering noticed between those subjects. Using as an example one such contemporary family that comes to us for help, we are asking you to consider with us the theoretical framework that underpins our clinical approach, the atmosphere aroused by transference and the work of symbolisation needed to promote effects by means of our interventions. Interpretation is one of the main tools that helps us in addressing the type of communication that is taking place between the members of a family.

The social group that gives us sense of belonging is an aspect of our reality and a trans-subjective universe that has a strong interference in the way in which our psychic life is built up and in the way in which our links are developed (Faimberg, 1985; Kristeva, 1995; Roudinesco, 2004). A sort of dialectic spiral takes place between individuality, the group and the social context. What was part of the ideology of family life, of childhood and the culture linked to them has undergone a very important change, giving way to new subjectivities with different difficulties (Puget, 2015) that need interventions from within a new *dispositif* (Foucault, 1984) that may allow the unfolding of the conflicts present in that structure. These changes produce immediate consequences in the nature of requests that families have for help and in the interventions required for them, and in the way these need to be carried out.

The family needs to be thought of as a group of egos that build up a field of unconscious manifestations of conflict and suffering (Bauleo, 1977; Berenstein & Puget, 1997). The inter-subjective context constitutes a setting in which different unconscious formations are found, resulting from the sense of belonging to a system of kinship, the daily shared routines, the shared meanings formed within a group, the affection that is experienced and the emotional experiences that take place within that grouping. The link binds these egos in an unconscious space that contains them. The family is an ensemble of places that these egos inhabit (Berenstein, 1989).

Although every clinical encounter has by definition a great deal of unpredictability, nowadays we find formations and ways of linking that, at least in their phenomenology, impose themselves as totally new phenomena. These new presentations can sometimes be perplexing and in many cases unsettling, since they put us off centre in the world of links with which we have been previously familiar, strange elements that feel foreign and make a particular impact on our minds (Puget, 2015). Relationships in which the ways of living, of looking at the world, of looking to the future and of dealing with suffering require us to think carefully in order to define our approach to intervention in a way that takes into account our experience of being thrown off centre.

In talking about the functions of being a parent, we will limit our discussion to interpretation, the theme of the conference. We feel that we can only deal with this issue, contextualised in the challenges posed to us by contemporary presentations, within the core of clinical psychoanalytical work with families.

Clinical case

This is a family comprising two women, Inés, who is 41 years old, and Patricia, 47 years old, who are parents of two boys, Alejandro, who is 16 years old and who lives now with his father but stays periods of time with Patricia and Inés, and Francisco, who is seven years old and who was adopted when he was 18 months old.

The reason for the consultation

Francisco's analyst indicates a need for family treatment. Francisco has been having psychoanalytical treatment since he was four years old. The reason for this treatment is that the boy and mother Inés have a bad relationship. He also had a delay in his psychomotor development and difficulty in potty training. Patricia says that they are only children and that she does not understand why Inés, who has such a good relationship with her older son, Alejandro, is so intolerant and has such a lack of comprehension with Francisco. Francisco was originally the son they had hoped and searched for. The relationship between Francisco and Alejandro as brothers is described as "wonderful".

Beginning of treatment

They describe how Francisco has disrupted their lives. The elder son, Alejandro, also had behavioural problems; he has provoked fights, even physical assaults, which have been directed at his mother Patricia and his father, due to the separation of the couple. Alejandro's father took on his upbringing when the couple divorced. Patricia did not take over Alejandro's care. He was then just three years old. Patricia and Inés only took care of Alejandro during stipulated visits. They said that they have managed his upbringing with no obstacles and in harmony, in spite of the difficult circumstances that surrounded the separation and their love union. Patricia began her love affair with Inés before her separation from Alejandro's father.

Patricia was at the time very depressed and "found a refuge in the happiness that she felt with Inés". She maintains that falling in love with Inés helped her to get over Alejandro's absence and not being able to live with him. Subsequently they became a couple. Patricia and Inés got to know each other in their work; both of them were involved in early childhood work. They have not legalised their relationship and resist doing so. Inés holds the fantasy that if they do so they could lose their freedom to love each other, fearing they would feel restricted by a more traditional type of relationship. Six years ago, they began to hopefully anticipate having a baby. Before taking the decision to act on this, there were months during which they experienced mixed emotions as they struggled to decide whether they should undergo assisted fertilisation or go for adoption. Finally, and "fortunately", they decided to go for adoption.

The analyst asks them why was it "fortunately".

Patricia says that they had decided that Inés should become pregnant, in order that she could have the experience of a pregnancy. However, when she was about to start the assisted fertilisation, she became significantly depressed. She took time to think about what was happening to her with the assistance of her own individual therapy, finally deciding that she would not be able to manage the *in vitro* fertilisation.

Patricia also made a series of comments which allowed us to pinpoint her fears about having a baby and in particular her fears related to inheritance. At times her comments about these issues had a touch of delusional thinking about them even though they were based on medical facts. She told us that when Alejandro was a small child they had a psychological consultation about him and were told that he had certain problems arising from hereditary traits and that in the long run he would have neurological problems. At that time Patricia's mother died.

As a consequence they decided that it was better to go through an adoption, which would make things easier since they could avoid the inheritance issue. That was the certainty they had in mind when they started looking for Francisco. Although this sounded somewhat mad it was how they thought they could deal with hereditary transmission and with their fears.

Inés went on to say that she had to do quite a lot of thinking to make herself comfortable with the idea of becoming a mother, as up until this point she declared "I had always been my mother's partner", a subject about which she had devoted many hours of thought in her analysis. When she met Patricia at work she fell in love with her and was then able to leave aside the intense relationship with her mother. When they decided to confirm their relationship, her family condemned her for "coming out of the closet". Inés never saw her family again and she doesn't know anything about them since then.

They also told us that they were both only daughters and that they both have several brothers with whom they have poor relationships.

At the end of these first interviews we decided to have an hour and a half session every week. The four members of the family group were invited to come, that is Inés, Patricia, Alejandro and Francisco. Patricia says:

> "The two moms and the two sons." "That's it." Inés approves Patricia's saying.

Beginning of the treatment

They both attend in a very anxious way because they say Francisco has been rejected at school. They describe the incident. Francisco has not been selected for the school football team and he was told: "Go back to your moms".

Analyst: Rejected?
Inés: Yes, because he has two moms!
Analyst: Because you are two mothers or two women?

Patricia answers immediately and says that this is a very open school, it is the parents of the other children, the ones that make the distinctions or it would be better to say there are some mothers who reject Francisco because of his coloured skin.

Inés says that they should think a bit more about what the analyst has just said because she has had a mother who suffocated her and that she sometimes feels suffocated when she has to behave as a mother. Patricia comments on another difficulty that they have had with their sons; they call the younger son by his original name (when they are at home they use this name and when they are away from home they call him by the Spanish name).

Session three months after starting the treatment and before Easter holiday

As Inés, Patricia, Alejandro and Francisco enter the consulting room, Alejandro makes a move to sit by Patricia's side but she tells him to sit somewhere else. A chair is left free by her side. This chair looks as if it could be for Francisco since glances are directed at him. He has a science book in his hands. It's a book for children about inventions.

Inés is still standing up, and comments, "It is cold". She makes an indication for the "children" to take off their coats. Alejandro and Francisco answer "No". Francisco says that he feels cold. Finally, Alejandro takes off his coat. Alejandro points out a page of the book that Francisco has left on one of the chairs, trying to divert Inés' attention as if he were trying to prevent the conflict that usually gains space between Francisco and Inés.

Inés loses her temper and in a tone of complaint says: Francisco is always like this; he always has to contradict me.

Francisco and Alejandro keep paying attention to the book.

Inés sits down in the empty seat by Patricia's side and she looks at Patricia waiting for her to say something to the child or to the children.

Patricia asks Inés to keep calm, that they are interested in reading the book.

Inés addresses the analyst and says: This is the usual way that Patricia tries to calm me down. She does so to prevent me from flaring up. But Francisco's manners show that he ignores me, I can't stand them or . . . .

Patricia interrupts her: It's much better that he ignores you so that the bad behaviours towards you are not repeated.

Inés cannot contain herself and reproaches Alejandro, the eldest son. She says that he always has his earphones on with music and that he protects Francisco who always does the same, so that she is always pushed again and again to break the rules. It is they, as parents, who fail. Inés gets more and more angry. She says that she thinks Francisco provokes these conflicts on purpose.

The analyst tries to highlight the present difficulties: Once again the same difficulties appear and there is not enough space in order to know if these are the same difficulties we have already seen, the same music, or if each of you is bringing a new song in. We are not able to see if there are new tunes between you.

Inés says that the music belongs to Alejandro and that a son should listen when an adult is trying to teach him, especially when this is the mother.

The analyst interprets that Alejandro and Francisco may be taking her words as an annoying noise and that it is not possible to know the reason for this argument. This is why they are coming to therapy.

After a silence Patricia says that the same thing happened last Sunday when they were coming back from a weekend trip.

They made a lot of food for lunch, some delicious beans. They decided that they would have the leftovers for dinner. Francisco, however, said that he would not eat them, that they were the left overs.

With great despair Inés tells Francisco: Nothing pleases you!

With increasing desperation Inés tells the analyst that she gives him lots of different foods and he always says "no", he rejects all the food and says that what she gives him is no good for him. He always wants fresh food. Patricia supports Inés, saying that she always offers plenty of food and always varied.

Inés says that his rejection drives her crazy and Alejandro says that the same thing happens to him; it drives him nuts when he sees Inés going crazy.

The analyst interprets that these complaints are provoked by what one gives to others who indicate that what is given is no good. Inés is a mother who gives, and Francisco does not want to accept it. She gives something and immediately expects the other to accept what she gives, but this does not mean that the boy is rejecting her. It looks as if mother and son have to accept what the other is offering, and this has to be accepted at once and unconditionally.

Patricia says that they don't know why Francisco does not want to accept what she offers; it might be because Inés is too insistent. What Francisco has said is that it is something already used. Perhaps he knows how to make Inés furious. She asks Francisco "Why is this so?"

Alejandro says that Inés does not understand what happens to Francisco and she only screams and yells and cries and looks at him in a crazy manner.

Inés starts crying and says that she shouldn't have decided to be a mother.

Patricia gets close to Inés and hugs her, and Alejandro says: It's not that bad.

Meanwhile Francisco grabs the book and takes it to Inés and tells her: You can read it.

The analyst shows them that they are all now functioning as if they were all mothers trying to make each other feel comfortable in this space.

Francisco looks at the analyst with surprise and smiles.

Alejandro: No, please, not more mothers!

Patricia: Inés wants to be perfect . . . and she shouldn't ask so much of Francisco nor of Alejandro.

Inés says that she doesn't understand anything but thinks that she's starting to understand part of what is going on between them.

This was the end of the session.

Conclusion

Up until now the focus of the case had to do with the common desire of the couple to have a child and the decision of how to conceive him, as well as the underlying issues that Francisco and Alejandro contribute to the construction of their subjectivity. The desire to have a child in order to build a family offers few choices and is complicated by the unconscious family structure the couple (who already have their mental constitution achieved) bring to the family: the parental couple who should help to open up life for their sons and instead create difficulties for them.

References

Bauleo, A. (1977). *Psychoanalysis and Groupality. Clinical Work with New Objects.* Buenos Aires: Paidós.

Berenstein, I. (1989). *Psicoanálisis de la estructura familiar. Del destino a la significación* (Psychoanalysis of the Family Structure. From Destiny to Signification). Buenos Aires: Paidós.

Berenstein, I., & Puget, J. (1997). *Lo vincular. Clínica y Técnica psicoanalítica* (Linkage. Psychoanalytical Clinical Work and Technique). Buenos Aires: Paidós.

Faimberg, H. (1985). *Psychic Transmission Between Generations.* Buenos Aires: Amorrortu.

Foucault, M. (1984). The Play of Michel Foucault. In: *Knowledge and Truth* (pp. 127–162). Madrid: Ediciones de la Piqueta.

Kristeva, J. (1995). *The New Illnesses of the Soul.* Madrid: Cátedra.

McDougall, J. (1993). *Alegato por una cierta anormalidad* (Plea for a Certain Abnormality). Buenos Aires; Paidós.

Monserrat, A. (2005). *Reflexiones sobre la actualidad en la familia, en a propósito de la Grupalidad* (Thinking About Family Nowadays, in Regarding Groupality). Buenos Aires: Atuel.

Palacios, E., & Monserrat, A. (2017). Contribution to the link perspective in interactions with families: Theoretical and technical aspects and clinical applications. In: D. Scharff & E. Palacios (Eds.), *Couple and Family Psychoanalysis: A Global Perspective.* London: Karnac.

Puget, J. (2015). *Subjetividad discontinua y psicoanálisis. Incertidumbres y certezas* (Discontinuous Subjectivity and Psychoanalysis. Uncertainties and Certainties). Buenos Aires: Lugar.

Roudinesco, E. (2004). *The Family in a Mess.* Barcelona: Anagrama.

Editors' prologue to the discussant perspectives

The contemporary nature of family psychoanalytic practice captured in the case presented by Alicia Monserrat Femenía and Elizabeth Palacios examines the dynamics of a family characterised by same-sex parents. The authors examine the links in this family, which are infused by unresolved dynamics in the parents. The authors conclude that it is not the sexuality of the parents, but their capacity to parent that is the clinical focus in contemporary practice. Affirming this view Carles Pérez Testor examines the way in which the authors address the lack of a parental mental space in this family and how the therapists attempt to repair this in a family whose dynamics are based on projections. Caroline Sehon, in her discussant article, incisively identifies the primitive nature of the defences in this family and discusses how interpretation in such a family can be seen as an attempt to transform a static, closed system into an open, dynamic system in which the family's interactional matrix might be re-patterned.

Discussant perspective

Carles Pérez Testor

The clinical material the authors have presented reveals the complexity of dealing with a newly reconstituted family that, following divorce, involves a homoparental couple and a sibling relationship resulting from an international adoption. In terms of the theoretical model from which my colleagues and I operate, parents are seen to be responsible for raising the family. In the 1990s the definition of a family which we proposed was:

> The family is the group in which one is raised and in which the basic and fundamental needs of its members are taken care of, in particular, those of children. It is a group in which the members are united, love each other, forge bonds, and help each other to grow and live like people in every dimension: cognitive, affective, relational, etc.
> (Font, Perez Testor & Romagosa, 1995, p. 86)

With reference to the case presented, the birth of the first child transforms the couple into a family. The family acquires the form of a group, a complex group in constant evolution, consisting of members in different phases of development, united by roles with inter-related and diversified functions. The ways in which parents implicitly or explicitly agree to carry out their parental roles depends on how they experience their relationship as a couple and how they have experienced relationships in their families of origin. The roles of the father and the mother are different and complementary. The mother and the father must "create an internalised system of relations, provide a framework for learning experiences and be a matrix that fosters the capacity of thinking" (Nicolò, 1990, p. 914). This requires an interdependent means of achieving containment in the group which has a single set of aims. The fundamental task of the family is fostering emotional and cognitive growth. The emotional growth of the family group begins with adequate emotional functions.

In accordance with the model of Meltzer and Harris (2013), there are family organisations that are based on emotional functioning which are founded on projection, yet in order to learn from experience, introjective emotional functions, which assist the ability to contain mental suffering, are necessary. The particular introjective functions that promote development are those involved in "generating love, promoting hope, containing depressive pain and thinking" (Meltzer & Harris, 2013, p. 68).

These functions make it possible to face and contain anxieties, identify and name feelings and conflicts, and to use the capacity to think, in order to achieve reparation for the perceived destruction one has caused and in the process develop a capacity for symbolisation. When the parental system takes responsibility for these adult emotional functions and assists in the development of thinking, the family is successfully organised and manages to avoid confusion and chaos.

When, however, projective emotional functions predominate in the family, it leads to "promulgating hate, sowing despair, emanating persecutory anxiety and creating lies and confusion" (Meltzer & Harris, 2013, p. 68). Consequently, the family structure breaks down, psychopathology manifests in the group, it loses its ability to carry out tasks of containment, anxiety becomes overwhelming and the group falls into disarray or resorts to using pathological defence mechanisms. Depending on its ability to integrate emotional functions and to keep a proper balance between introjective and projective functions, a family will be more or less successful in its ability to contain anxieties. Accordingly, from the standpoint of this model, this parental couple capacity will not depend on whether the couple are homoparental or heteroparental, but whether they are capable of carrying out introjective emotional functions.

This is the way in which the current family could be considered. That is, are Inés and Patricia able to perform these functions? In considering these questions when Inés is depressed and when she is about to embark *in vitro* fertilisation, she is incapable of identifying herself in the role of mother, which she associates as "suffocating" since she performed the role of her "mother's partner" until she was disowned because of her homosexuality. That is, her development moved from a symbiotic bond to a traumatic rupture. Now, Inés is unable to legalise her union with Patricia because of recurrent catastrophic fantasies.

Patricia is presented as being influenced by "*a prophecy*", according to which her son Alejandro "had psychological problems because of hereditary dispositions which, in the long term, would cause neurological difficulties". In terms of timing, this *prophecy* coincided with the death of Patricia's mother.

It seems that Inés and Patricia approached an international adoption against the backdrop of serious emotional difficulties, as individuals and as a couple both fleeing dangerous family legacies in order to accept an unknown, idealised adoptive legacy, which included the first eighteen months of their adopted son's (Francisco's) life experience, which was unknown to them. Francisco revolutionised their lives and Alejandro's as well, who protests over the separation of his biological parents by hitting Patricia who in turn responds with rejection and neglect. Alejandro was raised by his father.

(continued)

(continued)

The theme of rejection appears in the first family session. Francisco is rejected by the mothers at the school. One can imagine how this might affect an adopted boy who, one way or another, was abandoned by his biological mother and father, and subsequently rejected by his adoptive mother, Inés. He was a child who was subjected to identity confusion, and now has to answer to his Spanish name in public, and to his original name in private.

How is Francisco constructing his identity? How does he manage the experience of having a mother who tries to look after him and a mother who goes crazy? "No more mothers please," Alejandro says in a session three months into the treatment following a comment from the analyst. Alejandro situates himself as the spokesman (*porte-parole*) of the family and as the one who reveals the truth that nobody dares to put into words. He takes on the function of Tiresias in Sophocles' Oedipus.

The authors note that Alejandro thinks that Inés doesn't understand what's happening with Francisco. She only screams and cries and looks at him in a crazy manner. Faced with this evidence, Inés breaks down. Alejandro brings to light the fact that Inés and Patricia lack a "parental mental space", a space in the "couple's mind" that is ready to produce growth in the mental apparatus of their children (Perez Testor & Salvador, 1995). This concept is very similar to Benedek's "psychological field" cited by David Scharff (Scharff & Scharff, 1987) and to Nicolò's concept of "symbolic parenthood" (Nicolò, 2014), who notes "parenthood that conveys symbols and therefore determines filiation also allows the production of symbolic capacity" (p. 209). The homoparentality (Heymanns, 2016) is not the key problem of this family group. The material presented suggests that the focus to work on should be the reconstitution of the couple and adoptive parenthood since the relationship with Francisco is seriously damaged. The element of diversity could become a persecutory element which, in terms of projective identification, represents an externalisation of the internal persecution this couple seem to experience.

If it is possible to repair this "parental mental space" in family psychotherapy, Francisco might be able to deal with his future adolescence, which can be a very delicate developmental moment for children who have experienced international adoption, with more guarantees.

References

Font, J., Perez Testor, C., & Romagosa, A. (1995). Família i salut mental (Family and Mental Health). In: S. Doy, C. Campanera, & J. Teixidó (Eds.), *Atenció sanitària i entorn familiar* (Health Care and Family Environment) (p. 86). Barcelona, Spain: Departament de Sanitat i Seguretat Social, Generalitat de Catalunya.

Heymanns, P. (2016). Perspectives psicoanalítiques de l'homoparentalitat (Psychoanalytical perspectives of homoparentality). *Revista Catalana de Psicoanàlisi*, *33*(2): 75–91.

Meltzer, D., & Harris, M. (2013). *The Educational Role of the Family: A Psychoanalytical Model*. London: Karnac (The Harris Meltzer Trust Series).

Nicolò, A. M. (1990). Hacia una perspectiva psicoanalítica en el estudio de la familia y de la pareja (Towards a psychoanalytic perspective in the study of the family and the couple). *Revista de Psicoanálisis*, *47*(5/6), 908–922.

Nicolò, A. M. (2014). *Psicoanálisis y familia* (Psychoanalysis and Family). Barcelona: Herder.

Perez Testor, C., & Salvador, G. (1995). La dimensió familiar de la parella (The family dimension of the couple). *Revista Catalana de Psicoanàlisi*, *12*(1): 103–112.

Scharff, D. E., & Scharff, J. S. (1987). *Object Relations in Family Therapy*. London: Jason Aronson.

Discussant perspective

Caroline Sehon

Inés (41 years old) and Patricia (47 years old) met as colleagues and became lovers 13 years ago. With Patricia's divorce, Inés and Patricia relinquished physical custody of then three-year-old Alejandro to his father. Although the couple wanted to have a child of their own, they ruled out artificial insemination due to anxiety about "bad genes" and to Inés' fear of feeling smothered by a baby, just as she had felt in relation to her own mother. The couple ultimately decided to adopt, prompted by Patricia's fantasy that they would thus prevent the baby from inheriting their pathology.

Francisco was adopted at 18 months, and soon became the "identified patient" of this troubled family, which seemed mired in an endlessly re-enacted trauma. The intimate partnership was always on the verge of suffering some kind of collapse, for Inés and Patricia were unable to negotiate the developmental tasks of separation and differentiation. Mothers were characterised as needy and intrusive, while fathers were noticeable through their absence and were seemingly unavailable to help differentiate mother–daughter relationships. Adoption may have been an attempt to create an illusion of an intimate couple as much as a parental unit, but a parental fusion template prevailed.

Inés seemed to relate to Patricia as a transitional object that had allowed her to separate and differentiate from her mother, who treated her as a partner rather than a child. Possibly Inés was unconsciously drawn to Patricia in the hope of re-encountering her internal mother in more benign guise. In contrast, Patricia appeared to interact with Inés as if the latter were another child rather than a co-parent or intimate partner. Separation and differentiation seemed to be experienced as catastrophic for all family bonds – all members were destined either to merge with one another or to experience an absolute rupture. Apparently, the family lacked the capacity to build relationships between differences that were enriching and enlivening rather than depleting and destructive.

The couple described the family as one formed by "two moms and two sons". Such a cleavage along gender and generational lines reflects Inés and Patricia's pervasive tendency to engage in primitive splitting between "good" and "bad". For example, Inés and Francisco's relationship was characterised as permanently tarnished, whereas Alejandro and Francisco got along wonderfully. Or, the "bad" elements of the family system were aggregated, for example, when the couple decided that Alejandro's father should be the custodial parent, thus pairing a "bad" son with a "bad" father. These partitions express the family's rejecting object relationships; denigration and exclusion are preferred ways of dealing with overwhelming distress.

The couple is primitively organised around the defensive need to ward off incapacitating levels of affect by offloading badness or distress onto a person or group and, in turn, treating the recipient of their projections as a threat to the safety and vitality of the couple or family. Three months after the start of the therapy, we see in the session two boys with two women rather than two boys with two parents. Patricia does not appear to relate to Inés as a member of a parental couple organised around differentiated roles. Instead, she takes on a mothering role toward Inés.

Although the couple seems united around a common desire to rebel against the social traditions of a hostile world, this area of differentiation exists between them and society at large rather than within their parental boundary. Actually, this "us versus them" mentality may well have led them to join at the hip, consolidating their identity as a merged couple in the eyes of the children. Possibly, the couple feels the need to export this differentiation problem to their relationship with the boys, which partly accounts for Inés' divisive relationships with Francisco and Alejandro.

The analyst's second interpretation targets the family's insistence on repeating the same destructive patterns as a "closed system" without the psychic capacity to think and to develop creative and generative ideas that could infuse the old with the new (Fairbairn, 1958). Following Francisco's lead, both boys become captivated by a book on inventions. Could this object symbolise the growth potential sought by the children and attacked by the parents? Similarly, the siblings tune into music from "outside", regarding which the analyst interprets as follows: "Once again, the same difficulties appear and these don't let (in) enough space in order to know if these are the same difficulties we have already seen, the same music, or if each of you are bringing a new song in. We are not able to see if there are new tunes between you."

We might regard this interpretation as an attempt to transform a static, closed system into an open, dynamic system in which the family's interactional matrix might be re-patterned. Inés responds concretely and authoritatively. She blames Alejandro as the cause of the problem, without taking in the analyst's novel idea that the trouble exists within a link that has been unconsciously co-constructed by each family member (Scharff, Losso & Setton, 2017). The analyst continues to pursue this line of exploration, stating, "Alejandro and Francisco may be taking her words as an annoying noise, and that it is not possible to know what is the reason for this argument." Patricia confirms this hypothesis with her association to a replay of these dynamics on the way home from a weekend trip.

(continued)

(continued)

The third interpretation follows. The analyst states that Inés' complaints about Francisco's behaviour toward her "are provoked by what one gives to others, and these others show that what is given is no good." She highlights the boys' insistent rejection of the seemingly ideal feast, and thus their utter refusal to allay Inés' anxiety about being a "bad" mother. In essence, their objection represents a defiant act that would have been inconceivable for Inés to perform with her own needy mother.

Finally, the analyst interprets all family members' need to become mothers for each other as an unconscious strategy to defuse conflict. Perhaps the family aimed to open a space for Inés to protest against her feeling of having nothing to offer. In turn, the family drama unfolds. Inés has a tantrum, while the other three members rally round to reassure her.

To reach a deeper understanding of this narrative, it would have been very helpful to have access to the analyst's countertransference, which, in turn, would have offered clues to the transference. Given the family's need to enact and to evacuate rather than to think and symbolise their distress, the analysts would have likely had powerful countertransference responses, perhaps at times localised in their bodies. This clinical case example demonstrates the potency of a psychoanalytic approach to family work, even with very primitively organised families.

References

Fairbairn, W. R. D. (1958). On the nature and aims of psychoanalytical treatment. *International Journal of Psychoanalysis*, *39*: 374–385.

Scharff, D. E., Losso, R., & Setton, L. (2017). Pichon Rivière's psychoanalytic contributions: Some comparisons with object relations and modern developments in psychoanalysis. *International Journal of Psycho-Analysis*, *98*(1): 129–143.

Chapter 10

Fighting the darkness

A family in mourning

Janine Wanlass

Introduction

Families come into psychological treatment in many different ways. Sometimes a parent will call requesting family work, but often it is a symptomatic child that provides the impetus for the family to get help. Typically, interviews are scheduled with the parents, with the child named by the parents as the "identified patient", and with the whole family as part of an initial consultation. At the end of these assessment sessions a treatment recommendation is made, which may be for individual child work with accompanying parent consultation sessions, individual child work with periodic or regular adjunctive family work, or family therapy (Scharff & Scharff, 2005; Wanlass & Scharff, 2016). The family in the case described below, which focuses on interpretative work with unresolved loss, illustrates developmental differences in how children mourn and common challenges in working with grieving families (Bowlby, 1960; Freud, 1917; Garber, 2008; Green, 2013; Nagera, 1970; Sussillo, 2005).

Family case material

The family referred by a child therapist consisted of a 26-year-old mother, Maria, her six-year-old son Daniel and his four-year-old sister Sarah. After an initial assessment meeting with the family, the therapist decided to work primarily in weekly family treatment with the mother and children together and occasionally in adjunctive parent work with Mom. This was a family who were grieving a lost father and husband. It appeared that some of their issues with mourning involved their difficulty coming together in a shared experience of loss. Each member of the family seemed to hold an aspect of grief that kept others in the family at a distance. Moreover, it seemed that family work would allow them to own aspects of themselves projected into other family members and to face the "new" family they needed to become, which required them to let go of the "old" family they had lost. One of the children was experiencing difficulties in separation, likely to be linked to the failed mourning, which also seemed best addressed in the family context.

Background information

Maria called to make the appointment. She was worried that her children were having difficulty following the death of their father nine months ago. Maria reported that James, her high school sweetheart and husband of eight years, had died from an aggressive, rapidly progressing cancer. He was sick for about a year prior to his death, undergoing numerous chemotherapy treatments that ravaged his body but produced neither pain reduction nor slowed the progression of his cancer. Even in the phone conversation, Maria's anguish and grief could be heard in her voice, as she described the loss of her husband.

Parent intake session

The therapist arranged a first meeting with Maria, hoping to gather background developmental information about the children and some details about the family's response to James's death. She presented as a tall, thin, attractive woman, who looked depressed and fragile. As she spoke, however, the therapist felt strength, determination and a will to move forward with her life despite this enormous loss. She talked of conversations she had with James as he was dying, how he had encouraged her to marry again, a thought she could not bear to entertain at present. James had voiced his love for her and his dreams for his young children. The therapist was overtaken with feelings of sadness as Maria described this intimate goodbye. Maria mentioned her Catholic faith, which served as a comfort to her and her children and promised a chance to see James again in the afterlife. Her love for James was clear, directly expressed amidst tears.

Maria commented that James had remained as available to the children as he could during the course of his illness, refusing pain medication at times to keep him alert in playing and conversing with the kids. He died the day after Christmas. Maria noted that she was then in individual treatment, which helped her to cope, but she admitted that each day was a struggle.

Maria: I never planned to raise them alone. James was an involved dad. We married young, almost right out of trade school. We wanted kids right away. What am I going to do without him? He was the steadier parent, and now it's all up to me.

Additionally, she needed to find work, moving from her stay-at-home mom status to life as a working single parent. Maria noted that James's family was very involved with the children for the first six weeks after James died, but then they withdrew.

Maria: I think it's too hard for them. Daniel looks almost exactly like James. I'm sure that seeing him reminds them of losing James.

She expressed some anger about their withdrawal.

Maria: I could use their help, but you can only ask so many times.

When the therapist asked about Maria's family, she said that they were never close and that they disapproved of her early marriage. The therapist suspected there was more to this story, but Maria seemed reluctant to talk further. Maria reported that each child was planned, although her pregnancy with Sarah was more challenging than that with Daniel.

Maria: I was sick a lot, and it was difficult managing a toddler while pregnant.

The therapist was told that at birth, Sarah was small in size but healthy. Maria said that both children developed normally, displaying distinctly different temperaments.

Maria: Sarah has always been a very physical, active child, while Daniel is quiet, sensitive and shy. He never really bonded to Dr K (the children's prior therapist), who worked very hard to get Daniel to talk, but to no avail.

He's been so depressed and clingy since James died. He doesn't want to go to school. I had to force him to go into the classroom. I feel guilty, but I had to have some time to myself. Sarah has gone to preschool without a hitch, but she's angrier at home and often refuses direction. She was wilful before, but not nearly this angry. Sometimes I'm so impatient with them, and I feel bad. But it's all I can do to keep going. They both keep photos of their dad by their beds.

Maria cried silent tears as she struggled to compose herself. She then continued describing the children's development, but quickly returned to remarks about James's death.

Maria: I'm worried about both of them, but especially Daniel. He's just so withdrawn. He was so close to James, and the two of them would play video games for hours. That's all Daniel wants to do now. I've been more lenient with the rules about screen time. He seems so heartbroken, and Sarah is more defiant. She talks more openly though about her dad's death and what it was like for him to get sick. She remembers how he came to her last birthday party in a wheelchair, with a blanket wrapped around him.

Maria said that Daniel refuses to talk about his father, but that he sleeps with the photograph of James across his chest.

(As I listened, the room began to feel heavy and dark. I wondered about my capacity to manage this anguish, while at the same time feeling drawn to help this young mother left behind in a circumstance she never envisioned. Maria's memories of James were so vivid that he felt more alive than dead to me.)

When the therapist asked about prior treatment, Maria told her that the children met together with Dr K for about six months, during which time she had her own individual sessions. She commented that Daniel sometimes refused to go into the therapy room, clinging to her in the waiting room. Dr K would come out to speak with him, encouraging him to enter the playroom alone or with Sarah.

Maria: When Dr K tried meeting with him alone, Daniel would cry and refuse to leave my side.

She said that Sarah had no difficulty separating from her, but that she often engaged with the toys in an aggressive, destructive manner.

(During Maria's description, I felt an intense feeling of loneliness, as if this family that had once been close had shattered into pieces. I wondered if this replayed Maria's "distant" family. Perhaps it was a defence against a collective pain, too difficult to contain without an intact parental couple. I had the image of a family drawing with each family member represented as a small, stark, isolated figure in a separate corner of the page, longing to connect but without a path back to a family constellation.)

First family session

When the therapist went to the waiting room to meet the family, Sarah was reading a magazine aloud and pacing the floor of the waiting room. She looked up and smiled at the therapist as she greeted the family. Maria was talking to Daniel, who seemed sullen and non-communicative, his hands over his face. There was a slight irritation in Maria's voice as she tried to get Daniel to say hello.

Therapist: Hi Sarah!

The therapist sat down to Daniel's level while keeping her distance, sensing Daniel needed the physical space between them. Then she said Hi to Daniel as she stood up.

Therapist: Let's have all of you come into the office.

Sarah bounces into the office as Mom starts to push Daniel forward. (I am surprised by Mom's reaction, as I told Mom that I thought it would be helpful to meet all together. I remember that the children had met alone with Dr K.)

Therapist: You too Mom.

Daniel's face was not visible and his hair was hanging over his eyes. He enters the office reluctantly, holding Mom's hand. Mom sits on the couch and Daniel seems glued to her.

Maria: I told them yesterday that we'd be coming here after school, just like we did with Dr K.
Sarah: Yeah, Dr K moved to another hospital. Do you know him?

As she mentions this other loss, Sarah is wandering about the office, picking up a few toys and putting them down.

Therapist: You used to see Dr K and now you're coming here to see me. Some things are the same, like the time, but some things are different.
Sarah: Yeah, he had some of the same toys, like these animals. (She picks up a small plastic dog.) Ruff, ruff. But you have other stuff.
Maria: Daniel, go look at the toys with Sarah. (He shakes his head no.) You can't just sit here with me.

(I cringe as Mom says this. I sense that Maria is worn out and frustrated.)

Therapist: Your family has been through a lot of hard things.
Sarah interrupts saying: You mean our dad. He died!

Sarah takes her hand and makes a movement like she's slitting her throat. (I feel chilled. It's an angry, violent expression. I think about her earlier perception of a shattered family. Perhaps James's death felt like a violent blow, or maybe the children had wished for it at times, given his illness and agony. Mom looks startled by Sarah's actions but doesn't speak. I consider commenting on the style of Sarah's expression, but it seems too early. I don't yet know this family, so instead I respond in a very concrete way.)

Therapist: Yes, your dad died. (Daniel puts his hands over his ears.) Looks like that's hard for Daniel to hear about right now. You want to talk about it, and maybe Daniel doesn't want to right now.
Sarah: Well Mom said we can talk about it, but Daniel doesn't like me to.
Therapist: What do you think about that, about why Daniel doesn't want to hear about it?
Sarah: It makes him too sad. That's just like Mommy. I hear her crying at night when she thinks we are asleep. We used to have a Dad and now we don't. His name was James. Mommy says he's our angel now. (Sarah seems like the family spokesperson.)
Therapist: But Mommy and Daniel are so sad, too sad sometimes to talk about it.

The therapist can sense Daniel's interest in the conversation, but the therapist avoids looking at him. Mom seems less tense. She's holding Daniel, who is now sitting in her lap.

Sarah: Can we play with stuff or is this going to be like school, really boring?

She then picks up a couple of dinosaurs from the bin of animals and throws them across the room. They hit the wall. She moves to collect the dinosaurs, picking them up and looking at them. Daniel watches her, then looks at the therapist through his hair.

Sarah: They are all right!
Therapist: They slammed into that wall pretty hard, but they're okay?
Sarah: Yeah. Some animals get really hurt, but they can get better. Some can't, and they die.

Sarah announces this with no emotion in her voice. Daniel puts his hands over his ears again. The therapist notices that Sarah stays in constant motion, expelling affect in action without seeming to feel it.

Sarah: I want to play catch. Do you have a ball around here somewhere? (She looks around.) Here's one. (She slams it against the wall, making a very loud noise.)

Then she picks it up and throws it to the therapist, but with a great deal of force. The therapist catches it, more in an effort to protect herself than in a relational exchange.

Therapist: Wow that was a hard throw.

Sarah and the therapist throw the ball back and forth. (I feel Sarah's competitiveness, trying to make it so I will miss the ball. I can tell Sarah is pulling for my attention, trying to make sure I stay engaged with her. Daniel and Mom feel like family members on the sideline at an athletic event. I wonder, am I filling in for Dad?)

Daniel (whispering): She always does that!
Therapist: Throws stuff?
Daniel: Yeah, you gotta watch her or you will get hit by surprise. (The therapist is thinking of the father's death.) One time, she hit me right in the head. I didn't even see it coming.

Suddenly, Daniel is self-conscious, as though he has revealed too much. He hides his face in his Mom's coat.

Therapist: Surprises can be hard sometimes.
Daniel: Umhmm. Can we go now?
Sarah: Wait, I am not finished playing. Let's get the dinosaurs out again. (She drops the ball.)

(I feel anxious about ending the session, worried the family won't return. Intellectually, I know this reaction makes no sense. The family has followed through with treatment before. I wonder if she is identifying with Daniel's fear of separation.)

Therapist: Our time is almost up for today. What do you think about having all of you – Daniel, Sarah, and your mom – come to talk and play each week?
Sarah: Like we did with Dr K?
Therapist: Yes, and like we're doing today.
Sarah: With Mom too?
Therapist: With all of you together. That's a little different than what you did before.

(I notice myself not using the word family, as though saying the word would induce further pain. I am very aware of Dad's absence in this moment.)

Sarah: Okay with me, but I'm not the boss.
Therapist: Mom, Daniel?
Maria: I think that would be a good idea.

Daniel hasn't said anything. Mom looks at him, her impatience at his clinging again evident.

Therapist: I think maybe Daniel is still deciding whether or not this is an okay place to be, and that's okay.

The therapist next meets with the family for two additional family sessions and again with Maria alone. Maria wonders whether the therapist should meet with the children separately, something Dr K did in the past. The therapist says that she would rather keep the family together, because she thinks they each hold different parts of the grieving process. They are trying to find a way to be a family with a shared loss. Being together in the room concretely highlights the absence of James, and it seems that having the family all together is hard for Maria as well. The therapist also thinks that Daniel is not ready to separate from Maria, equating separation with death. Maria agrees to family sessions.

Three months later

In this session, it is notable that both children have started to shift their affective expression. Sarah is calmer and is able to stay with an activity and making up a story, rather than just throwing things about the room. Daniel begins to move closer to the toys, but is still reluctant to play. With guidance, Mom stops pressuring Daniel to engage, allowing him time and space.

The therapist is nonetheless very worried about Mom, who seems increasingly depressed as Christmas approaches. She meets with her individually for a parent session, and Maria tells her that sometimes it just feels unbearable. Maria misses James so much. She is exhausted by the children, yet knows she needs to be available and present. She feels pressure to get the house sold and move into a smaller, more finished space. They bought a home to fix-up, just before James became ill. Maria cries openly in the session. Gently, the therapist suggests that Maria's pressuring herself to move ahead, much like she was doing with Daniel, as though moving out would resolve the grief.

In the next family session, Sarah engaged Mom in playing with the dinosaur families, setting up homes for them to live in. She seemed to be playing out their own intended move, focused on keeping the families together, making sure the children stayed with their moms. The therapist comments that there were no dads.

Sarah: You know what happened to Dad, Janine (therapist)?

(I felt slightly reprimanded, like a child with a parent who tells them to stop pretending.) Reality crashed harshly and concretely into the play space. Sarah seemed to be trying to breathe life into mom, who was deadened by her grief. Daniel was reluctant to pick up any toys at first, but then shyly asked about the clay. Silently, he divided up the packages of clay into dark and light colours. He opened packages of each, first grouping the clay into piles of dark and light, labelling and counting as a means of binding his anxiety. Almost whispering, he said the dark and light were in a battle for survival.

The clay became Daniel's chosen medium for the next six–eight sessions. Each time, the dark and light battled. The colours crashing into each other demonstrated the battles. At first, the dark always "won", and he said there was no hope for the light. The therapist merely put words to the battle she saw in front of her, somewhat sparingly to avoid overwhelming Daniel. As she did so, he moved away from his mother, and closer to the therapist. Of his own accord, he started calling the clay dark and light *feelings*. As he mixed the clay together, she noticed he started to mix lighter colours with the dark, shifting the shade to a lighter hue. Sarah dropped her dinosaur play, where dinosaur families alternated between dinner, which was nurturing and pleasant, and community battles between dinosaur families. She was interested in what her brother was doing. For the first time, the children began playing together in the session. Daniel included his sister in this activity with the clay, a battle between light and dark, and then both children began physically pounding the therapist with the dark feelings.

Daniel said in one of these sessions: Here are the dark feelings. They are coming for you. They will get inside you!

Therapist (in a concerned tone): Oh, what will happen?

Daniel: You'll be afraid!

Sarah (dressed as Wonder Woman): You won't have any superheroes to save you . . . and you know what that means . . . (she again makes a violent move, pulling her finger across her throat like a knife) . . . you will die. (The pounding intensifies.)

Daniel: Right, you will die from the bad feelings. (The pounding continues for several additional minutes.)

Sarah (stands back and says): My daddy had a fight inside him. They put the good medicine in his tummy through a tube to fight the bad parts, but it didn't work.

Daniel drops the clay and distances himself from Sarah and the therapist, the movement from metaphor to reality too stark. The therapist sees his fear, and comments that it's hard to hear Sarah talk about their dad being sick and dying. He looks back at the therapist and nods. The therapist notices that while he is frightened, Daniel is staying connected to her. Sarah keeps talking about her father as Daniel retreats, both seemingly overwhelmed by "bad feelings". Daniel steps forward again, picking up the dark colours and pushing them against the therapist.

Therapist (to Daniel): Sometimes, it feels like the bad feelings are taking over inside you. You get afraid, and you don't know what to do with the bad feelings. (Daniel nods, and pushes them into the therapist more forcefully.) You want me to have them.

Daniel (interrupts): The dark colours, they can destroy you. I don't want them to hurt anyone else in my family.

At this point, both Daniel and Mom start to cry. She moves toward him and hugs him.

Daniel: I'm just so scared Mom. I'm so scared.
Maria: I know honey. I miss him too!

Daniel chokes up and can't talk. The therapist waits for a few minutes. Daniel looks at her. She feels he is pleading with her to find words for what he cannot.

Therapist: Maybe you want us to know that you're scared someone else in your family will die, like your Mom or Sarah?

He nods. Mom and Daniel are crying harder now. Sarah comes closer to them and makes fake crying sounds.

Maria: I don't want to die, neither did Daddy. I am planning to live a long time with both of you. To watch you grow up and get married.
Sarah: To our school sweethearts, like you and Daddy? (Mom laughs.)
Maria: To someone you love, who loves you. (She turns back to Daniel.) I know you're afraid of me dying. I can't promise I won't, because we can't always know what will happen, but I can tell you I don't think it's likely to happen.
Daniel: But it did to Dad.
Maria: Yes it did, and I'm so sorry that happened to our family.

The battle between light and dark went on for many sessions. The therapist was able to interpret their wish to locate all the bad in her to protect Mom and themselves from any further catastrophe. Daniel commented that he didn't really want it to get the therapist either, but he was worried about his Mom. Daniel articulated his worry that Mom's sadness might kill her, a worry he also had about himself. Sarah talked more openly about the process of her dad dying, which Daniel could now tolerate to a greater degree. Despite this the therapist thought Sarah was carrying the anger that the others could not voice, blocking her from feeling vulnerable and sad. She would cry "fake" tears, but she was stuck in her own way, more able to openly talk about James but without a range of feeling.

The therapist then decided to meet with Mom individually. She talked with Mom about her concern for Sarah, the way she was left holding the anger. She also noted that James was always presented as ideal, almost perfect. Mom could think about how she was so worried the children would forget him, prompting her to only talk about the good times and how much he loved them. The therapist thought she was talking about herself as well as the children. She commented that even good men are not saints. Maria laughed. The therapist noted that it is difficult to be mad at a saint, and Maria added, "Or at God for that matter." The therapist then understood how betrayed Maria felt by God; at the same time she was clinging to her faith for comfort. The therapist thought of Daniel's clinging.

It would take many months for the range of feeling to be shared across family members, but gradually, it evolved. Another Christmas passed, and this time the family stayed home to celebrate, rather than going away with friends to avoid difficult memories. The children made cards and candles to put on James's grave. The therapist learned more about their years with James, about times when he got mad at them as well as times they thought he was "so funny". Mom started dating again, and there was an adjustment as the children displayed both longing and ambivalence about accepting someone new. Fortunately, she chose a sensitive, mature man, who did not feel obviously threatened by the children's attachment to James. Treatment ended somewhat abruptly after Mom decided to remarry. Although the therapist was concerned about the short termination phase as a potential replay of their earlier loss, she had some confidence that this new family would manage the move forward, perhaps returning to therapy some time in the future as developmental challenges surfaced new and old difficult feelings and experiences. For the therapist, the treatment felt valuable yet unfinished, perhaps their way of leaving the trauma with her.

Conclusions

This family work represents a journey through mourning, somewhat incomplete in its duration and focus. It particularly illustrated the importance of interpreting play in family therapy. How Maria's earlier family issues were replayed in the current loss was not articulated or interpreted, nor was there any observation about the new family being formed, a blended family with a new Dad. I was very attached to this family. As the treatment ended, I felt pleased by the gains they had made, with their ability to acknowledge this profound loss yet find hope in the future. At the same time, I felt cheated, that the treatment had ended before I was ready. Now I was clearly identified with James, who had a life cut short with a family he dearly loved. We don't always get to choose our endings. Many questions remained unanswered in this therapy. Was this a good enough ending? Did these children have a good enough beginning to survive such a major life assault, as death of a parent? Was their loss of me processed well enough to prevent a traumatic re-enactment? Terminations in cases of family trauma often occur in traumatic ways. While recognising that fact is important, it does not necessarily negate the work accomplished. I suppose like James, I cannot know the future for this family, but I hold the hope for a "new" family moving forward while honouring the good and the traumatic in the "old".

References

Bowlby, J. (1960). Grief and mourning in infancy and early childhood. *Psychoanalytic Study of the Child*, *15*: 9–52.

Freud, S. (1917). Mourning and melancholia. *Standard Edition*, *14*: 243–258.

Garber, B. (2008). Mourning in children a theoretical synthesis and clinical application. *Journal of Psychoanalysis*, *36*: 174–188.

Green, V. (2013). Grief in two guises: Mourning and melancholia revisited. *Journal of Child Psychotherapy*, *39*: 76–89.

Nagera, H. (1970). Children's reactions to the death of important objects: A developmental approach. *Psychoanalytic Study of the Child*, *36*: 360–401.

Scharff, J. S., & Scharff, D. E. (2005). *The Primer of Object Relations*. Lanham, MD: Jason Aronson.

Sussillo, M. V. (2005). Beyond the grave—adolescent parental loss: Letting go and holding on. *Psychoanalytic Dialogues*, *15*: 499–527.

Wanlass, J., & Scharff, D. E. (2016). Psychodynamic approaches to couple and family therapy. In: T. L. Sexton & J. Lebow (Eds.), *Handbook of Family Therapy*. New York: Routledge.

Editors' prologue to the discussant perspectives

Janine Wanlass presents the reader with a very moving account of her work with a bereaved family, which highlights her skilful use of the therapeutic setting and her well-articulated countertransference with a family in which the father has died. Susana Muszkat, referring to Freud's seminal work on mourning and melancholia, affirms the utility of family therapy for such a family where aspects of the reaction to loss can be split off and projected into the children. She notes how the intervention helped to address the previously avoided transference challenges in mother's prior therapy. Daniela Lucarelli describes how Dr Wanlass' management of the therapeutic setting worked to address this family's presenting problems. In examining the process of therapy, she highlights the importance of the interpretation of the links between the mother and her children, along with the psychic work in the analyst, which was so well conveyed in her account of the work.

Discussant perspective

Susana Muszkat

Janine Wanlass is very open about her clinical impressions, thoughts and feelings. She also informs the reader about what she thinks of this particular family's organisation leading her to choose a specific setting to work with them. This highlights a significant number of elements about the work and opens up interesting discussion points about which I hope to contribute some ideas, specifically regarding the way the family links/dynamics operate in this family group, including the transference they established with the analyst.

In my experience working with families and couples, I often find that much of what is displayed by the children's difficult and unwanted behaviour or symptoms – especially when there is a so-called identified patient – can be understood as the result of unconsciously rejected and projected infantile aspects of *the parents onto the children*. Thus, children express metaphorically, through their symptoms, the difficulties encountered by the family. As a result, it is fair to say that if we pay close attention, children are often great co-therapists helping us formulate a diagnostic assessment.

Interestingly, it is also noteworthy that such rejected and projected aspects are paradoxically those elements that are often the same attraction factors responsible for bringing a couple together. The symptoms in such cases are the result of the non-metabolised beta-elements, or of regressed infantile aspects brought to the present, in the family links dynamics.

A good metaphor to convey this would be that of a play in a theatre, where each family member is stuck with a role, having to play it repeatedly in order to keep that specific family link functioning, thus, maintaining the painful, yet indispensable kind of symptomatic link.

The family dynamics, or the link, is, at one time, a product of this family's way of being together as it is the producer of their individual subjectivities. In other words, the family produces the link and the family members are products of their established link.

Consequently, taking the designated identified patient into an individual analysis would not only overburden this family member, but might also intensify and perpetuate the pathological characteristics of a given link. Separating one family member as the one in charge of the dysfunctional symptom – or the children from the mother in this case – will impede the integration of split-off aspects, reinforcing the idea that some feelings, ideas and thoughts are allowed, while others need to be cut off. This will often be maintained at the expense of a family member. In the case of the family presented by Dr Wanlass, this seemed to be the son's attribution, described as "so depressed and clingy and experiencing difficulties in separation". Was he the emotional spokesperson for expressing the pain in this family in mourning?

Moreover, was the daughter, the "other side of the coin", in charge of acting out the angry, aggressive, self-sufficient feelings in place of their mother? It is interesting to note that it was specifically the son's display of pain, that which was considered a symptom in need of treatment, whereas the daughter's behaviour was not interpreted as an expression of mourning as it did not portray a depressive tone.

Nevertheless, concurring with Dr Wanlass, I would agree in saying that the daughter was a prisoner in a role, as much as the son was. Having this in mind, I am in complete agreement with her for having proposed a clinical setting which took into treatment the family as patient.

Cesar Merea (2003) describes a level of unconscious functioning in the family, which he has coined as an *unconscious operative family functioning*. It is in no way to be taken as a form of collective unconscious, but rather a relational group dynamic which is not perceived by any family member, due to its unconscious character, and is played out unconsciously by all of them, becoming a communication pattern and producing effects (Merea, 2003, p. 107). This is an important part of the analyst's work: to make explicit the kind of family link dynamic, thus enabling them to see what they cannot.

Mourning and Melancholia

In Freud's (1917) well-known work, he distinguishes mourning from melancholia by affirming that while in the first, one knows what/who has been lost, in the latter, the individual does not.

The current family situation brought to us is undoubtedly a case of actual mourning, as the death of a parent, especially when in a family with small children, is a tragic event. The children have lost their loving and dear father. Maria has lost a husband, but perhaps also a parent in James and thus lost what seemed to be an idealised fantasy, where she re-created with James a perfect family, with the perfect house, the perfect children, with the high-school sweetheart, the prince, who would have promised that they would have lived happily ever after.

Transferences

Maria seems to be an orphaned child in search of parents. First, she has James, right out of high-school, who quite possibly was a repeated story of her family of origin from which she breaks away, being, so to

(continued)

(continued)

speak, completely substituted by James. Then, in her therapy with Dr K, it would appear that the analyst "responded" to Maria's transferential demands by proposing an analytic setting where the kids were seen separately. In doing so, the analyst relieved Maria of her inner painful unbearable aspects projected onto the children: the abandoned aspect (Daniel) and the arrogant, self-sufficient aspect (Sarah).

In the history provided, Dr K relocates during their first analysis, causing a new rupture, in a transferential repetition of what seems to be yet another loss and separation in Maria's life. Finally, in the middle of what was a very fruitful and helpful family analysis, Maria suddenly provokes an abrupt termination, as Dr Wanlass tells us, substituting the analyst with the new boyfriend, in an apparently new attempt to rebuild, in fantasy, the idealised family, now with the new husband and children. There seems to be little or no space, in Maria's mind, for failure, faults, the time and effort required for the construction of a new relationship, as the work of the analytic process they were going through with Dr Wanlass. Therefore, she narcissistically recreates a complete and fulfilled idealised infantile family.

By leaving Dr Wanlass abruptly, she re-enacts the splitting where the fragility is left behind inside of the analyst, who is, consequently the one who deeply feels the loss, again, a successful projective identification onto the analyst. The analyst reflects that she identified with James who "had a life cut short" and felt cheated, being suddenly cut off from family.

From my point of view, I see that the analyst was cut off by Maria – in one more unconscious repetition – and not by fate as was James. Consequently, the analyst was left with having to deal with the loss, doing the mental work that Maria refused to accept as hers. The past is not left behind in the past but, rather, it is actively present as Maria unconsciously repeats them in the links she forms.

Nevertheless, even if cut short, it is evident that a lot of work was successfully achieved, especially with the children. The analyst helped them bear a very tough situation in their lives and showed them a way through their grief and out of it. She was strong enough to face with them the challenge of talking about what they feared, sustain their grief inside of her, and relieve the children of their very fixed, inflexible roles.

References

Freud, S. (1917). *Mourning and Melancholia*. Brazil: Cosac Naify, 2011.

Merea, E. C. (2003). *Couples and Families: Extensive Psyche and Intersubjective Psychoanalysis*. Buenos Aires: Lugar Editorial.

Discussant perspective

Daniela Lucarelli

Dr Janine Wanlass' chapter suggests to me that she made "a journey *towards* mourning" with the family she presents. From the beginning, her countertransference seems to highlight the difficulties the family experiences in suffering their loss. I believe that Dr Wanlass had to deal with the difficult task of helping this family create the necessary conditions for them to carry on with their lives by working through, rather than trying to forget, their trauma.

I will try to go back over the analyst's narrative, starting from her initial decision to treat the whole family in a joint setting.

I consider that this choice was extremely significant; it was an implicit interpretation on the part of the analyst. From the outset, she recognised in the suffering of the individuals not only an intra-psychic dimension, but an inter-psychic one.

Dr Wanlass tells us that she also decided to arrange additional sessions with the mother, every now and then. I assume that she may have felt that the mother was the family member most in need. In this respect, the suggestion to occasionally meet the mother alone, outside of the family therapy sessions, may have also been an indirect response to the mother who seemed to remain on the sidelines, as if she did not recognise that she had difficulties as much, or perhaps even more, than her children.

If, on the one hand, we can consider that psychoanalytic work with the family should always focus on the continuous interrelation between the individual members and the family, on the other hand, we can think of the setting as an unsaturated area, a space created/found in the specificity of the encounter with the other. The creation of the setting is thus both a concrete and significant act which paves the way to a representational dimension that is not yet present (Lucarelli & Tavazza, 2012).

We can see how suffering has been fragmented in the psychic life of this family. It seems that each member, as well as the family as a whole, was unable to complete the psychic work of mourning. We know that families have the task within them, of carrying out psychic work, but this task can be hindered or made impossible by psychic suffering that cannot be worked through, either due to its intensity or to the level of the family's psychic functioning. In these cases, interpersonal defences may be produced (Meltzer & Harris, 1983).

It seems to me that this is what has happened to this family. Consequently, it may be extremely important to understand the mental life of this family in terms of inter-exchange and distribution of

(continued)

(continued)

suffering, that is, that we might focus our attention on the strategies adopted by the family group and on the links that the family members have jointly built together.

I would like to focus on a couple of points concerning the history of the couple.

The relationship was formed very early, during their adolescence. They married immediately, and also had their first child straight away. There is a possible connection between these events that suggests a very early need to create a supportive link, without experiencing discontinuity or separateness. Perhaps we can assume they formed a fused relationship. This may have brought Maria and James from a childhood dependency link to a marital one without, perhaps, a process of separation, individuation and a sense of identity.

It seems that they needed to be "one thing", to alleviate the emotional deficiencies of the past, to feel supported and to strengthen a feeling of self, that may have been too inconsistent and fragile.

While it seems that Daniel's birth could have become part of the couple's fusional link, Sarah's pregnancy may have introduced the "third party" which could not be integrated, as an internal third position was not yet formed.

Daniel seems to be the repository of the unresolved and dependency needs of Maria. Sarah, on the other hand, gives a voice, from the beginning, to the part of mother that has to deny those same needs; she has to do everything on her own and appears insensitive and omnipotent.

It seems that the fusional union of the family was then shattered into pieces without a separation process which would have facilitated mourning. Perhaps there had been no previous separation process in either member of the couple or subsequently in the couple; interpersonal defences were therefore recruited against an experience of loss that could not be borne.

It seems that Maria's continued functioning relied upon her two children, who represented parts of her self. Maria seems to have split the two aspects of dependency and autonomy of herself between the two children. Daniel seems to have carried her fragile part, in need of dependency and support; this part experiences the loss without being able to start a separation process. Maria seems to have rejected this part of herself. Sarah, on the other hand, seems to express her autonomy, as well as an omnipotent aspect that may represent Maria's ideal self. It seems that the children are crushed into partial representations of the family's self, preventing a variety of emotional states and experiences that are still present in the family from emerging: anguish, loss, powerlessness, anger, abandonment, fear of death, feeling of loss of self.

This family appears to have difficulties in integrating needs of autonomy and dependency, as well as feelings of aggressiveness and depression.

It would seem that the family's psychic functioning, with the loss of the husband/father, James, has returned to a more primitive level with attendant splitting. The family was unable to activate an integrated functioning, oriented toward a depressive experience. It was very important to hold family therapy sessions where the children could represent, through play, these split-off aspects of the family self. At the same time, they contributed to creating a sort of "oneiric family holding" so as to start a symbolisation and integration process (Ruffiot, 1982). Sarah looks much older than four. Through play, she represents very painful feelings that she must eject. She seems to be looking for someone onto whom she can project such feelings since her father is no longer there and her mother cannot perform her containing function. Sarah is the family's spokesperson. She exhibits adultomorphic defences. While the mother and Daniel try to stay away from a threatened feeling of pain, she plays Wonder Woman who looks pain in the face without apparently feeling anything and she makes the analyst feel that she is a "pretending child", whereas Sarah looks like being the one that needs nothing and can apparently face up to reality. Sarah is stuck in her position and cannot give room to other aspects of her self. This is why she is angry. She can also understand the transformation suggested by Daniel's playing when he is able to come out of his withdrawal.

The siblings start playing together. There is an important transformational movement reflected in their play. It expresses the birth of a shared ability at representation and the establishment of a transitional area. Moreover, the children begin making use of the analyst in a more marked way. They violently and concretely push their "bad feelings" into the analyst. The analyst is asked to fulfil that primary function of transformation, indicated by Bion (1962) as *rêverie*. She appears to have fulfilled this function for the whole family, so that along with the emotional experiences, now made conceivable, they could begin introjecting a warm and understanding object with whom they could identify. It appears to have acted as a container for the split-off aspects of the self of the various family members. This contributed to the reconstitution of the family *phantasmatic* unity, allowing each member to express more freely other aspects of their self.

Although Dr Wanlass did not explicitly interpret the links between Maria and her children, as she might have done, the analyst's mental work accompanied the entire narrative of the sessions. I think that this played a significant function in reactivating the family psychic functioning (Ruffiot, 1981). The analyst wonders about the sudden end of the analysis, considering it valid, but incomplete. I agree with her and I think that there is probably still a part of their experience that has not yet been transformed. We may think that Maria replaces her analyst

(continued)

(continued)

quickly with another object of investment, her new partner, replacing before separating as she perhaps did as an adolescent, as separating is still difficult.

References

Bion, W. R. (1962). *Learning from Experience*. New York: Jason Aronson, 1967.

Lucarelli, D., & Tavazza, G. (2012). La psychanalyse familiale: le setting analytique et ses variations (Family psychoanalysis: the analytic setting and its variations). *Revue Internationale de Psychanalyse du Couple et de la Famille (International Review of Family and Couple Psychoanalysis)*, *11*(1): 65–74.

Meltzer, D., & Harris, M. (1983) *Sincerity and Other Works* (pp. 387–454). London: Karnac.

Ruffiot, A. (1981). Appareil psychique familial et appareil psychique individual (Family psychic apparatus and individual psychic apparatus). *Dialogue*, *72*: 31–43.

Ruffiot, A. (1982). Le holding onirique familial (Family oneiric holding). *Génitif*, *4*(1): 25–43.

Chapter 11

The mess monster

Family therapy in the context of the arrival of a newborn brother

Antònia Llairó

Introduction

Family therapy during pregnancy, and in the first stages of children's growth and development, is an opportunity to deal with issues associated with first object relationships and as such has an important preventive function. This first stage of development is a crucial one on which the organisation of the child's physical and psychic functions are based. The pregnancy and birth of a sibling and the transition to parenthood are developments which are highly fluid and also offer many opportunities to reactivate previous insufficiently elaborated intra-psychic elements.

The conceptualisation of parenthood conflicts by Palacio Espasa and the Geneva team[1] (Geneva University Hospitals) provides a helpful understanding of the various dynamics that shape dominant object relationships. In the case to be discussed, one sees a depressive-masochistic type conflict that appears in a situation where the parents' grief is poorly elaborated. In such cases, the parents have experienced themselves as difficult children and usually have criticisms of their own parents.

Such parents tend to project onto their own children the image of the difficult child they had perceived themselves to be, as well as identifying with the inadequate parents they had experienced. They submit to the tyranny and aggressiveness that they project onto their children, converting themselves into martyrs, subject to the child's demands (Nanzer et al., 2012).

Case material

The therapist received a request for a consultation from the parents of a four-year-old girl who they say assaults, hits and bites them constantly as a result of trivial things, frustration, or sometimes for no apparent reason. The parents feel that they do not know how to manage this behaviour and are at a loss to find any motive or explanation for it. They feel that their daughter bullies them, sees herself as in control of them and has no respect for them.

At the time of the referral, the mother was four months pregnant, expecting a boy. It is the third pregnancy burdened with complex antecedents.

The first was an ectopic pregnancy and the mother had to carry the foetus for more than two months until it ended in a spontaneous abortion. The parents then tried for another child and the mother became pregnant with Sonia. During the postpartum of the pregnancy, the mother cried for three months. She explained with sadness how she was unable to manage when Sonia became agitated. Mother added that since the birth she had a constant, terrifying feeling that the child would die and was plagued by thoughts that she had died. She felt she had to repeatedly check whether Sonia was breathing. The therapist felt that the mother did not know if she could pick her up, as she feared she would reject the child because the previous loss had not been adequately mourned. As a consequence, she avoided making a link with the baby.

She nonetheless felt obliged to breastfeed her baby. She didn't want to do this, but her own mother told her "put up with it and carry on!" Remembering this the mother begins to sob. She describes a tyrannical mother. She doesn't recognise that her own mother is trying to encourage her to leave the conflict behind.

The therapist is interested in the mother's own experience as a daughter. When she was young, she was very obedient and caused no trouble. She cannot talk about herself and continues speaking about Sonia. She tells the therapist that since she was two years old, any time Sonia was told "no", there was a storm. Now, when the mother tries to pick her up, Sonia has violent reactions, including deliberately throwing things in a way that causes maximum damage. The therapist tries again to ask about her experience as a child. She says that she was very introverted, that things didn't go well for her and she didn't have the friends that she wanted. She suffered a lot. The therapist suggests that perhaps she thought that the same would happen to her daughter? The mother nods and starts crying. She says that during her current pregnancy she often cries but her partner is unaware of it. Her husband looks surprised but quickly confirms this. She is very frightened but hides her fears. She doesn't want anyone to know that she cries as she feels this is a weakness.

The therapist speaks to them about how important it is that the mother has been able to communicate in today's session, as it allows her husband to share her suffering. He says that she won't be alone, that he will be there to help her, thereby reinforcing his commitment to be present. The therapist also suggests a first family visit for the following week with Sonia. The parents ask whether they should tell Sonia the truth. The therapist speaks to them about being able to tell Sonia the reason for the consultation.

In summary, the mother has described herself as a victim of her daughter's tyranny and, at the same time, a victim of her own mother's tyranny. The mother expressed criticism of her own mother and towards her daughter upon whom she projects the image of a difficult girl and to whom she must submit. The mother feels alone and rejected: something that she fears and desires at the same time. It appears that for her the only way to avoid being abandoned is through victimhood.

First family visit

Sonia hides behind her mother and chews the head of an enormous rubber doll that she's carrying. She is dressed elegantly in an old-fashioned style outfit. The mother, in contrast, wears sportswear. Sonia doesn't speak. She looks at the therapist intently but doesn't respond to anything. She hides behind her mother's chair and bites the upholstery while staring at the therapist. Her mother scolds her. Sonia's face expresses hurt and she goes to the play table. Then she returns to play with us, bringing some rag-doll characters.

The mother says in a complaining tone that now Sonia wets the bed. I say that perhaps it's a symptom that requires them to take notice of Sonia. The therapist further adds that perhaps it could be related to a fear that the new sibling might cause her to feel excluded, that Sonia demands affection with bites and kicks. At this point, Sonia looks at the therapist who tells her that if she takes her hand she will help her to find her place. She helps Sonia to contain the anger that she can't bear. Sonia looks at the therapist intently without saying anything. She picks up some ragdolls from the set containing two grandparents, two parents and two children. She places the father, mother, and two children together on a piece of fabric. She repeatedly tries to put the grandparents together on a narrow bed, but one always falls off as there is no room for them both at the same time. When one is put onto the bed, the other has to make way. She alternates them, trying without success to make a shared space.

The therapist asks Sonia if she knows why she has come here and she remains silent. She adds that Sonia demands affection with bites and kicks and now in her game she shows me someone who is afraid of not having a place. Her father then explains that when Sonia has tantrums, he tells her that she is very ugly and that he puts her in front of the mirror, so she can see how ugly she is. The therapist suggests that if they talk about how ugly she is when she cries, perhaps Sonia will understand that they are criticising her need, as though having a need were something ugly and bad. She adds that the baby represents change, disorientation, and fear for Sonia, that these reactions are a mix of jealousy, rivalry and anxiety about the birth.

She further explains the need to elaborate a new situation that is now anticipated and that this should be spoken about. She notes that there are strong feelings appearing in Sonia related to tolerating a new sibling that has appeared before the birth, in fact, ever since the parents had decided to try for another child. The therapist notes that Sonia has had a lot of problems in the relationship with her mother and, therefore, the new baby is a rival before it is born. She points out that Sonia could integrate her kisses and kicks but that this would require the family to be involved in a process of understanding that they are in an evolving family conflict, one from which everyone could benefit. The therapist thus recommends ongoing family sessions.

The therapy process

The weekly therapy sessions swiftly provide containment for the family group. Mother is not so frightened and doesn't cry so much and Sonia stops wetting the bed. In the first session, the parents also talk about the meeting with Sonia's teacher, who highlights the demands that Sonia puts on herself at school. This raises the question of obedience. Is it possible to ask what being naughty means and whether this is experienced as a defect? The mother then tells the therapist how, as an adolescent, she would look daggers at her mother. She was unable to answer back but was able to direct furious looks at her. She recalls that when she was angry with her mother, she went to the cutlery drawer and put all the knives blade-up so that her mother would hurt herself when she opened the drawer. She half turns her head away so that she doesn't meet anyone's eyes and says, "I didn't want to hurt anybody!"

The therapist underlines the mother's rage that she hasn't been able to express before and links it with Sonia's externalised rage. The therapist points out the importance of being able to communicate and elaborate it and how the therapy will help to achieve this. The mother then describes an outburst of anger that Sonia had because she wanted her mother to take a newborn

Figure 11.1 The formless anxiety.

baby that they were visiting in her arms. At Sonia's insistence, the mother picked up the baby, who immediately began crying. So, the mother put her back down. While explaining this, she makes a gesture that we could consider rejecting and says that Sonia was beside herself. The therapist notes that Sonia might find it difficult to understand that her mother cannot hold a crying baby in her arms and that she might have even felt that her mother rejected the baby because it was crying.

The therapist thinks about the meaning this could have in Sonia's implicit memory; when a baby cries, it is rejected. During this session, Sonia draws the following picture.

Over the course of the therapy, the drawings express the anxiety and other feelings being worked on in the session. Sonia moves on from playing with the rag-doll characters to a toy telephone. The game allows the therapist to be put through to a baby that has apparently called and would like to speak to him. From communicating through action, we switch to a verbal exchange (see Figure 11.1).

Fear of chaos and misunderstanding

In one session the parents arrive and explain indignantly that when the father had let Sonia down from his arms, she tried to rake her nails across his face, and he consequently has scratch marks. This is discussed with the therapist along with the disorganisation generated in Sonia by situations that frustrate her. Suddenly Sonia says that the toy telephone is ringing, and she puts the receiver to the therapist's ear saying, "A child with no home is calling. They have destroyed his house." The therapist explains how she is telling her that her tantrums can destroy her house and how this expresses her fear of losing her parents.

Sonia nods and suddenly the mother associates: It's true that after a tantrum and kicking out a lot.

Sonia: You won't leave me alone, will you?

Here we see the "fear of losing the parent's love which would deliver them over helpless to the dangers of the external world" (Freud, 1940). The therapist states that it is important to say it, emphasising that it's because it's better that the parents set limits than letting anger destroy the parents' love.

Sonia, sensing her fear named, says: The monster is coming! Look out! Shhh!

We feel the need to be alert and silent. Sonia stays vigilant to protect us from the monster. We feel its disturbing presence in the room that could attack us but that Sonia is watching carefully. While the monster represents a threatening situation, the parents laugh and associate with a funny situation. Perhaps the parents only connect when Sonia makes them angry.

Sonia asks to do another drawing (see Figure 11.2) and says: It's the "mess monster".

Figure 11.2 The mess monster.

This character appeared associated with anger and dread which suggested the representation of an internal chaos, threats and turbulence in which affect is not differentiated. Within the conflict, there is a search by Sonia to be understood and to sort out a mess.

She looks for the relationship and it results in misunderstanding.

As Bion (1962) notes "The establishment internally of a projective-identification-rejecting object means that instead of an understanding object, the infant has a willfully misunderstanding object with which it is identified" (p. 308). This misunderstanding occurs in the here and now of the therapeutic relationship in the form of a monster. It acquires meaning, becoming a representation with a name that we can now use throughout the treatment. As such, it ceases to be a fear without a name, the "nameless dread" (Bion, 1962). The mother was then coming to term. There needed to be a one-month interruption to the family therapy. This is announced in the session.

Regression to reach contention

The family arrives at the following session one month later and the baby, a 15-day-old boy, is asleep, relaxed and satisfied in his pushchair. Sonia appears sleepy, faint and querulous. She closes her eyes and remains moaning and crying plaintively at the threshold. The therapist says to her that she is very sad, and she nods. The mother asks her to go in but Sonia doesn't move and can hardly stay on her feet.

The therapist tells Sonia she was expecting her. She hides her face between her mother's legs, and the mother pushes her gently to encourage her to enter the room. Sonia continues sobbing passively and her mother asks her to take off her coat, but the girl just stands there crying in terrible sorrow. The mother remarks that it has been like this for 15 days.

Everything has to be done for Sonia. She doesn't want to get dressed, shower, or eat. Often, she doesn't even want someone to help her. As soon as the mother takes off Sonia's coat, she falls to the floor. She huddles in the fetal position, continues crying and does not respond to anything or anybody. The therapist says that Sonia is very sad; we haven't seen each other for a long time. I have been looking after our things, just as she asked, while she couldn't come. Sonia goes on crying on the floor and the mother explains the problems she has had with her in an angry tone. The father adds that when he intervenes, Sonia hits and hits him. The mother asks Sonia to move onto the rug, and Sonia approaches a little. Sonia says her tummy hurts and she moans but she has stopped crying.

The therapist says that today we meet the baby who is very small, and Sonia is caught in a mess between the affect towards the baby and the aggressiveness that a rival stirs in the moments when she wants to be small like the baby and times when she wants to be big but doesn't know how. On hearing the therapist's words, Sonia gets up from the floor and goes to hug her mother. She opens her mother's cardigan a little and touches her breast. I continue, saying that with the arrival of her little brother, the mother is very busy, so perhaps Sonia feels her mother is not there for her.

Mother: It's true that sometimes when I have to breastfeed Sonia says, "Again?" and I say that he has to grow!

The therapist is interested in the baby, who sleeps and feeds well. While the mother is speaking, she reaches for Sonia's hand and says, "Come here". The little girl approaches and just as she's about to take her mother's hand, she hears a small cry from the baby and Sonia falls to the floor again. The therapist floats the idea that this could be coincidence, but the parents say that coincidence has got nothing to do with it. Sonia begins to complain of a tummy-ache again and moans.

Mother: Maybe we can make you some plain rice for your tummy.

Sonia nods and moans. They explain that Sonia comes to their bed at night and stays with them for a while, until she wants to go back to her own bed.

The therapist tells Sonia that it must be difficult to be alone in her room while the three of them are together. This is a mess. The therapist begins to list the messes that appear in Sonia's life these days; at mealtimes perhaps Sonia wants to be breastfed; when dressing, perhaps she wants the same care that the baby gets. The mother says she has offered Sonia the breast but she doesn't want it. Maybe Sonia is older now and does not want the breast, but she has the feeling that she still doesn't know what she wants. It's another mess!

The therapist talks to them about Sonia's regression as a call for affection and an attempt to find her place. She makes her demands through illness as she is allowed to complain about her health. If the parents look after her tummy, the care will help her find her place. Sonia listens very carefully as attention is drawn to this. The therapist emphasises the importance of her being able to express her distress so that her parents understand. If she says nothing, we will not know that she feels bad and is suffering.

Figure 11.3 The newborn baby entered in her world.

While the therapist is speaking, the mother's eyes fill with tears. The rage and exasperation have been transformed into tenderness. There is an atmosphere of understanding and a change in affect in the session. It could be understood that the distress has been taking shape over the course of the session. She has expressed her discomfort throughout the session, which moved from sobbing and non-specific moaning to the fetal position and then a pain centred on her abdomen. She is processing anxiety. After this situation, Sonia is able to integrate the game into her internal world and express herself through the drawing (see Figure 11.3). The newborn baby has entered her world and, in this world, she can express her sadness.

Sonia will have many tantrums and the parents' difficulties in understanding them and containing them will resurface. Sonia continues drawing progressively less terrifying, more structured monsters. At the same time, changes in three important developmental aspects are beginning to appear. Sonia starts to show expressions of shame and embarrassment when her parents speak about typical everyday situations with her. They are the barriers that mark the limits of her infantile sexuality. The family therapy allows these barriers to be formed in a benign way for the necessary repression (Tous, 1991).

Integration of Sonia's little brother into her internal world

In one session, Sonia sets up a game to introduce her little brother to all the characters in the sessions. Her internal objects greet the brother who enters this new world and is integrated into it. The brother is attentive to Sonia and laughs when Sonia directs her expressions at him. The mother rejoices at the good interaction between the children. The father develops a containing function. From a passive, irritating observer of the tantrums, he becomes able to feel his shame and confesses he had "tackled" Sonia. This image of tackling is transformed into the mental capacity to "placate". The hard father can become a strong father who can calm and persuade.

Elaboration of permanence

Suddenly, the family misses three sessions for different reasons. Sonia arrives at the following session hiding behind the pushchair and stays hidden. She does not want to greet anyone. She doesn't move toward us. She has had some big tantrums, but unlike the previous ones, Sonia can end the tantrum crying and letting her mother approach her, hug her and finally console her.

The therapist thinks about the days Sonia has been absent and says how difficult it is to recover contact with her when she has distanced herself after so long without any sessions.

Sonia: I thought you weren't here!

She expresses the tragedy of forgetting, of abandonment, of death. Based on this utterance, we are able to approach each other once more.

Therapist: Perhaps Sonia is uneasy about having lost contact.

On hearing her anxiety named, Sonia begins to make a circle around ours and moves around in a peculiar way. Then she needs to have a wee, then a poo, then asks for water. The therapist moves closer to tell her that we will have to put everything away soon and she exclaims that they cannot go as we haven't had lunch and she starts to prepare the food.

From this session onwards, there is a game of hide and seek at the beginning and end of each session in which Sonia experiences, in words of Winnicott (1965), the joy of being hidden and the disaster not to be found. She plays with the absence, with loss and the pleasure of being found.

Discussion

Throughout the family therapy process, the parents modify the relationship with Sonia. They submit less to the tyranny and aggressiveness that they project onto the little girl. The father continues exercising the firm, containing role and establishes a more trusting relationship by setting limits. The mother acquires some insight into what she projects onto Sonia. At the same time the interrupted pregnancy, current motherhood and the baby on the way are elaborated.

This is a therapeutic function of the sessions that allow Sonia to evacuate and then nourish herself. The images that emerge in the session allow emotion and representation to be connected in the shared emotional experience. Sonia's tantrums are disappearing and her anger turns into conflicts where she can complain. When she doesn't get what she wants, she can cry and be sad. The mother can then console and congratulate her while Sonia can express her desire to be big, to grow, and begin to occasionally help her mother. The mother can say, with satisfaction, that she is lucky with Sonia because she helps with the baby and cooperates. A libidinal aspect appears in the relationship and I feel their enjoyment as I tell them about it.

Conclusion

The articulation of the misunderstanding with which Sonia is identified opens a path to a triangular relationship and the inclusion of the brother. The family therapy offers a space for thought and containment in which the family can reflect and connect with emotion and sadness, followed later by finding pleasure in the relationship. Nevertheless, Sonia still has some character traits and rebellious aspects that make it difficult for her to put up with frustration. These developmental aspects that were highlighted and were strengthened through treatment gave a confidence that other current or future messes could also develop in a healthy way.

References

Bion, W. R. (1962). The psychoanalytic study of thinking. *International Journal Psycho-Analysis*, *43*: 306–310.

Freud, S. (1940). An outline of psychoanalysis. *International Journal Psycho-Analysis*, *21*: 27–84.

Nanzer, N., Knauer, D., Palacio Espasa, F., Qayoom-Boulvain, Z., Hentsch, F., Clinton, P., Trojan, Le Scouezec, I. (2012). *Manuel de psychothérapie centrée sur la parentalité* (Parenthood Centered Psychotherapy Manual). Paris: PUF.

Tous, J. M. (1991). Una contribució a la comprensió psicoanalítica de la vergonya (A contribution to psychoanalytical understanding of the embarrasment). *Revista Catalana de Psicoanàlisi*, *VIII*(1–2): 65–81.

Winnicott, D. W. (1965). *The Maturational Processes and the Facilitating Environment: Studies in the Theory of Emotional Development. The International Psycho-Analytical Library*, *64*: 1–276. London: The Hogarth Press.

Note

1 Nanzer, Kanuer, Palacio Espasa, Qayoom-Boulvain, Hentsch, Clinton, Trojan, and Le Scouëzec.

Editors' prologue to the discussant perspectives

The chapter by Antònia Llairó illustrates with a very evocative case example how the birth of a sibling can offer many opportunities to reactivate previous, insufficiently elaborated intra-psychic elements. Introducing the concept of the *Arrivant*, Sonia Kleiman, from the perspective of link theory, considers how a starting point with such a family may best start from a position of uncertainty rather than origin and causality. Juan González Rojas then describes how the resulting *inter-fantasmatisation* in this family is a response to something shameful, which cannot be thought about, and how effectively the therapist utilises the daughter's drawings as a starting point of representation, or *figurability*.

Discussant perspective

Sonia Kleiman

The presentation prompted me to reflect on a number of theoretical–clinical ideas: firstly, to think about how one distinguishes between a way of thinking that focuses on origin, causality and determination, and a way of thinking that has manifold starting points and is based on indetermination and uncertainty; secondly, to differentiate between a way of thinking that starts from the centre, and a way of thinking that starts from multiplicity; and thirdly, how to distinguish between thinking about links and thinking from a link perspective.

The clinical material begins with the idea of an "arrival". This is an eloquent term that does not refer to birth. It leads me to Derrida's concept of *arrivant*[1]. That is, there is an event that arrives and is excessive; it cannot be accounted for fully by previous experiences. It is an arrival that involves all participants. What arrives is new. Memories and representations resist the newness of the *arrivant*. In the current case it is possible to see that almost everything that is happening at the emotional level is an effect of the mother's painful memories of her own mother. What is about to arrive is disturbing because it brings with it uncertainty. Causality and determinism eliminate newness and refer to what is about to arrive at an origin in a different time and space that is tied to other relationships. Both in clinical practice and in a family, the *arrivant* demands that we make room for the unprecedented. There are multiple theoretical perspectives from which to address the construction of emotional life in families. Theories are reference points that enable us to continue to think. In terms of current scientific thinking, the idea of determination has been challenged by new points of view arising from different disciplines such as physics, philosophy and mathematics. Science has thus opened its doors to the random, to complexity, and the event and uncertainty.

Related to learning in childhood, this is perhaps not so indelible as we used to believe. This is a cause of great relief. Is psychoanalysis also willing to adopt the idea that not everything is necessarily ruled by causality? In the current case, the parents come to the analyst with a particular demand. How do we respond to this request for help? Are these parents interested in finding out what's wrong with their daughter or what's wrong with them? Is it a request to curb the behaviour of a child that causes them unease or could the parents' description of the girl's behaviour serve to describe the couple's relationship? Does the consultation involve them, or is there a strong motivation to think that the problem lies with the girl or in the approaching birth of someone who is not only a sibling but also a child?

(continued)

(continued)

Psychoanalysis inquires into the fuller nature of the reason for seeking help, not just the symptom presented. It thus examines every possible ramification of the presenting problem. In the current presentation, the analyst is confronted with a four-year-old girl whose reactions cause despair along with a mother and wife who cries and says she's lonely; and a father, and husband, who claims he has not noticed anything but will provide support in the future. Immediately, one wonders how this issue of providing support is part of the things happening.

The parents seek help because of the girl, but the analyst thinks that it is important to see them as a family. This decision may be based on two different premises. The analyst may, by doing so, strengthen the parents' focus on the girl and view them as "supporting" her or may rely on a link logic that centres on the family functioning. Such logic entails thinking that the family, in its way of forming as a family and the way members relate to each other in its multiple variations, has resulted in the current production, the actual problem.

The focus then becomes the family link, not the identified child. This is how Berenstein (2010) explains it:

> Link theory decenters subjects by placing them in a group. There are two consequences to this approach. Subjects are dislodged from their central position and, as a result, the notion of center is canceled because inherent in this notion is a quality of uniqueness and hegemony. Looking at the family involves displacing oneness, homogeneity in order to give the family a different, new meaning from the point of view of heterogeneity. A significant implication is that the way is opened for a different way of listening.
>
> (p. 13)

Thinking about the presenting problem from this vantage point means that our listening will be directed to the family's link production. Link production alludes to the conscious and unconscious work performed by the members of the link; it refers to the ways of being and of affecting each other emotionally, as well as the impacts of this.

This approach demands that we separate identities and family roles and plunge into the experience of the sessions, into the ways in which family members inhabit family situations, into the unexpected, kaleidoscopic ways in which effects of presence develop among them. The girl-symptom, the girl who does what she is not supposed to do, the girl who provokes a disturbance, who is disobedient and aggressive, the girl who explodes could be considered from the perspective of the family as a whole – their emotionalities, atmospheres, corporealities. Through her hyper-visibility, the girl exposes what has been rendered invisible.

Considered from this perspective, is the father emotionally present in the sessions, or is his absence the reason for his absence from the narrative? If, instead of thinking of individuals, we could think in terms of a scene – of identities, genders, kinship places, uncertain futures – three-dimensional images would surface that depict actions: people talking, playing, being physically engaged. Perhaps, then, our ideas of what may be happening between them would be unexpected rather than certain, would involve questions rather than predictive hypotheses. We would blindly negotiate the signs appearing in the sessions.

The clothes the family wear, which are perceptively noted by the analyst, speak of their functioning. In addition, their fights, complaints, pain, play, drawing, also provide rich material which creates a multifaceted scene which engages the analyst in a type of cartographic, not just archaeological, journey of remembrance. It is not the same thing to approach the girl from the vantage point of psychopathology or history, both hers and her parents', as it is to approach her from the perspective of the power of her behaviour. She plays, draws, moves, spits, shows, conceals, suffers, recovers, pees on herself and bites. Unawares, she and her parents create an emotional intensity in the family's functioning that should not be prematurely terminated or interpreted. Rather, these affects demand a place as they express the family's ways of being together as well as the impacts of this experience and how the family members belong to this link.

It becomes clear that the girl, by her behaviour and her influence on the family, rescues her parents from inertia and indifference. From this perspective, her behaviour is not a rebellion but a powerful means to engage everyone, including the analyst, in the task of exploring what is going on in this family, and build a space with them. In this regard, it would be interesting to find a way of thinking with the family about their difficulties which acknowledges how their history and their current situation could have interacted in such a way as to produce a productive discontinuity that may give rise to new experiences.

Reference

Berenstein, I. (2010). Toward a family clinical practice. *Virtual Course: Theory and Link Clinical Practice* (Online Course, Link Theory and Clinical Practice), unpublished.

Note

1 I did not translate this term because Derrida's translators have left it in French. "*Arrivant*" refers to the person/event that arrives/happens unexpectedly and is also the present participle of the verb "to arrive". Derrida uses it to allude both to people (immigrants, strangers) and events.

Discussant perspective

Juan González Rojas

The case presented provides a clear account, both in terms of its theoretical referents and in its description of the development of a clinical process. It is a well-articulated narrative which describes the clinical objectives, the setting and the therapeutic focus. In the global context of family intervention, it could be compared to "group" and "in group" therapy, where there is an oscillation from one to another while developing and building the group intervention and moreover the group.

In the family presented Sonia's behavioural symptomatology reveals the difficulties and vicissitudes arising from the original attempts to establish the primary link, secure attachment and a dual unit that provide a symbiotic base from which to develop (Bleger, 1975; Fonagy, 2004). The behaviours that the girl exhibits are not understood by her mother, and even less by the father, and are like hieroglyphs needing to be deciphered. They appear to depict something strange or at risk of being expelled, something that in its repetition seeks understanding, something about the place, or the non-place of Sonia, as the family scapegoat.

There is a metaphor that needs to be elaborated in the family's story that represents a search for its re-signification. It is felt to be something that cannot be integrated inside nor outside, that is both accepted and rejected, actively or passively. It represents something that has not been able to be elaborated or put into words, either by the mother or the couple, which threatens to become an unmentionable, and could later be an unthinkable experience for Sonia. It has neither an inscription, nor a verbal representation. Projective identification, cleavages and splits all point to those difficulties in integrating within the family what remains dead inside or outside the family skin, its relational family psychic apparatus, or genealogical envelope (Anzieu, 1990).

The construction of the mother and daughter relationship, which has become a warped dual unit, has become a knot in the fabric of the family. The weaving of this fabric through words, affections and representations sheds light on their difficulties in separateness and in symbolising the associated particular and shared defences. It has resulted in an *interfantasmatisation* (Eiguer, 1987) whereby Sonia bites, hits, makes herself noticed, hides, regresses, advances again and, where her mother out of her own obsessive fears speaks of what she has not been able to integrate, that is, the trans-generational influences and her own experience with her parents. It also includes the role of a powerful and retaliative grandmother, who seems partnerless and a grandfather whose suspicion of helplessness added to the grandmother's anger.

The knot of the here and now of those conflicted in the family therefore connects to an historical genesis, through the common family *fantasmatic* leading to the hypothesis concerning the difficulties of the way links are structured in this family, both in the couple partnership and in the bonds between other members in the family. These are difficulties that also represent an emerging threat to fraternal bonds.

The paternal lineage does not feature in the story. It is as if it is in the shadow with the figure of the grandmother from the maternal lineage being dominant. Related to this, the mother's place in the family is in conflict. Sonia's place is also consequently filled with anguish. This seems connected to perceptions and traumatic sensations recorded in her first psychic experiences with her mother which are unprocessed and linked to her body self.

The shame linked to the unspeakable, trans-generationally transmitted symptoms, in a waterfall of repetition, seeks the exoneration of guilt and shame, and the liberation of this woman's desire to be a mother. The symptomatology manifested in the family's strange behaviours, about what is not linked, reveals something sinister, ominous, and which seeks elaboration (Berenstein, 1984).

The resultant sealing and partial foreclosure as defences in this family do, however, succumb to the intervention and the therapeutic setting. The search for representational expression to put into words that which will enable the removal of primitive anguish from the body through Sonia's drawings becomes a focal aspect of the treatment. Thanks to this, it is possible for Sonia to elaborate her place in this family in a way that does not threaten her psychic development. It seems likely that such representational work with the drawing of the parents by Sonia was equally useful to the parents, as it helped them define their own space so that they could re-work the unhelpful pacts and contracts inherent in their relationship (Aulagnier, 1975).

Fantasies helped to contain the aggression of the maternal rivalry with her child with whom she is identified (Bergeret, 1984). The therapeutic process, however, helped to access the child that had been killed off in the mother and allowed for the mourning of her own mother. In the work towards this transformation everything forms a staging of the shameful experience, which generates a duel between the *renegation* of the loss and the successful and unsuccessful pathological defences.

Therapeutic progress did, however, facilitate mourning, which allowed for individuation and differentiation between the mother and Sonia. This lack of individuation had previously retarded the development of a helpful super-ego in Sonia. Sonia's bizarre behaviours can be seen to represent a "message in a bottle" of the difficulty of imaginative development. She had not been able to symbolise and put into words

(continued)

(continued)

what her parents failed to symbolise which had maintained an enigmatic experience in the family (Kaës, 2007). The construction of the *figurability* (representation) through the drawing was the first resource marshalled in therapy to establish a link of communication in words, images and affects which until then had been non-existent, previously blocked by the parents' collusion in forming *de-negative pacts* which were related to feelings of shame.

References

Anzieu, D. (1990). *Las envolturas psíquicas*. Buenos Aires: Amorrortu.

Aulagnier, P. (1975). *La violencia de la interpretación, del Pictograma al enunciado*. Buenos Aires: Amorrortu.

Berenstein, I. (1984). *Familia y enfermedad mental*. Buenos Aires: Paidos.

Bergeret, J. (1984). La violencia fundamental. *Revue Francaise de Psychanalyse*, 6.

Bion, W. (1980). *Experiencias en grupos*. Buenos Aires: Paidos.

Bleger, J. (1975). *Simbiosis y Ambigüedad*. Buenos Aires: Paidos.

Eiguer, A. (1987). *El parentesco fantasmático*. Buenos Aires: Amorrortu.

Fonagy, P. (2004). *Teoría del apego y psicoanálisis*. Barcelona: Espaxs.

Freud, S. (1972). *Obras Completas*. Madrid: Biblioteca Nueva.

Kaës, R. (2007). *Un singular plural*. Buenos Aires: Amorrotu.

Chapter 12

The mystery, the turbulence and the passion of infantile phantasy in the couple

Whose pain is it – a shared internal world of unmourned objects

Karen Proner

Introduction

Donald Meltzer's theory of the "aesthetic conflict" brings a very different emphasis to the Kleinian developmental theory. It presents the beginning of mental life as having a more positive valence, away from frustration and absence as the initial driving force to development and towards a more complicated look at the nature of the earliest relationship to a "present" object. The theory with this emphasis, if accepted, can greatly influence the way in which we work with our patients. This chapter will focus on the way in which his theories of infancy have influenced my own work with couples. The extended view of the Kleinian theory that Meltzer offers provides a more challenging and complex way to work with couples.

The aesthetic – a paradigmatic shift

Beginning where Meltzer does, Melanie Klein's baby is seen to be born with a rudimentary ego which involves a capacity to feel anxiety and psychically protect itself. Klein's newborn has a rudimentary capacity to relate to objects in external reality and in phantasy, although the differentiation of internal and external is at first very limited. Klein's baby's early ego lacks cohesion, alternating between integration and disintegration. According to Klein the death instinct makes an infant attach immediately to an object which in turn makes the infant feel fearful and in the presence of an uncontrollable and overpowering object. Klein never speculated about prenatal life. In his *Studies in Extended Metapsychology*, Meltzer (1986) makes a plea to shift from theory making to model making. He notes:

> The field of the fetus may not be as wide as the field of an adult but its boundaries still include a vastly complex source of sensory data from the mother's body and beyond. Light, sound, vibration, changes of gravitational orientation, temperature and acceleration all impinge

> upon it. Its aqueous medium is more like the forests of the sea than a fishpond in the garden. Furthermore, as regards its equipment, for lack of convincing evidence to the contrary, we must consider the fetus fully equipped though as yet inept at utilising its apparatus and devoid of a teacher. Even here we cannot be absolute for in a very cogent sense the nature of the equipment teaches its own use. The very fact that the fetus can get its thumb into its mouth places it in a position to explore both sides of the relationship; of thumb exploring mouth, as well as mouth investigating the uses of thumb. The heart of the narcissistic organisation is thus available to be juxtaposed to the wealth of object relations. Observations and imagination become necessary, limited by the fact that one can never with certainty know what the other (the object) feels, experiences, thinks, wants, hopes or fears.
>
> (p. 16)

Meltzer wrote this when he already had begun formulating his ideas on the aesthetic conflict. Is he saying that the aesthetic conflict begins before birth in the "heart" of the organisation of the fetus' experience? He suggests that it is the only way you can encompass the mother's impact on the baby, that is, psychic development is profoundly influenced by the complexity of intrauterine life which impacts on the baby's imagination and capacity for exploration and emotional response. Meltzer thus conveys the importance of appreciating the infant's extraordinary aesthetic sense which he believes is there before birth. He also makes clear that this sensual pleasure is not just on a quantitative level but a qualitative level.

> How then may the bombardment of color form, and patterned sound of such augmented intensity as greets the newborn, impinge upon his mind? I claim with some insistence that this is the aesthetic sense; certainly the human baby is alive to the beauty of the world and to its inevitable fragility.
>
> (Meltzer, 1986, p. 28)

Using Klein's and Bion's theories he restates that it is not just the mother's body that is the "world" but the mystery of her mind that impacts on the baby. He further takes from both theories and states that when the beauty and the mystery arouse the wish to know the object, it also arouses the negative emotions: minus L (Love), minus H (Hate), minus K (Knowledge) (Meltzer, 1988).

I became interested in this earliest relationship not only through Meltzer's most evocative writing but through a particular infant observation of a newborn, presented in one of my infant observation groups. This experience inspired subsequent interest in this earliest phase of development and inspired an article which looked at what Meltzer would call the early ethological bonding process, which he linked to his ideas of later defensive adhesive types of identification. I was intrigued with the normal aspect of these processes (Proner, 2000). Bowlby (1969) had described the necessary bonding in attachment. However, it was developmental researchers who brought a detailed understanding to these speculations about early life. The area that interested me was the area that psychologists call "interactional synchrony". I quote from my article:

> The idea is that we are born with an instinctual propensity to imitate. Our body moves when we emit sounds. The listener will engage in a corresponding synchrony, body, and sound. It is clear to researchers that it is not motivated by physiological needs as in order to be fed, but is a pleasurable experience in and of itself resulting in a beautiful linking of the reactions of the two, a synchronied "dance" between the mother and infant. It is clear that it is a part of the infant seeking companionship, and the preface to language development – the pleasure in responding and being responded to. This very primitive form of synchronous response creates an illusion of oneness, which brings mother and baby together in an orchestrated attunement that is the prerequisite to being in a position of projective receptivity. In other words, this proto-mental synchrony precedes projective identification which is the next step in the movement toward mentation. It is commonly thought that a mother's reverie brings forth this attunement.
>
> (Proner, 2000, p. 58)

I suggested that this instinctual synchrony acts as the catalyst for mother's reverie; the mother's mind further enables, in Bion's terms, a metabolising and containing function. I ask in this article:

> Is this synchrony the first step of the dance which brings the baby's and the mother's mind in a primitive responsive juxtaposition, the most basic element needed for the container-contained functioning, the proto-mental elements of identification? For the mother, it is a preface to feeling identified, "in love" with her baby. For the baby, it must feel like "fitting", the opposite of inchoate. Perhaps the repetition of this "fitting sensation" might eventually become the "binding" that Esther Bick (1968) calls "skin". Ainsworth (1967) says that the attachment is not constructed from overt patterns of behaviour, but instead by what she terms "internal" experiences, which are built into the nervous system as a result of transactions with the mother and expressed as "expectancies". Hofer (1984) speaks of the regulating action of internal representations of object relationships on "biological systems" lying in the generation of expectancies. Are these proto-mental elements the real "song and dance" of development that Meltzer talks of, the needed duet for the reciprocal relationship between mother and baby?
>
> (Proner, 2000, p. 28)

Meltzer, in describing this relationship, draws our attention to the earliest, crucial and most painful moment in development. What is it about the nature of this pain that makes it is so powerful? Is it that the "fitting" of the mouth–nipple or that eyes are experienced as "holding" eyes that is so exquisite in its completeness that the sense of interruption or ending is so palpably present? Meltzer might say that this provides the earliest and the primary experience of displeasure or frustration. He would argue that mystery and the unknowable mark the beauty of the experience. This moment bears the nature of all subsequent object relationships. The mother can help to mediate the infant's experience for, hopefully, she too is lost in this rapture, one which is crucial for the subsequent structuring of the baby's defences, her emotional responsiveness, and in particular her "passionate response".

Meltzer and couple psychoanalysis

So what does the nature of this early infant development have to do with our work with couples? It relates to the beginning of life for each member of the couple and how this early experience influences coupling. It therefore reminds us of how complex our work is because things like a reciprocal relationship, empathy and the capacity to tolerate not knowing what the other is feeling, and the elements of dependency and intimacy and bearing the real inconsistencies of real relationships, start at the beginning of life. In fact, this is so commonly accepted as an idea that we don't really think about it very much in our work with couples. The enormous complexity that the early infantile experience of each partner brings to the couple's relationship, especially in how it influences their intimacy and sexuality, is evident and its understanding provides unique challenges for the couples therapist.

Many of Meltzer's writings are filled with interesting thoughts and concepts relevant to couples work. For example, his article "A psychoanalytic model of the child-in-the–family-in-the-community" (Meltzer, 1976) is rich with relevance for our work with couples and families, especially the influence of the community on the couple and the family. He refers not to the external community, but the community of the internal world as constructed in the minds of the individuals. In referring to what he calls the "family organisation" he provides a dynamic description focused on the titular roles of all aspects of family life: the parents, the baby, the preschool child, the adolescent, the grandparents, etc. He sees that the level of mental pain able to be tolerated by the family is reflected in the family "growing", being "stabilised", or "regressed". Meltzer outlines the functions of any or all of these classical roles in family life as generating love, promulgating hate, promoting hope, sowing despair, containing depressive pain, emanating persecutory anxiety, creating confusion, thinking. He sees that these functions tend to be delegated to the individual members of the family, bringing them into conflict with their opposite number. He terms "functional dependence" as describing the situation where a member of a dyad attaches to another in order to have the other perform a function for them. The function can be assumed or imposed. Perhaps the most psychotic constellation of these functions is when they are avoided and carried out by no one, which causes an atmosphere of chaos with an associated sense of catastrophic anxiety. He points out that such family organisations are best understood in a highly dynamic model which assumes some flux. Meltzer points to the need to work with two models in our interventions with couples: "a momentary state", but also as "a general tendency".

In the same article when Meltzer explores "The family organisation" he divides the family types into: the Couple family; the Matriarchal family; the Patriarchal family; the Gang family; and the Reversed family. To demonstrate the value of his ideas, I will explore what he calls the couple family. Meltzer outlines four introjective functions of the couple family: generating love; promoting hope; containing pain; and thinking. The capacity of the couple to perform these functions will require their periodic withdrawal into privacy which is supposed to be sexual and mysterious. He notes that the times when the couple is obliged to be apart produces a hovering "Sword of Damocles" atmosphere. While their conjunction arouses a constant expectation of the new baby member of the family, the history of their courtship is of mythological interest to the dependent members giving form to their hope for the future.

He further emphasises in his exploration of this model that the catastrophic anxieties to do with dependency land on the mother, although the father may be greatly loved. Any sense of inadequacy in the mother will be shifted onto the father. The mother is seen to take the projections but the father is the "end of the line for mental waste". Interestingly, he understands that the great vulnerability for the couple is the death of a child or a fetus. It is more devastating than dealing with an ill child. The death of a child may have been felt in the shared unconscious phantasy of the couple, as if they could not perform the basic function of keeping the children alive. I want to make it clear that although Meltzer in this article goes back and forth between meaning in the internal world and the external world, I believe he means that it involves the infantile internal world of each of the couple. It is the area in which we can promote learning and working through. He notes that the ability for the couple to face loss lies in the unique identity of each individual. I think he means an identity that is based on phantasies, firstly about the mother's body and then "mother's babies" (Meltzer, 1976).

Clinical example

To illustrate these issues I would like to describe a clinical case that was presented to me in Rome at a conference held by the Italian Society of Psychoanalysis of Couples and Families. I am very grateful to Dr Ausilia Sparano for her permission to share with you her clinical material. This is a consultation in a Neonatal Intensive Care Unit.

It is a consultation with a couple who had just given birth to a baby who was one of a pair of twins where the other twin died. The couple also had an 18-month-old boy who was showing separation anxiety and sleep problems. Their premature infant was placed in an incubator after birth with no contact with mother. The parents had not had any trouble getting pregnant and through infertility treatment they were able to conceive their firstborn son and later, twins. The small fragile twin was named after mother's childhood friend Eliza who had died at 13 years of age. The stronger twin was named Aurora. The small twin died soon after birth and Aurora was fighting to survive when the consultations began.

What was striking in Dr Sparano's description of the consultation were the details of their present history: of their problems with their early sexual relationship and their difficulties in conceiving. In a parallel way this was followed with a very long description of their history which consisted of a world of attachment objects who had suffered greatly from the loss of the capacity to keep their babies alive. Mrs B's father was described as having projected her anxieties into her as a child. She was described as a mature woman, with a voice of a teenager who described an "ideal (childhood) family life", but one in which her father would never "let her go out of the house". Her paternal grandmother, a very anxious and depressed woman, had lost one of her six children at birth. Mrs B's father was the youngest child. His older brother died in a car crash at 18 years of age. Another brother suffered from panic attacks. The grandmother, who lived with Mrs B's family, died when Mrs B was eight years old. Dr Sparano reported: "It seemed that the common link that connected her to her paternal family is the anguish for the loss that takes different forms as anxiety, panic, somatisation and obsessive control." She noted that the main theme of her infantile family seemed to be "we need to all remain close because something terrible could happen: the danger outside the family was always present." It seemed to me that Dr Sparano was describing an uncontained "nameless dread" (Bion, 1967) that had been recycled through the generations. One can see this phenomenon particularly in families with holocaust histories or very traumatic histories marked by major losses. Mr B's family also had similar generational unprocessed loss. His mother lost her firstborn, a girl who died a few days after birth; he never knew the reason for her death because his mother no longer spoke about it. Her next son, Mr B's older brother, never left home and lived with his mother with no other emotional life. Mr B described her as a mother who was shut in her own pain and not able to express affection to her sons. His father was absent and no doubt avoided things by always working. In summary, these are two families suffering adverse consequences related to the loss of children yet dealing with their anxieties differently: Mrs B's family through obsessional (controlling) defenses, and Mr B's family by splitting and denial.

Mr B was very motivated to work on these anxieties. He had suffered in the presence of a mother who was emotionally cut off and unable to respond.

He experienced this again with his wife's state of mind and worried about the effect on the children. He requested psychological help. The consultation was marked by a splitting in the function of the couple. Mrs B was focused on twin phantasies and mourning the dead baby and in effect all the dead babies, in particular, her dead childhood friend.

As described by Dr Sparano, the couple appears to have enacted the grief-stricken couple they both suffered from as children in the presence of the unconscious of their parental figures. It is noted by the therapist that "Mrs B repeats in an exhausted and monotonous voice her anguish for the dead child in long monologues, cries and repeats." Mr B says little, often appears absent, looks around: "almost seems estranged". Dr Sparano sees her task as creating a psychic shelter to contain what she calls "the destructiveness of the pain and create the capacity for awareness of the psychic contents related to both birth and parenting by linking the past losses and the present ones." The therapist refers to a "destructive pain" that mother was suffering. Dr Sparano seems to understand the unconscious (survivor) guilt of Mrs B. She also understood her need to have a baby as part of an "omnipotent phantasy" one which required not only great effort but the support of IVF. Perhaps the mother unconsciously felt that she could bring the dead babies back to life as in her naming of her vulnerable twin Eliza. Was this to enable her to get rid of all the dead babies in all the depressed mothers' minds? She was eager to tell Eliza's parents of her plan. However, now Eliza is dead and she is not able to let her go. Letting go can feel like forgetting. Mother is not able to forget. Perhaps to her it would feel that she would lose all the infantile babies and then risk losing the infantile mother as well.

Discussion

This material highlights how complex and difficult our work is in helping our patients mourn. In couples with complex identifications and projective identifications it can seem an impossible task.

Returning to the end of Dr Sparano's presentation Mr B presents a dream in which he was on a beach. He notes that maybe Mrs B was there but he could not remember it too well. He says:

> It was almost night after sunset, and he walks toward a very dark side of the beach where there is a kind of fence. It is dangerous to get close to it and yet he is driven by curiosity and together with another person (a person he had never had contact with) he tries to see what's beyond it. Meanwhile, he observes the sea; suspended on a rope are two children who are about five–six years old who are able to stand perfectly in balance as acrobats heading to the dark side of the beach without feeling they were in danger.

Mr B says that the children could represent his children and that the dark side represents the pain and suffering that makes their lives hang in the balance. Mrs B is very distressed and seems unable to think about the dream. According to her this dream only seems to confirm the fact that because of them, their children's lives were hanging in the balance and were thus in danger. It is clear here that the associations of this couple reflect a split in that Mr B seems ready to work on things, but Mrs B feels overwhelmed by guilt and feels she is to blame.

The therapist interprets that the quality of suspension in the dream could be viewed as a characteristic of pre-term birth. She suggests that the sea may indicate the children's struggle between life and death. She also suggests that the rope could be seen as linked to the tubes attached to premature babies to support their breathing and feeding. The fence was linked to the cerclage because of the uterus incontinence. Like their pre-term babies these parents had also prematurely felt pain and uncertainty. They had been children who were exposed too early to pain and uncertainty without a safety net that could protect them from these feelings. They didn't feel able to contain their fear, nor those of their children. Mr B appears very moved by this interpretation and his eyes fill with tears. However, Mrs B stares into space.

It seems that this interpretation managed to make contact with Mr B, who presented the dream. However, it seemed to leave mother more alone than ever with what may have felt to be the unthinkable guilt about "who killed the babies". After all, it was her uterus that continued to drop babies out or did not take in the eggs. Just as her father suffered, she too suffered as a girl in the presence of his anxieties. Now she suffers as the mother who seems unable to protect her babies.

My thought about this dream is that it could be interpreted in many ways, on an individual level perhaps as a dream of the suffering of one of the members of the couple, Mr B. As such, it could be used to enhance communication between Mr B and Mrs B so that Mrs B could understand her husband's unconscious. Alternatively, it could be used to bring the dynamic of the couple into "base relief" where it could be examined and the anxieties therein better understood. What was communicated to me first was the uncertainty that Mr B expressed in the dream: was he with Mrs B or not? The dream seems to question if they are together in this dangerous darkness that is encircling the beach, perhaps in the same way that he felt as a helpless child with parents whose depressed mind threatened to encircle him. Perhaps Mrs B knew that feeling too. Is there anyone there to help with these unthinkable, unspeakable unknowns? Why do babies die? Perhaps Mr B feels the fence to be like a structure that prevents him from getting close to his wife and her depression and sadness in the same way that he felt as a child with his mother's sadness. There was perhaps a terrifying mystery of what is inside her mind. Mrs B too may have also felt her father's anxieties and dread, fenced off by idealising, controlling family defences. The two children are indeed suspended by their shared backgrounds on a rope in a kind of acrobatic act to not feel or think together as the father seems to be focused on keeping the live babies protected and mother seems immersed in keeping the dead babies from disappearing. The danger is the madness which feels like the nameless dread they both experienced as children in the presence of parents' minds, which were not functioning and not knowing. This state generates what Meltzer refers to as "catastrophic anxiety".

Dr Sparano worked with this couple over the three months that Aurora was hospitalised and worked with mother over the eventual "kangarooing" and feeding of her infant. The baby began to suck and feed and mother began to feel the life and responsiveness of her baby and the baby began to thrive.

Conclusion

We can ask at this point again: Where is the pain? Whose pain is it? In response to that question, we can feel relieved that these parents have accepted treatment and have begun the process of recovering parts of themselves in the process of becoming parents to their two children. Meltzer notes that pain can be "transported" easily among group (family) members, mostly in unspoken ways. Although Aurora quickly recovered with the help of the "incredible emotion" of the kangaroo method and gained weight, an interesting observation of the parents struck me. The parents described Aurora as a "very reactive baby". "Even if she has a stiff neck and difficulty in muscle tone, she seems to be searching for contact." It seems that her mother sees something and feels something in holding the baby. Does she see her vulnerable baby search for an object? However, something in the baby's body curiously stiffens and does not allow the mother to hold her. I think of Bick's (1968) understanding of the role of the mother's mind and body providing a primary skin for the baby in the early days of life. Bick understood the use of the body to hold itself if uncontained.

One could say that this physical characteristic of the baby dates from her premature birth and time spent in an incubator. Being contained by a machine is different than being held in the arms and mind of a mother. Or could one say that the pain of mother's and father's losses is felt in the body of the baby as a loss of a container for the baby's experiences? Is this a primitive form of internalisation? Can the inter-generational pain of unheld babies be so concretely lodged in the body of Aurora? It is too soon to know. On a hopeful note for the future: at the end of the eight sessions, during this period of hospitalisations, the mother contacted the therapist to continue to work with her on "mourning her child and the inner part of herself". The process of working through mourning brings hope for this next generation.

Acknowledgement

I would like to express my appreciation to Dr Ausilia Sparano who has been very generous in allowing me to use her material to illustrate my ideas. She has written her own article which can be found in *The International Review of Psychoanalysis of Couple and Family*, Number 16–1/2017. ISSN2105-1038). It is entitled "Suspended on a rope. The family unconscious as seen in a consultation with the parents of a preterm neonate".

References

Ainsworth, M. D. S. (1967). *Infancy in Uganda: Infant Care and the Growth of Love*. Oxford, UK: Johns Hopkins Press.

Bick, E. (1968). The function of the skin in the early object relations. *International Journal of Psychoanalysis*, *49*(2,3): 484–486.

Bion, W. R. (1967). *Second Thoughts: Selected Papers on Psychoanalysis*. London: Heinemann.

Bowlby, J. (1969). *Attachment and Loss: Vol. 1. Attachment*. New York: Basic Books.

Hofer, M. (1984). Relationships as regulators: A psychobiologic perspective on bereavement. *Psychosomatic Medicine*, *46*: 183–197.

Meltzer, D. (1976). A psychoanalytic model of the child-in-the-family-in-the-community (with Martha Harris). In: A. Hahn (Ed.), *Sincerity*. London: Karnac, 1994.

Meltzer, D. (1986). *Studies in Extended Metapsychology*. Strathclyde, Perthshire: Clunie Press.

Meltzer, D. (1988). *The Apprehension of Beauty*. Strathclyde, Perthsire: Clunie Press.

Proner, K. (2000). Proto-mental synchrony: some thoughts on the earliest identification processes in a neonate. *International Journal of Infant Observation*, *3*(2): 55–63.

Editors' prologue to the discussant perspectives

In her presentation of a case she supervised, Karen Proner elucidates how Meltzer's understanding of infantile development can inform our clinical practice with couples. In particular, she suggests how the complexity that the early infantile experience of each partner can influence the couple's relationship, especially in terms of intimacy and sexuality, and how an understanding of this provides unique challenges for the couple's therapist. She also discusses Meltzer's ideas about the impact of the death of a foetus or a child on a couple's relationship. Amita Sehgal, with reference to recent research findings concerning loss, takes up the issue of this impact by examining the case presented, and thinking about the role of the analyst in being able to contain the grief of the parents and understand it by paying attention to the mirroring of affect between the partners. Anna Romagosa Huguet next provides a link theory perspective to the material presented, especially noting the impact of trans-generational links. By creatively referring to Dali's painting of the *Angelus*, she also notes how important the third position, which the analyst represents, is to the facilitation of the mourning process in such a couple.

Discussant perspective

Amita Sehgal

Meltzer's theory of "aesthetic conflict" is a model of psychic development (Meltzer, 1986) that begins with the infant's first response to its mother. Meltzer believes the infant's initial response to mother's sensual beauty, "the dazzle of the sunrise" (Meltzer & Williams 1988, p. 29), is almost immediately replaced by the "tormenting uncertainty" (Meltzer, 1992, p. 61) about what is inside her, the unknowable contents of her mind. Meltzer uses Bion's schema of affective links, Love (L), Hate (H) and Knowledge (K) which, according to Bion, form the basis of one's relationships to one's objects, to define the infant's aesthetic experience. The infant's attempt to manage the tension created by the seemingly incompatible combination of L, H and K towards the aesthetic object can be unbearable and forms the nub of the aesthetic conflict (Fisher, 2000).

Meltzer's concept suggests that the infant is intensely preoccupied with the contents of the mother's mind. In addition, Bion's idea of maternal reverie indicates mother is interested in what is in her baby's mind and makes herself receptive to her infant's communications (Bion, 1962). In the current chapter, Proner proposes that mother and baby's mutual interest in the contents of each other's minds bestows a reciprocal receptivity to projections, creating an illusion of oneness.

With these ideas in mind Proner develops the concept of interactional synchronicity, our innate propensity to imitate, and projective receptivity and extends it to adult couple relationships. She reminds us that both partners in the couple were once infants in their families of origin, each importing into their adult relationship patterns of behaviour that had been influenced by a combination of mirroring their parents and by being the receptacle of parental projections.

Proner illustrates Meltzer's view that the death of a foetus or a child has a tremendous impact upon a couple's relationship, with a clinical example of a couple where both partners had grown up in families grieving the loss of a child. The couple themselves had undergone lengthy fertility treatment and were dealing with the trauma of losing one of their twin babies. Proner asks how we, as couple therapists, might help such a couple mourn the death of their child, especially given their developmental histories.

Infertility investigation and treatment expose the most intimate area of a couple's life to public scrutiny. The route to becoming parents in such a way can be emotionally challenging as conceiving a child through fertility treatments can generate stress and tension and "stir up complicated emotions of inferiority, humiliation and shame"

(Cudmore, 2005, p. 301). It can also have an alienating effect upon the parents because of conscious or unconscious phantasies about who is the destructive partner (Mattinson, 1988).

As couple therapists it is important for us to explore the couple's experience of, and the meaning the couple attribute to, their history of being unable to conceive naturally. This is especially relevant when working with couples such as the one described, where the partners had to deal with the double grief of the loss of their ability to create their own baby, as well as losing a much-wanted baby.

The distress of being parents dependent upon medical assistance to not only create their babies, but also to keep them alive, would be painful to acknowledge. All three of their children, their 18-month-old son and their twin newborn daughters, were conceived through medical intervention and they relied on the medical team to keep one daughter alive (in an incubator) and watched helplessly as doctors failed to save the other twin. One can imagine that, for this couple, the lack of control and ensuing feelings of helplessness and despair would have been hard to bear. Their anger and frustration generated as a result of these experiences would most likely have found expression within their relationship.

Recently conducted studies suggest that a child's death can cause both cohesive and detrimental effects on a couple's relationship (Albuquerque, Pereira & Narciso, 2016). The researchers found that variables that influence the outcome of how a couple manages the loss of their child include the cause and type of death and the pre-death nature and quality of the relationship. These variables can also impact on one partner's ability to communicate openly with the other and can create a congruent grieving response (where both partners can grieve together) or an incongruent one (where they grieve in isolation within the relationship). They also found that another factor that impacts upon the couple's ability to process the trauma is the capacity of the individual partner's family of origin to process trauma (Albuquerque, Pereira & Narciso, 2016).

In the case presented it seemed unlikely that Mr and Mrs B's loss could be talked about openly in their families of origin, as there might have been uncomfortable feelings concerning the capacity of women to create babies and keep them alive. Mr B's mother was emotionally unresponsive to her children, herself still being shut in the pain of losing her own daughter who died at birth. That is, Mr B lost a sibling and grew up with his mother's depression and with parents struggling to mourn the loss of a child. Mrs B's mother seemed to have been absent and not talked about, and Mrs B's father had lost two siblings and had himself grown up with a depressed mother who continued to live with her son and his family during Mrs B's early childhood. Mr B grew up

(continued)

(continued)

with the direct experience of infantile death and maternal depression and Mrs B grew up living with her depressed grandmother whose children had died and a father who held onto her tightly.

The couple's history is significant given that we know that the body imitates the affective states of others and infants learn emotions through observation and imitation. This is facilitated by mirror neurons present in the brain (Gallese, 2003; Scharff, 2014). Whilst this could be a source of enjoyment and pleasure, as in the case of maternal attunement, it could also be a source of pain when faced with maternal mourning and, in the case of Mr and Mrs B, possibly influenced the way they learnt to cope with infant death.

From the material presented I found it hard to ascertain the quality of the couple's relationship prior to their child's death. It would also have been helpful to have some idea of the couple's own associations to the dream which they brought to their therapy. The dream made me wonder whether there might have been a psychological division of labour in this couple whereby the wife experienced the emotional pain of the loss, and her husband supplied the support, energy and hope of moving on from it. I had also wondered if the husband might have been more susceptible to being lost in grief himself, having lived with maternal depression due to infantile death, and whether this shared unconscious split served a protective function for him. If this is correct, and where material from another session might have helped elucidate this idea, then this way of organising the relationship might have helped to manage the immediate grief. If not carefully attended to, however, this functional division might have also led to a dysfunctional split where each partner felt isolated from the other.

In working with Mr and Mrs B, the mirroring role of the therapist as the attuned caregiver might also have been of particular significance. The therapist's non-verbal cues and responses are not subject to conscious control but are channels through which affective signals are transmitted and received (Clulow, 2014). The ability to withstand and understand the couple's grief by paying attention to the mirroring of affect between partners was possibly also very important. That is, by being attuned to unconscious inter-subjective communications and the shared emotional climate generated in the session, the couple therapist could, in this way, have facilitated an holistic processing of grief in this couple.

References

Albuquerque, S., Pereira, M., & Narciso, I. (2016). Couple's relationship after the death of a child: A systemic review. *Journal of Child and Family Studies*, *25*(1): 30–53.

Bion, W. R. (1962). *Learning from Experience*. London: Heinemann.

Clulow, C. (2014). Attachment, affect regulation, and couple psychotherapy. In: D. E. Scharff & J. Savege Scharff (Eds.), *Psychoanalytic Couple Therapy: Foundations of Theory and Practice* (pp. 44–58). London: Karnac.

Cudmore, L. (2005). Becoming parents in the context of loss. *Sexual and Relationship Therapy*, *20*(3): 299–308.

Fisher, J. V. (2000). A father's abdication: Lear's retreat from 'aesthetic conflict'. *International Journal of Psycho-Analysis*, *81*(5): 963–982.

Gallese, V. (2003). The manifold nature of interpersonal relations: The quest for a common mechanism. *Philosophical Transactions of the Royal Society of London Biological Sciences*, *358*: 517–528. London: The Royal Society.

Mattinson, J. (1988). *Work, Love and Marriage*. London: Duckworth.

Meltzer, D. (1986). *Studies in Extended Metapsychology: Clinical Applications of Bion's Ideas*. Strath Tay, Perthshire: Clunie Press.

Meltzer, D. (1992). *The Claustrum*. Strath Tay, Perthshire: Clunie Press.

Meltzer, D., & Williams, M. H. (1988). *The Apprehension of Beauty: The Role of Aesthetic Conflict in Development, Art and Violence*. Strath Tay, Perthshire: Clunie Press.

Scharff, D. E. (2014). Aggression in couples: an object relations primer. In: D. E. Scharff & J. Savege Scharff (Eds.), *Psychoanalytic Couple Therapy: Foundations of Theory and Practice* (pp. 59–70). London: Karnac.

Discussant perspective

Anna Romagosa Huguet

Karen Proner offers us an interesting reflection on the influence of Meltzer and Bion's theories regarding aesthetic conflict and early links, as well as discussing how childhood development studies have influenced her conception of psychoanalysis and working with couples, an influence with which I can identify.

Meltzer, Bion and later others initiated a construction of a model of the mind's aesthetic dimension based on the theory of aesthetic conflict. This includes the ability to play, to form images, to dream and to narrate. Subsequent theorists have expanded these ideas with Pistiner (2007), for example, suggesting that the mind's aesthetic dimension includes three specific domains: that of sense, myth and passion.

In discussing the current chapter, I would like to add some ideas concerning the relationship between early childhood and a couple's relationship. Firstly, the couple creates a space, a kind of nest or cradle, for the inner baby each of them has inside (the intra-psychic baby), and for the baby, they create from their shared unconscious fantasies (inter-psychic). This is shaped by their respective family and social histories (trans-generational links). If the couple can contain the unconscious baby, it propels their growth as a couple.

The container–contained model (Bion, 1963) allows us to understand the importance of the reverie function, an active transformation that works like an emotional digestive apparatus and which stimulates the ability of the baby to tolerate difficult emotional experiences. The members of the couple seek containment and see each other as a potential container, but the deficits of their respective containment function may mean that these are repeated in the next generation.

The couple relationship itself also implies the formation of a "link" between the two subjects, which in turn constitutes a new relational field that is an unconscious co-creation of the couple. This new formation that we can call a dyad involves a couple state of mind (Waddell, 2002; Morgan, 2018) and is a third position (Britton, Feldman & O'Shaughnessy, 1989), a symbolic third that they both not only create but also modify and maintain in a dynamic process that offers the possibility of solving conflicts and growing as a couple.

The author presents her supervisee's clinical material, that of a couple who has lost a child. The author asks: Whose pain is it? This reminded me of the story of the Catalan painter, Salvador Dalí, and the painting *The Angelus* by J. F. Millet (1859). The painting, which was popular in many French homes, represents a couple of peasants in a field who have interrupted their work to pray to the Angelus. Dalí felt such a strange and disturbing sensation when he observed this painting in his childhood, as if there was a great latent burden in it (Dalí, 2006, p. 28). Finally, he related it to the myth of the castrating woman and the death of a son. Indeed, the representation of the death of a child is hidden in the painting. Years later, Dalí (2006) learned from a friend of Millet that between the two peasants, he had actually painted the coffin of their dead child, but he covered it with a new coat of paint. The otherwise "inexplicable" anguish created by the two lonely figures would be hard to account for. With the absent element explained, one can see that they are in fact united by the absent argumentative element, "vanished as inside an upside-down collage" (2006). A brother of Dalí died at the age of three, a year before Dali was born, and had the same name as he. The new "delirious drama" that emerged from *The Angelus* appeared objectively and "the same associative systems had to sprout, however not in the formal field but in this other, much more unattainable and complicated one: that of representations and psychic phenomena" (2006, p. 28).[1]

I would now like to discuss the clinical case that was presented. Firstly, there is some background information that shows that Mr and Mrs B have been shaped by unresolved traumas in their respective families of origin. It is shown how both their defensive systems link. From this one can hypothesise a shared unconscious fantasy of the couple: that we can resurrect the dead children. The death of their baby, however, destroys this fantasy. Each of them handles the pain of this and the underlying anxieties in a different way. Mourning the death of the child often has different manifestations in the mother and in the father. Mr B seems absent, although he is concerned about his wife and children and seeks therapeutic help. Mrs B, on the other hand, expresses (with grief and a repetitive speech) her pain about the death of the baby and for all the losses in her family's history. The loss is omnipresent and the therapist comments on the "destructive pain" suffered by the mother. At this time there is an inability to represent the traumatic experience that the couple cannot integrate emotionally.

The reality of death appears to have shattered the fantasy of being an omnipotent couple capable of saving all babies. Now these parents feel that their relationship has led to a catastrophe and they lose their couple state of mind. This is not a conflict with the other, but rather within their relationship, because the union of their minds and bodies has ended in a catastrophe. The therapist must be able to metabolise this and the author notes how difficult it can be for therapists to help couples elaborate their grief.

The author asks: How should we approach this couple's pain for their child's death? Bion considers Passion (P) as a component of the links L (Love), H (Hate), K (Knowledge). Passion is an emotion experienced

(continued)

(continued)

with intensity and warmth, without violence, and that can be shared. On the contrary, negative links or anti-links (–L, –H, –K) are dispassionate links (–P). Grimalt (2012) differentiates understanding from Bion's concept of com-passion, which has the meaning of two minds that share emotions with all their intensity. We can understand the couple and imagine their suffering, but this is not the same as sharing it, experiencing it at first-hand, registering it emotionally, thinking about and processing it, assuming the functions of containment and reverie. Our countertransference offers us the possibility of approaching this catastrophic atmosphere whilst acting as moderators of pain, stimulating the couple's capacity to transform it.

Returning to the case, the therapist reports a dream of Mr B that represents a change. Dreams are potential generators of meaning which favour the development of the mind's aesthetic dimension as well as a digestive function. When the couple can dream, the trauma appears as a problem that can be expressed and offers us the possibility of thinking about it.

I will now share with you some ideas that the reported dream suggested to me. In the dream, Mr B firstly doubts if his wife is there. (Having lost the couple state of mind, they feel distant; they cannot trust one another enough.) He sees himself walking towards the dark side of the beach (the trauma). Despite feeling that it is dangerous to go there, Mr B tries to see what is in the dark, perhaps because he is accompanied by a stranger (the therapist). This provides the possibility of exploring the pain in which they are submerged and leaving the desperate defences that lead them to collapse. Mr B says that the dark side could represent their suffering and the children–acrobats suspended on the rope, their children. Mrs B cannot relate to this because she is overwhelmed by pain and guilt. The dark side makes me think of a "no-container" couple and the image of the children balancing catches my attention. Acrobats defy gravity and work hard to master jumps and pirouettes, so they can land on their feet, avoiding a catastrophe. A couple link always involves a capacity to maintain and recover balance. This, however, involves hard work, like that of the tightrope walkers.

I agree with the author when she suggests that the dream could be interpreted in different ways. This allows for a further important question: How can we better help the couple in such circumstances? Do they have to continue swinging on a tightrope or can we throw them a lifeline? The therapist's interpretation of premature birth seems to isolate the mother and increase her sense of guilt. Thinking about the concept of the shared physical space that the dream introduces seems to me to be more helpful. The author also reflects on this idea.

It seems that focusing on the couple and family link can stimulate the containment of anxieties and favour the creation or recovery of parental abilities in this regard. It appears that it can help them find a third position from which to observe their relationship and to be able to elaborate mourning. The future will depend on their ability to stay in a reflective and contained state. There is a clear link between mourning and creativity and the dream appears to be a manifestation of the work of mourning beginning.

In the event of a child's death, how can the state of mind of a creative couple that allows containment and reverie be maintained? The death of the child is a devastating catastrophe that threatens to annihilate the couple state of mind as a result of the difficulty of integrating such an experience emotionally and rationally. It involves a loss in the identity of couple and family and often leads to mutual recriminations or projections of anger and pain. The "third position" is lost and it will be necessary to find it in order to be interested in life once again and to recover creativity and vitality.

A child's death threatens the couple as it generates anguish and an unbearable pain. It often requires a therapeutic intervention. The identity of the couple and of the family needs to be reorganised, along with the restoration of parenting with their remaining and future children. That is, the work of mourning does not only include the painful experiences of loss, but also the loss of a parental container function.

In the case presented, the three-month treatment bears fruit. The fact that baby Aurora is evolving well allows the couple a feeling of being a "creative couple". The therapist has a mental space of a couple, a third position from which she can observe and think about the couple. The couple are able to introject this and the therapy promotes the development of a container–contained relationship which is beneficial for both members of the couple.

References

Bion, W. R. (1963). *Elements of Psycho-Analysis*. London: Heinemann.

Britton, R., Feldman, M., & O'Shaughnessy, E. (1989). *The Oedipus Complex* (The Melaine Klein Trust). London: Karnac.

Dalí, S. (2006). *El mito trágico de «El Ángelus» de Millet* (The Tragic Myth of Millet's Angelus). Barcelona: Tusquets. (First edition in 1963 in French Language.)

Grimalt, A. (2012). Traumes preconceptuals: l'assassinat de la ment i el self oblidat (Preconceptual traumas: the forgotten self and the murder of the mind). *Revista Catalana de Psicoanàlisi*, *XXIX*(2): 69–88. Available at: http://www.raco.cat/index.php/RCP/article/view/307330/397303

Morgan, M. (2018). *The Couple State of Mind: Psychoanalysis of Couples and the Tavistock Relationships Model* (The Library of Couple and Family Psychoanalysis). London: Routledge.

(continued)

(continued)

Pistiner, L. (2007). *La dimensión estética de la mente, variaciones sobre un tema de Bion*. Buenos Aires: Ediciones del signo (*The Aesthetic Dimension of the Mind: Variations on a Theme of Bion*. London: Karnac, 2009).

Waddell, M. (2002). *Inside Lives. Psychoanalysis and the Growth of the Personality*. London: Karnac.

Note

1 Dalí had the laboratories of the Louvre Museum examine the painting with X-rays and it was confirmed that in the precise place he had indicated there was a first layer of paint with a black mass that looked like a small coffin.

Chapter 13

Reflections on interpretation in contemporary clinical practice with family and couple links

Lia Cypel

Introduction

A major and complex issue in clinical practice, which has relevance to the topic of interpretation, is the diversity of theoretical approaches and their respective challenges. At the centre of this issue is the increasing interest in link theory, an approach to couple and family psychoanalysis that requires the analyst to tolerate and deal with the impact of her own subjectivity. Analysts engaged in dialogue with colleagues who have diverse frames of reference are recognising the importance of dialogue among a plurality of perspectives. Wisely, they are not seeking to deny the incompatibilities or differences that emerged, but to become enriched by them. This attests to the vitality and creativity that can be found within the contemporary thinking and practice in couple and family psychoanalysis at a time of significant socio-cultural transformations.

Paradigmatic shift

A shift from an individual psychoanalysis to a link psychoanalysis perspective and the dialectical relationship between them has required a significant amount of research and development. This encompasses the continuing elaboration of psychoanalytic concepts that may be suitable and useful to approach the family and couple links. All these developments have resulted in discoveries that continue to expand the analytic framework. This has revealed unexplored areas that, according to some authors, may open up new potential meta-psychologies. These developments in the theory and clinical practice with the psychoanalysis of link configurations may also contribute to expanding the concept of the human psyche from an individual psychoanalysis perspective to one concerning mutual exchanges. Consequently, it is essential to include the notion of inter-subjectivity in the clinical dimensions of observation and analytic elaboration in both approaches.

A willingness to be open to such contemporary ideas connects to what we might call the analyst's "internal setting". This refers more particularly to analysts' genuine and ethical disposition and related ability to be subjects and experience the impact of their subjectivity in the link, as well as to understand the impact of societies which are undergoing marked changes. This requires of the analyst sensitivity and care to distinguish between psychoanalytic transformation and one resulting from non-psychoanalytic influences. A failure to do this can otherwise see the analyst lose her psychoanalytic identity and setting. Contributions to our discipline that respect the psychoanalytic method in this way deepen its specificity and render it especially suitable to interpret the anxieties of present-day society.

All of this suggests the value of an approach to interpretation that focuses on the different links that impact on couples and families. In this regard, the way in which the clinical setting becomes constructed depends primarily on the analyst's internal analytic stance, her "internal setting", and the sense of herself which derives from her own personal and professional experience and her own analysis. The nature of the unique clinical situation that develops also depends on the theoretical framework she brings, one which will express her adopted model of the unconscious functioning of the mind (in the individual or the link context). In other words, it will determine the focus her analytic listening will take in the clinical situation, which in turn will shape her observations and interpretations.

Since there are manifold possible variables and combinations of such ways of listening and observing, there will also be many and diverse ways of constructing a therapeutic link with any particular couple or family. Each will have its own conceptual reasons and will be based on the analyst's personal truths, which become activated in the moment to moment of the psychoanalytic process.

The link approach entails a conception of psychic reality as being somewhat ineffable with multiple dimensions in constant motion and whose manifestations tend to consist of unpredictability, uncertainty, and contradiction (which coexist with their invariants). This means that understanding can only be approximate and relative. The resulting unconscious link field (transference or non-transference), be it a couple or a family link, would, therefore, become a complex, multidimensional and multifactorial system, with endless possibilities of transformation in relation to its internal (intra-subjective) and external (inter-subjective) realities.

The question thus becomes, where do such theoretical ideas lead one clinically? An approach using link–psychic change implies that the goal of our analytic work, by way of analyst container/reverie function, is a focus on the development of our patient's ability to think and learn, through the link unconscious emotional experience, in the unique reality of that specific ongoing session. From this perspective emotional experiences cannot be conceived of in isolation from relationships, from links, be it between patients with an analyst or patients with each other. Following Bion (1962), we know that thinking always involves the alternation between integration and lack of integration, binding and unbinding in relation to the mind's natural movements (internal links) as well as to external links. These links are all indispensable for the expansion of the psychic container, which evolves through breakups (crises, separations).

It is precisely this process that allows a new integration, a reorganisation (whether of thoughts or of the link arrangement) between two or more individuals that will make room for, or enable the advent of, a new psychic fact, of the unknown, of the unpredictable. Otherwise, we would be faced with the saturation, the endless repetition of the link, and thereby with the impoverishment and loss of link members' ability to think and know themselves and the other(s).

Interpretation

Focusing on interpretation, the analyst following a link theory approach would no longer be one from whom we would expect interpretations that offer final truths. From the link vertex, interpretations seek meanings, not causes. The aim is a psychic change in the link that involves the expansion of both patient's and analyst's minds, rather than a narrowing of observation, thinking and feeling. There are no explanatory conclusions, only possible conjectures. Analysts establish relations between clinical facts and connect psychic events, but continue inquiring, dealing with doubt and, therefore, questioning themselves and their patients, leading the latter to interrogate themselves and their truths, hitherto unshakeable thoughts. In this way, patients are able to adopt a reflective attitude and think about their participation in the resulting link conflict. From this perspective also, the interpretations offered by the analyst are always those that are possible at each particular moment and represent a partial aspect of an inaccessible, unknown totality.

A questioning position wherein the analyst expresses her awareness of their relative lack of knowledge about a couple or family and her ability to tolerate this (analysts must know that they do not know) should be initially and primarily between her theoretical framework and clinical practice. In this way, an interchange between theory and practice would be ensured that would facilitate a mutual feedback and revitalisation between the two. This process is indispensable for grasping clinical facts through hypotheses in our search for meaning.

To put it differently, analysts would leave aside their omnipotent locus of supposed "absolute knowledge" and make space for the link emotional experience that develops during the session. This then expands interpretation beyond the transference, by enabling contact with the emotions contained in the link, which facilitates an awareness of the experience of the subjects in the links.

As a consequence, the analytic link process does not evolve in a linear and predetermined way. Instead, cause and effect give way and make room for the unpredictable, a field in which the psyche is viewed as extensive, open, in continuity/discontinuity with another/others, and with the external, sociocultural world.

In this scenario, subject and link, and subject and environment, are mutually determined; they continuously re-constitute each other and generate a living unconscious which promotes a subjectivity process in every member of a link. As Käes (2007) has put it, "not one without the other, nor without the link that unites and contains them."

Family and couple link psychoanalysis, then, has probably become a most favourable site for debate concerning inter-subjectivity and on the construction of subjectivity, since links are primary depositories of current social malaise and individual symptoms of this malaise appear as ego syntonic with social values. It is important to point out, however, that according to this view, even though the link context provides the primary vantage point, the individual is still taken into account. Thanks to the link setting, each can be understood in terms of two dimensions, the intra-subjective and the inter-subjective, which are both in a dialectical relationship with each other. One dimension corresponds to unconscious individual psychic reality, with its affects, fantasies and representations (contained in object relations), which can flood a patient's link(s) with transference projective identifications. The other dimension is that of unconscious link psychic reality, with its structuring of unconscious alliances, pacts and collusions, tied to the current singular link situation.

Both dimensions can interact and alternate in search of a balance that will always be unstable; one or the other dimension may prevail. It is, however, the one that most characterises the unconscious link configuration which will become the focus of the resulting interpretation. Link dynamics may also present different stages of emotional development, from the dominance of narcissism to a stage where the recognition of alterity is found, expressed by the greater or lesser complexity of the link(s). Analytic listening will identify the clinical material to be interpreted as a "selected fact" (Bion, 1962).

The intersubjective dynamics are expressed in the joint discourse (the chain of associations produced during the session), where each link member re-signifies the other's speech. In this discourse it is important to identify what constitutes the core of the intersubjective dynamics – the elements that grant meaning to the affects, fantasies and defences that permeate verbal and nonverbal communication between link members.

This notion of a psychoanalysis of dialectical linking, which also takes into account intra-subjective dynamics within the realm of inter-subjective unconscious dynamics (that is, that can interpret the transference repetition of the past as well as the new and unknown aspects of the present in the link, depending on the situation), is essential for the validation of the psychoanalytic approach. These aspects are emphasised in order to reflect on our current clinical practice along with some related issues of interpretation.

Link psychoanalysis, as has been described, may be of particular contemporary value given what it has to offer is different, foreign to what the sociocultural environment provides, needs and demands. Focusing on links will enhance an individual's ability to know himself and others and to grow emotionally in a way that will be useful in his everyday life.

Such an approach to treatment involves the analysis of issues connected with choice, responsibility and the capacity to form and maintain links. Moreover, the space of containment/reverie of the analyst, which is also the space of transference interpretations, is the one that promotes the emotional experience needed to learn about the patient's current relationships. In this way, analysts might be able to trigger transformations in a patient's links and their related subjectivity.

Link psychoanalysis would thus fulfil its destiny by going against the grain of the sociocultural flow by "being a plague" so to speak. It also would seek the new and would go in the direction of the unknown. This refers to the unprecedented newness that is part of each member's link emotional experience, not to the currently "instituted new". Link psychoanalysis would, in contrast, offer an "old new" that is reinvented by the force of the rapprochement between subjects and their genuine truth as human beings.

As has been repeatedly stated, contemporary subjectivity is shaped in a social environment that favours the dissolution of individuals into a globalised mass culture that threatens our privacy, our individuality, and the construction of independent thought because of the fragility of interdiction. As a consequence, individuals experience great difficulty in tolerating frustration and psychic pain. Therefore, what patients reveal to us, very often and in different ways, is the need to work on link deficits rather than conflicts.

How do analysts work with links in which symbolic capacity is precarious and which have developed in a society that greatly favours regression to a narcissistic area and indiscriminate incorporation rather than introjection? How will emotional link maturity be achieved without introjection, which facilitates the differentiation between internal and external worlds, fantasy and reality, self and other? Why should we address these links, which are stereotyped and endogamic (Lévi-Strauss, 1962) and function with a dual logic? Is it in order to know that such conditions, which structure the quality of the link and provide subjectivity to the members of the link, are harmful to their psychic development?

Links found in borderline functioning where there is an excess of narcissism, where there are cracks in "support links", or where there are aspects of psychic that remain unrepresented, require psychoanalytic work, not just with what has been lost, but also with what never existed. In such circumstances, interpretations are very often perceived as persecutory.

Such links often need a more comprehensive approach that includes, in addition to transference interpretations, interpretations that may reach areas of repetition without an object and which make it possible to tackle identity issues and problems associated with an empty internal world.

Bleger (1967) states that in these cases a very rigid frame becomes a depository for the most primitive aspects of the link, albeit in a "mute" way, and these aspects tend to remain outside the analytic process and are neither analysed nor interpreted. They are not talked about; they belong in the realm of the sacred and cannot be touched by words.

What would the analyst's role be in such a situation? What would interpretations be like under these circumstances?

Further considerations regarding the interpretation

Let us recall first that the locus and function of the analyst may be seen as having an objective side, tied to a somewhat rational reflection (Green, 2008) and a human side, that of the real, subjective, reflective person of the analyst. This is related to the evocation of the analyst's own life experience, including her own analysis and hence her own unconscious.

Interpretation, in turn, involves the analyst's listening and her countertransference. Analytic listening is not a rational accumulation of information or knowledge, but a process that is also linked to the unconscious. Analysts seek to place their own ego in a state of suspension, that is, they enter into the experience with a couple or family without memory or desire (Bion, 1967) in order to enter into the production of metaphor with the couple or family associated with their unconscious link reality during the session.

Countertransference, a somewhat vague notion but yet an essential analytic tool, constitutes another dimension of the inter-subjective analytic situation that involves the analyst's ego. It has nothing to do with her *knowledge* of theory in the performance of her function. Rather, it concerns her *conviction*, or I would say her *faith* in the unconscious, which stems from her emotional experience of it.

Perhaps what generates transformative interpretative effects in very dysfunctional links is what happens in moments of real presence, of intense engagement of the analyst, which tend to materialise in the session as experiences such as "I found myself speaking" (i.e., I did not realise I was speaking). That is, something emerges. It is as though the analyst's unconscious and her experiences in relation to it would configure a verbalised content.

Paradoxically, it is necessary to know a lot about psychoanalysis in order to be able to forget it. In the obituary he wrote for Ferenczi, Freud (1933) announced himself against the mechanisation of technique and the intellectualisation of interpretations. Underlining this point in his article "Recommendations to physicians practicing psychoanalysis" (Freud, 1912), he states that analysts must be in a position to use their own unconscious as an analytic tool.

These notions are important to include because they refer to important dimensions of our clinical experience that are part of the core of the emotional experience of a couple or family that unfold in the session, wherein verbal and nonverbal contents are processed by the analyst's reverie function. It is mainly by way of these experiences that link members gradually co-construct helpful metaphors which are essential for interpretations to be assimilated.

Couples and families react to an interpretation in such a way that its action gradually modifies or institutes meanings, which can generate transformations in their links. They are interpretations that become possible only at a particular moment in time. They are partial hypotheses of a whole we know that is inaccessible. Moreover, they lead to new inquiries that are compatible with the investigative/reflective position of the analyst at first, and later to all parties in the clinical situation who are searching for a psychic link, whose modification could facilitate psychic change.

Prat (2014) suggests that we define the status of interpretation based not on its form, but on its effect, both on the psyche and on the analytic process. The form of the interpretation would thus be viewed as that which facilitates communication with couples and families and constitutes a specific vocabulary, between verbal and nonverbal language, "the language of success" (Bion, 1967), and which is in harmony with a patient's level of symbolisation.

Ferro (1997) in turn claims that interpretation is no longer considered something that is like having a dictionary at hand: one which makes it possible to pinpoint a meaning. Rather it is viewed as a proposal of a meaning that is never exhaustive but is always taking shape, "unsaturated" as Bion (1967) puts it.

This "hypothesis" uses the couple's emotions as a springboard to arrive at new, more complex and clearly defined meanings which in turn transmit affects to both members of the couple (Ferro, 1992).

Ferruta (2002), for his part, speaks of an "interpretive construction" and Roussillon (2005) of a "psychoanalytic conversation". Others suggest adopting versatile, singular settings, using figurative images for deficits in symbolisation.

At the same time, we cannot forget something that is crucial, that is, the analyst's personal style, which has always been a determining factor. Rather than what analysts say, it is often who we are that affects the analytic process. This refers to the ways in which one articulates divergences and convergences, our unconscious and natural ways of being, including our rhythm and tone, our intuitive nonverbal and body language. From this perspective, clinical practice of link psychoanalysis has a theoretical basis that allows us to address the unconscious experience of the most primitive world of an individual through a psychoanalytic inquiry in both directions: into the role and effects of these experiences in the link field; and into the kinds of subjects that the link is forming and maintaining.

Conclusion

Working with links in couples and families can be seen as essential to effective interpretation, a central characteristic of the psychoanalytic methods. The justification for link psychoanalysis with couples and families is that by creating favourable conditions for them, analysts can work through the dynamics of their links which restore individuality as an attribute of the emotional growth of links between members. In this work solving conflicts is not the only important outcome. With the conflict as a starting point, we aim to build psychic structures that will allow patients to deal creatively, to the best of their ability, with today's shifting world and with social diversity in a way that is democratic, respectful and true to themselves and to others, while remaining meaningfully integrated to their existential time and space.

References

Bion, W. R. (1962). *Learning from Experience*. London: Heinemann.

Bion, W. R. (1967). *Second Thoughts*. London: Heinemann.

Bleger, J. (1967). Psychoanalysis of the psychoanalytic frame. *The International Journal of Psychoanalysis*, *48*: 511–519.

Ferro, A. (1992). *The Bi-Personal Field: Experiences in Child Analysis*. London: Routledge.

Ferro, A. (1997). *L'Enfant et le psychanalyste* (The child and the psychoanalyst). Paris: Eres.

Ferruta, A. (2002). Une interprétation qui construit le sujet: l'aventure du processus (An interpretation that constructs subjectivity: The adventure of the process). In: J. J. Baranes & F. Sacco (Eds.), *Inventer en psychanalyse: construire et interpréter* (Invention in Psycho-analysis: Construction and Interpretation). Paris: Dunod.

Freud, S. (1912). Recommendations to physicians practicing psychoanalysis. *Standard Edition*, *12*: 109–120.

Freud, S. (1933). Sandor Ferenczi. *Standard Edition*, *22*, 227–229.

Green, A. (2008). *Idées Directrices pour une Psychanalyse Contemporaine* (Guiding Principles for Contemporary Psychoanalysis). Paris: Presses Universitaires de France.

Käes, R. (2007). *Un singulier pluriel* (A singular plural). Paris: Dunod.

Lévi-Strauss, C. (1962). *La Pensée Sauvage* (The Wild Thought). Paris: Pion.

Prat, R. (2014). A roupa nova da interpretação (Interpretation's new clothes). *Revista Brasileira de Psicanalise*, *48*(2): 33–46.

Roussillon, R. (2005). La conversation psychanalytique: un divan en latence (Psychoanalytic conversation: A couch in latency). *Revue française de psychanalyse*, *LXX*(2): 365–381.

Editors' prologue to the discussant perspective

Lia Cypel presents a stimulating theoretical discussion, which describes how an inter-subjective perspective has influenced contemporary approaches to couple and family psychoanalysis and discusses the implications of this for technique. In relation to interpretation, she notes that an approach that stems from a theoretical framework of inter-subjectivity focuses on interpreting the links in couple and family relationships where interpretations are focused more on meaning than causation. In taking up the idea of the dialectical relationship between the analyst and the couple which ensues from a link theory perspective, Barbara Bianchini notes how such an approach is characterised by uncertainty and unpredictability. She notes that, from this perspective, transference also acquires a broader meaning. In particular, that it is part of an emotional field with its own specific and potentially transformative functioning.

Discussant perspective

Barbara Bianchini

Lia Cypel's chapter focuses on the role of interpretation as it has developed as part of the "Link Theory" approach to couple and family psychoanalysis. Her premise is that the shift from an individual to a link psychoanalysis perspective, and the dialectical relationship between them, is undergoing a significant period of research and development. She maintains that this is contributing to a shift in the concept of the human psyche from an individual psychoanalysis perspective to one that emphasises the impact of interpersonal relationships. Consequently, many psychoanalysts have found it helpful to introduce the notion of inter-subjectivity to their clinical observation and methods of psychoanalytic elaboration. Such an approach takes into consideration ineffable psychic reality, with its numerous, continuously changing dimensions, which are characterised by unpredictability, uncertainty and contradictions that allow it to be only partially understood. From this perspective unconscious couple or family links are seen to be complex, multi-dimensional systems, with infinite possibilities for the transformation of internal (intra-subjective) and external (inter-subjective) realities.

The author consequently believes that the goal of our analytic work is to effect link/psychic change, through the analyst's container/reverie functions, seeking the development of the patient's ability to think and learn through the link. This process allows a new integration and organisation between the individuals concerned that can lead to the creation of new psychic facts, making room for the unknown and the unpredictable.

One wonders if the author's proposition is to introduce to couple and family psychoanalysis a point of view that enables an understanding of the phenomena observed in both the internal world and the interpersonal one. Her chapter proposes a two-fold psychoanalytical investigation: on the one hand into the role and effect of the unconscious experience of the subject's most primitive world in the field of the link, and on the other into the type of subjects that shape and maintain the link.

I believe that in our practice it is not only a question of privileging one of the two aspects – intra-subjective or inter-subjective – or of trying to integrate them both, but also of creating something new or destroying things previously created. In the session, therefore, the analyst, containing and sharing emotions, is mainly concerned with the theme of change and with the repetitive forces that obstruct it. The analyst should forego his/her certainties and try to generate previously un-activated functions and encourage new modes of being.

The couple relationship is thus not seen to be static and needs to continually recreate itself. It exists as a permanent process that is maintained through the creation and destruction of something beautiful and important and a constant oscillation between hope and containment of the confusion and suffering caused by depressive and persecutory elements. In this way the couple relationship and each partner are allowed to grow within their co-created links.

In the consulting room we are able to facilitate the development of new thoughts and emotions. In this way the couple's potential is not only about recovering what happened in their past and what is happening in their present, but also about looking creatively about what is possible in the future. In each session, emotions are either created or avoided. We face the fear of creating and the despair of being continually under attack from preconceived ideas. It is thus a process of retrieval, recreation and overcoming the abandonment of the beauty of the emotions.

This process strongly connotes the emotional intensity of the ever-expanding analytic field, precisely because each partner, their relationship and the analyst constantly communicate at both an unconscious and conscious level. The co-created beauty in the analytic session can therefore activate and create new possibilities. In this setting we try to give importance not only to that which is said and interpreted, but also to that which is "done".

Seen from this perspective the transference has a broader meaning, that is, an affective and emotional involvement that accompanies every experience. An interweaving of reciprocal transferences and of respective identities gives rise to something different: an emotional field with its own specific functioning, irrespective of its initial elements which is much more than the sum of its parts. An encounter between individuals creates something which is radically different from that which each person separately represents. Subject and object are not consistently distinct from each other but, from a functional point of view, can be considered reversible. Here I am referring to Ferro and Basile's (2009) potential field in continual expansion, where all possible worlds brought into being by the analytic session can take shape. As Ferro (2013) notes, this model looks only fleetingly at the contained, but focuses instead on the development of the way the mind functions and on those qualities of the mind that can be developed. The shared experience is that of allowing emotions, affects, thoughts and characters to circulate in the presence of the analyst (he/she also too has a place in the field), who guarantees and safeguards the setting and promotes within it a sort of oneiric activity.

The author also makes relevant reflections concerning interpretation, one of the fundamental tools of analysis. In particular, she considers how

(continued)

(continued)

we can work on the stereotypical, narcissistic links that do not lead to introjection. She believes that it is necessary to adopt an approach that, as well as including transference interpretations, also includes interpretations that may reach areas of repetition without an object and enable us to tackle issues of identity and the problems associated with an empty internal world. In describing the qualities of interpretation required in cases of this nature, the author makes reference to Ferro's (2013) concept of saturated and unsaturated interpretation, and to the importance of the analyst's involvement and style.

To these concepts, I would also add the development of the analyst's emotional participation in the process of creation and destruction, with the intuitive insights that derive from his/her inspiration. Meltzer (1976) said that intuitive insights were a result of "the aesthetic component of experience, the 'beauty' with which material and formulations cohabit, blossom and bear fruit as a thing apart from ourselves" (p. 141), separated from the analyst and the patient, but which belong to the field of the analyst and patient.

For this reason Ferro (personal communication) compares saturated interpretation to traffic lights, where red means stop, and green means go, creating no-through roads and compulsory routes, while unsaturated interpretation is like a roundabout that illuminates the process, that keeps it moving and from which one can choose various roads, none of which is unequivocally signposted, providing infinite routes to new possibilities of imaginatively overcoming conflict and misunderstanding, without any no-through roads.

Each instance of communication is considered to be the narration of what is created in the consulting room between the minds of the couple and that of the analyst. This leads to the illumination of mutual interaction, "characters-facts-narratives are deconstructed, made insubstantial and re-dreamed in order to develop a capacity for thought" (Ferro, 2013, p. 181, personal translation).

References

Ferro, A. (Ed.) (2013). Modello onirico della mente. In: *Psicoanalisi oggi*. Roma: Carocci editore. (Dream model of the mind. In: *Contemporary Bionian Theory and Technique in Psychoanalysis*. London: Routledge, 2018.)

Ferro, A., & Basile, R. (2009). *The Analytic Field: A Clinical Concept*. London: Karnac.

Meltzer, D. (1976). The delusion of clarity of insight. *International Journal of Psycho-Analysis*, 57:141–146.

Epilogue

Timothy Keogh and Elizabeth Palacios

The conference from which these papers were drawn was held in Madrid in 2017. It was an exemplar of conferences that have begun to bring couple and family psychoanalysts and therapists together, particularly over the last decade. The conference, like others, presented a wide range of perspectives about the practice of couple and family psychoanalysis and was both enriching and challenging. The challenge not only resulted from the logistics of communicating complex clinical and theoretical ideas and concepts across language barriers, but from different viewpoints about what is seen to be transformative in couple and family work.

These differences have derived out of the culturally rich soils in South America, Europe, Britain, North America and more recently the Australasian region. The resultant cross fertilisation has had a catalytic effect on theorising and advances in clinical practices, all at a time when the interest in this particular form of psychoanalysis has surged.

As an applied form of psychoanalysis, couple and family assessment and intervention have challenged the traditional psychoanalytic approach found in individual work from a number of vertices, including the setting, the definition of who the patient is and the approach to interpretation: The focus of this book. As explicated in a number of chapters in this volume, this is related to an awareness that in couples and in families the focus of interpretive work is not only on the relationship between patient and analyst or therapist, but also on interpreting which goes on in the here and now between members of a couple and within a family. Theoretical advances which have highlighted the importance of what the analysts/therapists bring to the therapeutic relationship have been found to be of particular relevance to couple and family work. In the link theory framework, the actual presence of the analyst/therapist and the imposition this creates on the relationship that she enters into with couples and families have become very valuable concepts.

The notion of the link as a co-created entity to be understood and analysed sits comfortably with developments in thinking about couples and families, which has regarded them as representing the intersection of sets of internal and archaic object relations. This in turn has confirmed not only the importance of the countertransference of the analyst/therapist, but also the reverie in which she engages, which allows for a selected fact to emerge which can inform interpretations that are subsequently made. Current approaches to couple and family psychoanalysis therefore emphasise this rich matrix of transferences (or links) to the analyst/therapist and within the couple and members of the family, along with multidirectional countertransferences, in the here and now of the session. The focus is on how couples and families come to form the relationship or links they have, their nature and the defensive purpose they serve.

The same factors that have been identified as important to creative coupling and generative families have also been central to the developments that have been taking place amongst theorists and clinicians. That is, the *other*, as initially foreign and alien, has ultimately been able to be tolerated, resulting in a creative movement in this applied area of clinical psychoanalysis. This, as Puget notes in her discussant perspective in this book, does not come about by trying to make the otherness of ideas the same as one's own, but from being open to the change that their difference presents. This is an important issue as human history is replete with the brutality and savagery resulting from responding to otherness by trying to control or annihilate it. In terms of issues facing our current world, our profession sets an important standard in this regard.

In couple and family work an ability to be open to relationship or link-based interpretation presupposes a certain level of psychic development, which either allows for a level of toleration of difference and a capacity not to feel threatened or engulfed by it. The issue of primitive mental states in couples, in particular, highlights that interpretation, whilst a workhorse of technique, is not the only aspect of psychoanalysis that is transformative.

Moreover, we are reminded from the deep exploration of interpretation within couples and family psychoanalysis that this book represents that psychoanalysis has other powerful and potentially transformative tools at its disposal. It is important in this regard to remind ourselves that as with individual patients, we often see very narcissistic couples and couples who have underdeveloped psychic structures, even to the point of lacking a viable psychic skin. In these circumstances we can feel confident in aspects of psychoanalysis such as the psychoanalytic frame and the psychoanalytic stance and the transformative containment that they provide.

Whilst all these advances in theory and practice have taken us into new and helpful directions, one is nonetheless always mindful of the enduring concepts that Freud articulated for us which stand the test of time in all forms of psychoanalytic endeavour. In particular, one is mindful of the value and the power of the unconscious that provides a strong link among all psychoanalytic professionals.

In conclusion, it is worth noting that whilst psychoanalysis has sometimes been regarded as the impossible profession, in reading some of the powerful accounts of work reported in this volume, one is reminded of the importance of human bonds to happiness and peace and thus what a privilege it is to be able to work to restore and enhance them.

Index

Readers interested in accessing the case studies by the names of the patients will find them listed as subheadings under a main heading, "case studies and vignettes".
Page numbers in italics refer to information in figures.